# John Bentley Mays

# emerald city
*Toronto Visited*

Photographs by
## Richard Rhodes

**VIKING**

VIKING
Published by the Penguin Group
Penguin Books Canada Ltd, 10 Alcorn Avenue, Toronto Ontario M4V 3B2
Penguin Books Ltd, 27 Wrights Lane, London W8 5TZ, England
Penguin Books USA Inc., 375 Hudson Street, New York, New York 10014,
U.S.A.
Penguin Books Australia Ltd, Ringwood, Victoria, Australia
Penguin Books (NZ) Ltd, 182-190 Wairau Road, Auckland 10, New Zealand

Penguin Books Registered Offices: Harmondsworth, Middlesex, England

Printed and bound in Canada on acid-free paper ∞

**Canadian Cataloguing in Publication Data**

Mays, John Bentley
Emerald city

ISBN 0-670-85356-9

1. Toronto (Ont.) - Description and travel.
2. Toronto (Ont.) - Social life and customs.
3. Architecture - Ontario - Toronto.   I. Title.

FC3097.3.M38 1994     971.3'541     C94-931421-8
F1059.5.T684M38 1994

All the texts in this collection first appeared, in shorter and considerably different form, in *The Globe and Mail*. Grateful acknowledgment is made to Thomson Newspapers Ltd. for permission to reprint material which appeared first in *The Globe and Mail.*

All photographs appearing in this book were taken by Richard Rhodes.

*to Erin*
*city kid*

# ACKNOWLEDGMENTS

The earliest versions of all these pieces appeared as "Citysites" columns in *The Globe and Mail,* and I must acknowledge the guidance of my senior editors Katherine Ashenburg and Karen York, from whom the idea for this weekly feature came; William Thorsell, editor-in-chief of *The Globe and Mail,* an unfailing source of ideas and encouragement; and the several editors on the arts desk who helped hammer my thoughts into publishable form. Little here is exactly as it was in the newspaper. For helping me in this work of rethinking and rewriting, I am indebted to Jackie Kaiser and Meg Masters, the book's editors at Penguin. Lee Davis Creal, my agent, has been an enthusiastic advocate and adviser at each step. I am also indebted to Mary Adachi for her fastidious and helpful copy editing of the manuscript.

My special gratitude goes to Richard Rhodes, who created the remarkable portfolio of photographs found in this book, and to David Olive, whose acute commentary on an early draft of the manuscript nailed many an imprecision, pointed me down avenues of thought hitherto unnoticed, and saved me from committing more than one error of fact and judgment. As for the mistakes that survived David's scrutiny, and any others, I take full responsibility.

Throughout this book, I have sought to acknowledge every source, personal and literary, in the text itself. At the end of the volume is a list of books and articles which provided facts, or informed my thinking on each topic, or opened my eyes to a site, style or place I had not noticed. There is also full bibliographical information on works cited in the text, for readers who wish to follow my paths deeper into the forest of cultural forms and meanings. Absent from the notes, however, are references to a handful of indispensible reference works always at my elbow during the writing of this book, and constant resources of fact and guidance: Patricia McHugh, *Toronto Architecture: A City Guide,* 2nd edition, Toronto: McClelland & Stewart, 1989; Eric Arthur, *Toronto No Mean City,* 3rd edition (revised by Stephen A. Otto), Toronto: University of Toronto Press, 1986; Robert Bothwell, *A Short History of Ontario,* Edmonton: Hurtig, 1986; and Alan Gowans, *Styles and Types of North American Architecture: Social Function and Cultural Expression,* New York: HarperCollins, 1992. If there is one group of writers whose works I have plundered while grievously underacknowledging throughout, they are the city reporters of *The Globe and Mail,* whose stories, throughout our 150 years of publication, add up to an extraordinary archive on urban occurrence and process. The useful phrase "Depression Modern" has been borrowed from the title of Martin Greif's *Depression Modern: The Thirties Style in America* (1988).

There are also a number of people whose names appear never or rarely in the text and notes, but whose contribution of collegiality, friendship or personal example should not go unrecognized. Thus, my special gratitude goes to Anne Collins, Richard Handler, Antanas and Snaige Sileika, Adele Freedman, Anita Fonda, Gianni Vattimo, Anne Gibson and Ken Winters, Adrienne Fonda and Jean-Phillipe Finkelstein, Larry Richards, Robert Harbison, Robert Everett-Green, Anne and Robert McPherson, Stephen Godfrey, Marie Day and

Murray Laufer, and the Venerable the Archdeacon of Trafalgar.

Thanks, also, to Laura and Antonio Bechelloni, Michael Valpy, David Sobel and Susan Meurer, Diana Birchall, Andrew Lipchak, Jack Diamond, Philip Johnson, Witold Rybczynski, Dennis Reid, Miriam Pretty, Ivar Kalmar, Cheryl Rief, Roald Nasgaard, Scott Jones, Diane Burchmore, Jane Walker, the Reverend Jane Watanabe, Beth Potter, Allen Moore, Robert Hollands, the Reverend Philip Hobson, the Reverend Brian Freeland, Eberhard H. Zeidler, Michael McMahon, Terry Fenton, Dr. John D. M. Griffin and Dr. Cyril Greenland, Randy Sorensen, Peter A. Gabor, Richard Stromberg and other researchers at The Toronto Historical Board, the staffs of the architecture collection and the John P. Robarts Library of the University of Toronto, the Metropolitan Toronto Reference Library and the library of *The Globe and Mail,* the University of Toronto Bookroom, Pages, Ballenford Books and the Bob Miller Bookroom; and the staff and bookshop of the Canadian Centre for Architecture. I am also grateful for the many critical and informative letters and phonecalls from readers of the original articles.

Two people, however, deserve my gratitude more than any others, because of their unfailing love and loyalty: Margaret Cannon, my wife; and Erin Anne Bentley Mays, my daughter, to whom this book is dedicated.

John Bentley Mays
Toronto
September, 1994

# CONTENTS

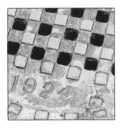

## Pleasures in Places

## Modern

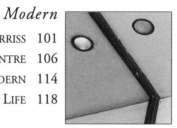

## Shopping

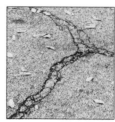

# emerald city

# INTRODUCTION

## Finding the Emerald City

I arrived in Toronto, by bus, on a blazing day in August, 1969. Though I had been living only twenty miles across Lake Ontario, in Rochester, New York, I imagined Toronto to be a quaint old fishing village with a large and famous university settled improbably in the middle of it. This misperception—not less absurd, because unquestioned—is not unusual among Americans, who tend to have odd ideas about Canada in any case. Upon stepping out of the bus station on Elizabeth Street, I was astonished to see, almost at once, the dark towers of the Toronto-Dominion Centre rising into the white-hot summer sky.

So I went to my nearly bare flat in the north-Toronto neighbourhood of Deer Park, spent one night there, and set out the next day on the first of many pacings-off of the city, just to find out what sort of place I had come to.

My route that first day out took me on a wander southward down the broad declining slope of the lake's ancient, higher shoreline, towards the city and the Toronto-Dominion towers, on the horizon. But instead of heading directly downtown, I drifted south-westward, through the old village of Yorkville—thick with hippies in lovebeads and tie-dyes, and with suburbanites in town to shop Yorkville's boutique circuit—then across the Gothic campus of the University of Toronto, and thence into the narrow streets west of Spadina Avenue, among the gamy-smelling, thronged vegetable stands of Kensington Market.

I ended that first day in Toronto on the hot, dusty western-waterfront grounds of Exhibition Place, where the 1969 edition of the Canadian National Exhibition had just opened.

I had loved state fairs since childhood—and had not yet learned of Toronto's peculiar anxiety about *this* fair—so it seemed like the most natural thing on earth, to take those spectacular rides churning against the sky, and plunge into the sweaty human surge teeming up and down the Midway. My best memories of that day are of the dense mix of delighted screams, rock and funk, barkers' barks and pig-squeals, bingo calls and laughter from the canvas-top beer parlours, the pneumatic hiss and gearbox clatter, all hanging like a bright, deliriously toxic cloud over Exhibition Place.

Only years afterwards, I found that here, on this site of rides, spectacle and façades, of fanciful pleasures and of architectural memories—dreams of Crystal Palace and Brighton Pavilion—*here,* and not in the city's more obvious centre, in the skyscrapered financial district around King and Bay, Toronto had begun.

The only reminder of that foundation visible today is an inconspicuous monument standing on the south-west corner of Exhibition Place, where the petting zoo and kiddie rides are installed during Ex time. Near that plinth of stone, in the winter of 1750, French carpenters and masons under the Marquis de la Jonquière built a small wooden trading post, which was called Fort Rouillé by its builders, in honour of the current colonial minister in Paris.

The population of Jonquière's little settlement, in its decade of life—the fort was burnt by the hopeless French after the British defeat of Fort Niagara in 1759—never numbered

*Ferris Wheel, Conklin Midway*

more than about fifteen souls, mostly soldiers and kitchen help. It appears that no Christian priest ever went there. But though small and short-lived, the memory of the little palisaded camp lingered in Toronto's folk imagination and fireside tales for more than a century. And it seems to have cast a certain spell on the ground that has never quite gone away.

Though ideal for both, the grounds around what Torontonians called "the old French fort" would never be used for farming or habitation. Rather, the place would remain forever martial and jovial—a zone of tentative dwelling, offering only temporary solace, and standing as an emblem of the grand ambitions of nations and peoples, like any military post on far frontiers. So it was after 1787, when the British bought the place from the Mississauga Indians, having decided to make it part of the military compound of Fort York. And so it remained after 1878, when the Victorian garrison turned the vacant site over to the Canadian National Exhibition, as its permanent home.

Industrial and agricultural fairs, festivals of modernity that sprang into existence in Europe and North America with the coming of industrialization, had been held in Ontario as early as 1820, but only on an itinerant basis. By the 1870s, however, the Ontario railroads had created the arteries necessary for the rapid pulsing of people into Toronto and out of it, and the city's growth created the centre of gravity for the province's accelerating economy. The Exhibition acquired its first permanent home on the site of the old French fort in 1878, and presented its first edition the following year.

From the beginning, the Exhibition, like the burnt fort that preceded it, was a representation of a distant empire—not a political realm, but the metaphysical imperium of modernity, radiant with promise of abundance and wonders. The thousands drawn from their Ontario farms and small towns by the magnetism of those early fairs came not only for the show, but for a taste of this coming apocalypse of modernity.

And they entered through an appropriate monument, the Princes' Gates, a tribute to the victory of industrial democracy, and the imperial British loyalties of the common man.

It was at dusk that day, standing alone in the Princes' Gates, looking east along the lakeshore towards the Modernist tall buildings at the city centre's present heart that I got a first hint of Toronto's peculiar conflict over its own urbanity, its struggle with modernity. To this day, on the mental map of the city I carry in my head, the Gates is the dividing line between these two options for a city style Toronto cannot choose between: small-town British Victorianism, with cliquish fidelity to class, the old school tie, the anachronism summed up by the persistence of an agricultural fair in a metropolis of millions; and the American, hard-driven high Modernism symbolized by the downtown towers, with all they express of the yearning of at least some Torontonians to escape the parochialisms of the past, and enter full secularity.

This conflict, between the weight of tradition and the weightlessness of Modernity, is a theme in this book, probably because it is the central theme in my life. I was born into a Southern American family with deep roots in the land and the traditions of living on the land; yet from the age I knew anything, I knew I would be cutting those roots, little by little, and breaking loose from the South and whatever destinies it held for me. It was not possible for me to know then that the project lying before me was Modernity itself, unfinishable, in ways incomprehensible, at times unendurable. But even in the darkest hours of loneliness, I have never imagined the initiations, the understandings, of the Modern condition to be anything other than the only intellectual and moral tasks ultimately worth embarking on, and carrying through to the end.

Which brings me to the title of this book, and its source—not in the book, by the way, but in the movie version of Frank Baum's *Wizard of Oz*. As a child, during the war years, I saw it again and again, while never then (nor now) understanding it. The whole film is Dorothy's quest to get back to Kansas. But since Dorothy had the supreme good fortune to be picked up by a tornado from a drab black-and-white farm and set down in a prismatic country of endless delights, adventures and surprises, what could she possibly find to do, once back on the farm? Why would *anybody* want to go back to Kansas after catching a glimpse of the delightful and busy Emerald City?

The best thing to do was, or should be, (I believed from childhood onward) to keep riding the tornado for as long as possible, in hopes of being dropped into some desirable Oz. So it was that I came to Toronto in 1969, to teach for three years at York University and then, so I thought, to catch the next tornado out of town. It took me some time to figure out that this was to be no short stop, but a home-coming, and the discovery of the Emerald City I had been looking for since I was high enough to look over the cotton on my father's plantation.

This is a reporter's book, and an account of coming to Modernity, Toronto's and my own. It is not history. Though it is about Toronto places, the book will, I hope, be used as a guide to discovering and thinking about any place, in any city. It is hence for any stranger in metropolis, including those born in one; and especially for anyone who has ridden, as I have, what E. M. Cioran called civilization's whirlwind from agriculture to paradox.

# *Thinking Places*

*July, St. Clarens Avenue*

# The Port Industrial District

Wherever I've lived, I have always had a thinking place. The first was a shaded gulley, lined with blackberry bushes and wild roses, water-gouged into the red Louisiana dirt at the edge of a cotton field near the house in which I spent my earliest years.

More recent thinking places have included a sunny hillside in North Carolina; the dapple-shadowed dirt under a bridge over the Genesee River in Rochester; a cold room, open to the sky, high in the stone stump of an ancient Irish church's ruined belltower.

So it was that, not long after coming to Toronto some twenty-five years ago, I soon found myself a thinking place. It's in a desolate, declining downtown zone known as the Port Industrial District, just east of Toronto's inner harbour, and within clear sight of the skyscrapers at the city's centre of gravity. It is bounded on the north by the cement colonnade bearing up the Gardiner Expressway, on the south by Lake Ontario beach park frontage—now deprived of its once-panoramic view of the lake by the long artificial finger of the Leslie Street Spit—and, to the east, by a sewage-treatment plant.

Most of the district today is a low, dead-flat version of what's now called an industrial park, traversed by straight broad avenues—laid out to serve much grander buildings than

the ones that actually got built—and pierced by murky rectangular tanker slips. Apart from the port facilities, little rises
far above the district's level damp floor of landfill, except huge
mounds of road salt shrouded in black plastic sheeting, tall
cylindrical tanks built for chemicals and heavy oils, and the
poetically boxy, angular hulk of Ontario Hydro's Richard L.
Hearn thermal generating plant. Most of the off-street parts
of the district are paved by oily, rubble-strewn earth or dotted
with forgettable buildings, survivors from the final years of
Toronto's Industrial Age.

In 1969, cargo tonnage at the Port of Toronto attained a
record level of 6.3 million tonnes, and has been declining ever
since. What's left is a strange landscape, the home of tanks and
concrete emplacements and ageing factories, cranes and chimneys and silos; and a temporary stop for Great Lake tankers,
lying still and low in their slips. Only one strip of the District,
running parallel to the lakeshore on a long ridge, the last
memory of an ancient sandbar, is still wild, thick with poplar,
sycamore and willow and with dense, prickly undergrowth,
and busy with marsh and shore birds.

The district is not appealing aesthetically, nor should it be.
Urban thinking places shouldn't be tourist attractions, lest the
sightseers make you forget the reason for being there. Or,
much worse, lest some earnest, environmentally and historically conscious government—municipal, provincial, federal—
decides to turn it into a park. Which decision, of course,
would bring in its train the baleful works of "improvement":
paved walkways, good lighting throughout, well-maintained
toilets, and lots of finger-wagging laws about proper human
and pet behaviour. As matters stand now, it's not park; and
within this wilderness of trees and rust are many places to be
alone and think, into which one can disappear completely
from the crush and rattle of urban existence into a shady nook
and consider life, fate, some specific decision or the world—all
within a ten-minute drive of the hectic middle of Toronto's

financial district. If not picturesque, this industrial district is graced with a subtle melancholy that is peculiarly right for thinking things through.

To get a sense of what I'm talking about at its most enchanting, you need only cycle or drive down there late one afternoon, just before night has begun descending on the incandescent city.

Find your thinking spot—a sun-warmed concrete slab beside the inner harbour's Eastern Gap, or a log alongside a damp footpath snaking through the marshy dense foliage near the shore, or some crumbling concrete wall near a battery of oil tanks—and watch the ghost-mist from the vanished marsh upon which the district was built rise over its ramshackle buildings, and the pools of oily water gleam with the first cold light of the rising moon.

At such a lonesome moment, the mind may drift towards the things of which ruins have always made people mindful: mortality and the brevity of life, the decay of what Dame Rose Macaulay, in her book *Pleasure of Ruins,* calls "the stupendous past." In the presence of the rusting bones of Toronto's once-vivid port, one naturally inclines to think about the futility of worldly ambition—individual ambition, surely, but also that of the civilization to which we've fallen heir.

Tumbledown castles, vine-enshrouded monasteries made eerie by screech-owl and bat, fragments of once-mighty temples raised to gods no more adored, have long occasioned reveries of this sort. Rusting petroleum tanks, little boarded-up cinder-block boxes slowly tiring and crumbling, junked trucks littered here and there like fallen, ancient animals in the evening mist—these, too, speak to us of the world and ourselves at dusk. The ties with a powerful element in Toronto's past, as incarnate in its artifacts, has been cut; loading cranes have been left to go still and die, concrete grain elevators demolished, once-magnificent factories swept away. The connection of such built objects with more traditional ruins, I believe, is in the poignance we feel whenever witnessing a great dream—in the case of the Port Industrial District, the tough, ambitious idealism of heavy-mechanical capitalism—slowly falling victim to the impersonal forces of time and obsolescence that have overcome all cultures of the past, and will overcome every person in the end. "A monument of antiquity is never seen with indifference"—so wrote Thomas Whatley in 1770. "No circumstance so forcibly marks the desolation of a spot once inhabited, as the prevalence of Nature over it."

However delicious such reflection may be, it has the side-effect of dulling one's curiosity about the hard history and real archaeology of a site. It's the uneasy sense of that anaesthesia that prompted Henry James to call his own seeking after ruins "a heartless pastime; and the pleasure, I confess, shows a note of perversity."

Had I not been assigned a weekly *Globe and Mail* column about city spots, I'd probably be still indulging in the pleasures of my favourite ruins and wastelands, and still as ignorant about them as ever. But among writing's many gifts to the writer is a dissatisfaction with impression and reverie, the commonest of temptations leading to horrible journalism. You don't have to spend much time typing away, before the hankering to get past the Jamesian "perversity" sets in, and you want the facts of the site. I was fortunate to find, early in my descent into the obscure history of my thinking place, the illuminating work of Toronto architect Jeffrey Stinson, entitled *The Heritage of the Port Industrial District.*

Like a good art critic, in Baudelaire's famous definition, Stinson is "passionate, partial, political." Whether his topic is a tank farm and hydro pylon, or a popstand on Cherry Beach, or the long row of trees lining Unwin Avenue—the paved road just north of the lonely, thicketed ridge where the best thinking places are—Stinson writes with pleasure, attending to details dilettantes easily overlook. As we might expect from a student of the recent proletarian past, Stinson cautions against the unthinking knock-down of old industrial buildings, and rises to indignation at the snobbery embodied in the tired but still-entrenched Victorian Brick school of heritage, with its fixation upon the noble residences of our dead betters, and its aversion to the industrial operations our ancestors built and worked in. Only yesterday, a right-thinking urbanist like Stinson would have shunned those heavy-industrial belchers of smut and leakers of poisons in our midst. Their few fans (including me) had to go to Buffalo in order to get the whiff and feel of naked industrial might, and the human culture generated by it. But as Toronto companies have vanished or fled to cheaper climes, leaving their dilapidated homes behind, this non-nostalgic sort of urban scholar has arisen, concerned with local building's immediate past, and devoted, as earlier heritage folk were not, to remembering the great industrial age *here,* as it slips away into long twilight.

If nostalgia obliterates history, or at least dulls the desire for it, Stinson's pleasure is in the precise and definite. As we learn from his report, done in 1990 for the Toronto Harbour Commissioners, the first Europeans to take up residence on the original town site of Toronto looked out on a large near-lagoon, separated from Lake Ontario by the Toronto islands archipelago, and, just east of this calm sheet of water, on to a spacious marsh lying behind a long sandbar. The source of this wetland was the Don River, which gathered its waters from the high forested plateau and lower lakeshore terrain north of the lake, and carried them south, ever more broadly and slowly, finally emptying them into the great marsh.

By Victorian times, after the city had put down lasting roots in the stiff glacial clay by the lake, Torontonians had taken to escaping the summer's heat at cottages on Fisherman's Island, as the sandbar dividing marsh from lake came to be called. There, for some years anyway, they could enjoy respite from Toronto's blistering late-summer heat, the delight of the long sandy beach, the stalking of the marsh's innumerable waterfowl.

*Left Turn, Commissioner's Road*

But even before the turn of this century, the wastes generated by Toronto's burgeoning industries and population had already taken a near-mortal toll on the Don River system as a whole, and the marsh in particular. The once-luxuriant fen had thickened into pestilential sludge. So it was that the Toronto Harbour Commissioners was summoned into existence by growing protests from the public against this festering stew—as well as by calls from industrialists for new land near downtown, and better marine facilities than those afforded by the inner harbour up to that time. In 1911, the commissioners were handed 1,385 acres of polluted marshland, and the daunting job of cleaning it up.

Which they promptly set about doing. By the end of 1912, city council had approved the commissioners' plans and by 1914, the work had begun: draining and filling the marsh with sludge, sand and dirt; engraving deep, broad shipping canals; constructing docks and wide paved roads, storage and docking amenities, connections to railways tracks. At the same time the renovation proceeded, a strip of public beaches and parks and bridle paths a thousand feet wide was being developed along the four miles of District lakefront, bringing into existence North America's first harbourfront reconstruction to take into account a city's need for both profit and fun.

Stinson's style of archaeology is notable for its sensitivity to the varied uses people have made of this place. Activities the author catalogues range from the mass-production of shells from scrap metal by an army of workers during the First World War to weekend cycling, and the serious back-seat sex that's still an important use of the dead-end roads of the District year round, and the production of a modern industrial port culture, joining humans and machines into a vivid whole.

Though a preservationist at heart, Stinson is also level-headed. He does not want the District frozen in place, turned into a theme park of Toronto Past, or an open-air museum of industrial archaeology. At the same time, he warns against any plan that does not mandate an adequate time-period for considering the possibilities of reuse offered by sturdy, workable abandoned buildings. Stinson does not hide his anxieties about developers who have exquisite, immaculate, computer-generated visions of a "perfect, money-making future" that would simply displace the untidy industrial zone with soaring condominiums and manicured parks.

Barring an unending depression of real-estate values in Toronto, it's probably only a matter of time before the suburban-biased Metro politicians and the land developers do indeed strike a deal to arrest the decay, purify the soil and put up bright new office blocks and condominiums and public housing on this site, so temptingly near downtown, and so blessed with uninterrupted, breathtaking views of the skyscrapers.

When I think of that, the perverse Jamesian resident in my ruin-seeking soul returns. I think of the loss of my refuge—which is a need, not just a diversion—and of the sites of thought to be lost by my anonymous compatriots, the many other lonely twilight walkers I have sighted on my visits to the Port Industrial District. Gone will be a certain free balm for the soul's inner noise, now so easily and quickly available on those broad avenues, where pools of waste water so beautifully catch and set shimmering the glow of our skyscrapers in their oily mirrors.

## THE JOHN INGLIS PLANT

In November, 1989, the last washing machine rattled off the assembly line at the 108-year-old John Inglis plant on Toronto's Strachan Avenue, just north of Exhibition Place, just south of King Street West.

The 650 workers who still had jobs at the end of the factory's decades of decline exchanged phone numbers and farewells over coffee, then punched out for the last time. And for the first time in more than a hundred years, the sprawling nine-hectare site suddenly became what it has been ever since: a dead zone of weedy gaps and unpeopled buildings, some vast and imposing, others mean, and yet another space of gloomy quiet in the once-mighty manufacturing district west of the downtown skyscrapers, along the lakefront railway tracks.

Only one mechanical object continues to animate the eerie stillness of the site: a high electrified sign adorned with the Inglis logo, and treating both inbound and outbound commuters on the Gardiner Expressway to a robotically flashing message of moral uplift. (Sample exhortation—it changes every day—: "Speak ill of none, but speak all the good you know of everyone.") A connoisseur of melancholy urban sites, willing to take an afternoon to kick around Inglis's rubble-strewn parking lot, will find much worth savouring in that scatter of structures. The red-brick Victorian Romanesque of an old jail incorporated long ago into the complex, for example; and the main plant's titanic modern pavilion, its horizontal walls made of glass framed in steel and reinforced concrete.

A forlorn majesty suffuses the site, confirming—as only once-great abandoned factories can—the truth of *sic transit gloria mundi*. Not even the tall sign with its moralizing electric message breaks the spell. It is a poignant reminder of the theory, dear to the hearts of Victorian colonial industrialists of the sort who founded Inglis, that an allotted burden of the rich was to raise the Common Folk's ethical standards and self-respect, by example and by education.

Yet along with eliciting regret for well-nigh vanished capitalist humanitarianism, the Inglis sign reminds us of the people who were the objects of this concern, the workers who toiled at this and the other industrial emplacements once so common in Toronto's downtown. Inglis produced indelible memories, sad and happy, it's worth recalling, as well as washing machines and such. It was a site of desire and narratives, the secret histories so easily dispersed when plants shut down, and of which the extant buildings, for all their impressive emptiness and wistful grandeur, never whisper a word.

"No matter how many new factories are built, no matter how many new jobs are found, the culture in the plant cannot be re-created," Toronto labour historian David Sobel and researcher Susan Meurer have written. "Workers' culture is the mortar between the bricks, the stuff that holds workers together, the salve that makes the hardness and roughness of daily work in a factory bearable."

The quote comes from what its authors call an "intelligent scrapbook"—a compilation called *Working at Inglis*, and underwritten by United Steelworkers of America local 2900, intended to preserve in words and pictures what traces remain of workers' culture at Inglis. A specialist in applied technology and communications, Sobel says that the project gave him the unexpected opportunity "to understand what a closure is all about." The project is partly an act of remembering, partly resistance to the forcible destruction of the past strongly linked to closings. As an automotive plant manager told Sobel: "Historical information about employees is non-value-added information, so we destroy it." Burrowing through the heaps of old ads and in-house publications and photos of Inglis workers toiling, boozing, dancing and striking which have survived loss and active suppression, one discovers the richness of that experiential tapestry woven at Inglis over the course of a century. The loom was the physical equipment itself, on which the working culture was formed. Inglis was always a zone of continuously changing technologies and ceaseless transformations of metal into myriad useful objects, from the day it opened at its present location in 1881. Early on, it made the engines and pumps for Toronto's 1883 massive expansion of water distribution; later it produced factory turbines and home water heaters, shells and howitzers, and, during the Second World War, 186,000 gas-operated Bren guns.

And forever easing the human hardships and hard work at Inglis was the salve of working-class culture, the chief interest of Sobel and Meurer. As many as twenty thousand people toiled in the plant during the era of Bren gun manufacture, but also fell in and out of love there, became enduring friends on the assembly line, and, after work, went over to the Palace Tavern on King Street to plan strikes and company shindigs, to cry the blues, to tell stories or just have some fun. Many of these workers were single young women, drawn from Canada's Depression-crushed towns to Toronto's war-inflated industrial operations. Many soon found their way to the Inglis Girls' Recreation Club, where friendship circles, "socials," cabaret performances, dancing lessons and other pleasures provided an antidote to the loneliness of city living and the monotony of the assembly line.

Now the charm of such memories is perilous, simply because nothing can be more effortlessly sentimentalized than the cultural life of a vanishing work force—especially when its artificiality and ideological function are forgotten or conveniently ignored. A bit reluctantly—both are leftist romantics at heart, even though they know better—Sobel and Meurer do remind us that the sedatives for homesickness provided by the long-vanished Recreation Club helped "reduce absenteeism and prevent (out-of-town immigrant) workers from returning...home," and kept the workers' energies focused on the industrial process.

Such strategic "culture" is something many urban wage-earners nowadays may have a hard time recognizing. Instead of taking anodynes provided by the plant, the post-industrial workforce provides its own, in our choices of distraction, movies and television shows, travel destinations, home-improvement schemes, consumer products. As surely as the Recreation Club kept the newly urbanized Inglis girls in line, so do expensive entertainments keep the informational proletariat of the late twentieth century—*us,* that is—mobilized, persuaded, and properly disposed towards management. All moments in the history of industrialization have had characteristic methods of shaping a reliable work-force—methods which, like Inglis's working culture, seem especially liable to be forgotten and disregarded when the process requiring them shuts down or is superseded.

Much of the value in a separate project, based on a heap of brief silent films Sobel unearthed while rummaging through the National Archives of Canada in Ottawa, lies in its unadorned recollection of this ideological grease, and how it has been marketed and applied. Though documentary evidence about these pictures is scarce, the basic information about their intent and target audience can be deduced from the seven shorts compiled by Sobel's Labour History Images Group in a video package called *The Moving Past*. All were made by the government of Ontario's now-disbanded Motion Picture Bureau, between the First World War and the Crash— a period notable for the remarkably rapid influx of rural folk into Toronto's industrialized workforce, and the intensification of mining activity in Ontario's north. *Her Own Fault* (1922), about the deportment of young female employees at Toronto's Gutta Percha Rubber Co., is aimed at young women new to both city life and the mechanized workplace. *Life In Mining Camp* (1921), on the other hand, is a direct appeal to out-of-work Toronto labourers—veterans returned from the war in Europe to recession and hardship—to forsake the big city and head north, where the pay is good and so's the grub. *A Story of Stone* (1924) is a lofty hymn to the nobility of stonework, from dusty quarry to sculpted quoin, from the building of Solomon's Temple to that of a neo-Gothic government office tower at Queen's Park; and seems to have been made to lure older school-kids into construction and associated trades.

But however various the audiences they were shot and edited for, however different the cinematic styling of each, all seven films gathered in *The Moving Past* nourish an attitude of compliance and conformity, satisfaction with one's place in the swiftly changing army of industrial producers, and admiration for assembly line and the rationalization of work.

The agenda is easiest to see (and comes across funniest) in *Her Own Fault*. This little melodrama about two newcomers to industry shows the rise of delightful Eileen, who leaps out of bed early, does calisthenics at morning "rest period," is not ashamed to wear glasses as she mass-produces shoe heels, and enjoys embroidering and chatting with the other girls during lunch break. She is humble, industrious, contented, and she spends her evenings in healthy recreation, such as canoeing with her friends.

Eileen's demonic opposite is Mamie, who gobbles her food, wears spike heels and is too vain to wear glasses (even though she needs them). Because she's "too nervous to rest" in the evening, Mamie flings herself each night into orgies of dance-hall shimmying. In the end, as the caption tells us, "both girls get what was coming to them": Eileen, a promotion and, it's hinted, a beau; and dissolute Mamie, tuberculosis and a pink slip.

The other films are more subtle, and some are beautifully crafted. Both *Silver Mining in Ontario* (1919) and *Making of an 8" Explosive Howitzer Shell* (1918) present heroic, pulse-quickening portraits of complex production. The brilliant film about the Howitzer shell, by the way, is less documentary than avant-garde rhapsody, a jagged song to precision military technology and—the true object of worship—the robotized workplace.

Sobel's works of recollection address (though they occasionally become complicit with) the tendency of contemporary academics and some white-collar labourers to romanticize Inglis beauty pageants, the passion of its union's strikes and other aspects of disappearing working-class culture. They do not encourage as much critical attention as they should to the facts and ideological lubricants of post-industrial work-life.

At their best, however, these projects remind us of the odd way historic methods of mind-moulding slide into oblivion, and they rebuke a trend among urbanists and the architecturally interested public towards a purely formal appreciation of former plants.

They are Parthenons, our Colosseums, the architectonic climaxes of our industrial civilization's physical mark upon the world, and, as such, sites saturated in thought and memory. While Ruskin would doubtless be horrified at the use to which I'm putting his words, factories finely illustrate the dictum, pronounced in his essay on memory, the sixth of *The Seven Lamps of Architecture:* "There are but two strong conquerors of the forgetfulness of men, Poetry and Architecture; and the latter in some sort includes the former, and is mightier in its reality." So while not opposed in principle to swooning at the rusty front gate of a dilapidated vacuum-cleaner plant, or admiring in timeless aesthetic bliss a harbourside grain elevator whose day is over, I agree with Prince Charles—who would, like Ruskin, be scandalized to know he'd been put among the factory fans—that "when a man loses contact with the past he loses his soul. Likewise, if we deny the architectural past—and the lessons to be learnt from our ancestors—then our buildings also lose *their* souls."

The sort of research being conducted among former Inglis employees can provide a useful corrective—or addition—to the formalist forgetfulness afflicting current industrial preservationism. The ideal candidates for this salvation are retired work-environments which appear to have been sanitized by a neutron bomb—every brick and mullion and spandrel intact and subject to inspection and criticism, but devoid of memory, of *thinking,* and of every trace of the cultural fabric people spin around machines in the architecture of production.

Of course, a dead factory is very often a thing of remarkable beauty. Gazing across an immense, silent shop-floor cleared of machines and noise, lit only by afternoon sunshine slanting through curtain walls of dusty glass, anyone with eyes to see would be moved by the clear flow and austere elegance of modern manufacturing space. Yet in all such appreciation for the purely architectural and engineered, there lurks a spirit of pastoralism, of reluctance—especially stylish among architectural connoisseurs at the present moment—to accept the ceaseless ripping down, tearing up and rearranging things that every great and living city is very much about.

Surely, we need it all. An appreciation for the material craft which has given us the industrial infrastructure of modern life, and artifacts to support this appreciation. And also the awareness that abandoned factories, in addition to their often magisterial and tragic beauty, were once sites in which men and women, managers and wage-slaves, bosses and minions, together created durably interesting narratives of conflict, technique, human agency and human cooperation.

## CANADA MALTING

"Our eyes are constructed to enable us to see forms in light," wrote Le Corbusier in his famous 1923 tract *Towards a New Architecture,* then decreed: "Primary forms are beautiful forms because they can be clearly appreciated."

To illustrate his point, he littered his pages with photographs of Canadian and American grain elevators, and thus touched off a fascination with North American silos and such—the functional spin-offs of industrial process—not dead among urban visionaries to this day. The buildings of Le Corbusier and other pioneers of heroic Modernism "were explicitly adapted from these sources," architect Robert Venturi has written, "largely for their symbolic content, because industrial structures represented, for European architects, the brave new world of science and technology," while buildings referring to the masterpieces of the past did not.

Heavy production facilities still cast a spell, though less as mentors than as victims. Perhaps it is in our nature to want to spare victims, including architectural ones. In any case, the affection for North America's decrepit, abandoned and doomed industrialization is today as fervent as ever, at least among the watchers, guardians and students of built form.

Toronto's port facilities, once the pride of our inner harbour, provide an excellent example of the dynamics of this desire.

With the decline in Great Lakes shipping from the end of the Second World War into the 1960s, the grimy industrial emplacements on Toronto's inner harbour were doomed. Recognizing this, in 1972 the federal government, hand-in-glove (as usual) with developers on to a good thing, stepped in to "save" our waterfront—i.e., knock down almost everything in sight, and sponsor the "renewal" of the former industrial zone as an upmarket condominium market and recreational and "cultural" fantasy-land.

Whereupon the second sort of concern with the older architecture kicked in, inspiring urban archaeologists, architectural historians and the heritage people to join forces in efforts to spare examples of vanishing port industrial culture. They saved very few reminders of Toronto's historic orientation towards the Great Lakes marine highway; so today, much of the passion is focused on the Canada Malting complex on Bathurst Quay, one of the only defunct industrial plants on the inner harbour to have so far escaped the wrecker's ball.

The harbourside complex is not old. The silos were put up in 1928 for the storage of barley, hauled in on Great Lakes ships, for transformation into malt. In 1944, the plant capacity was doubled, to meet increased demands for booze and other malt products, and buildings continued to go up until 1961. But even though Canada Malting is no antique, the cracks and pocks and water stains on the grey concrete cylindrical shells, the ignored fine brick cornices on the germinating house, the unchecked shrouding by vines of a *Moderne* office building in the shadow of the tall silos, even the burned-out boat slowly rotting on the grounds, all make this ruin an affecting artifact, and help explain the outlay of time that has gone towards saving it.

In early 1988, only weeks after the factory's November, 1987, shutdown, Toronto City Council struck a committee representing a number of keen public and private interests, to look at possible futures for Canada Malting. In September, 1992, some forty architects, artists, urban planners and historians gathered in Toronto to ponder the future of the former storage and processing facility, then the property of the federal government, and since deeded to the City of Toronto.

In the late summer of 1993, city planners issued their most specific call to date for plans to "restore, reuse and maintain" the complex. By that autumn, a number of proposals had come in, most obviously unfeasible, a couple—one, to turn the silos into recording studios, classrooms and other facilities for musical production and study; another, to make a kind of *son-et-lumiere* out of it all—were felt by city officials to have promise. Everyone is united in a belief that the silos should be saved, that is; some people even have ideas that might work. Nobody, to my knowledge, has come up with anything that would save the taxpayers the expense of just forgetting about Canada Malting altogether. Demolition is estimated to be a $3 million job, according to planners, and would sweep away one of Toronto's best examples of an original North American building type. The other would be mothballing, which would cost about $1 million for starters, consume some $38,000 a year in maintenance, and give the taxpayers nothing in return, except an old artifact, continually in need of face-lifts and cosmetic touch-ups, to look at.

While, in principle, I favour the recycling option, I am not optimistic that an economical reuse for these buildings will ever be possible.

Now, before anybody pops a copy of the Toronto Historical Board's *Silos Can Be Re-Used!* into an envelope and posts it to me, let me say I've got a copy already, and find both the THB's two examples of redeployment wanting.

Exhibit A is the Quaker Square Hilton in Akron, Ohio, the handiwork of Curtis & Rasmussen Architects. Finished in 1980, this project involved the conversion of thirty-six former oats silos and related buildings into a hotel and commercial and retail mall, three restaurants and four nightclubs, all under the same roof. Unlike any such fun paradise that might get built on Bathurst Quay, however, the Hilton is downtown, not on a windswept jut of landfill, separated by an expressway from Toronto's bright lights—though, to be sure, the advantages of a downtown location in Akron is offset by surroundings so depressed and depressing that few Hilton visitors venture outside its maze of shops and clubs and rooms. Sources both inside and outside Akron's hotel business have described the Hilton to me as an island resort in a sea of nothingness. But what tourist or business traveller would ever want to stay on isolated Bathurst Quay, with myriad hotels in the very midst of downtown Toronto's shops and cultural attractions?

In any case, the mid-1990s is not the time to raise the hotel option. According to John Hamilton, spokesman for the Metropolitan Toronto Convention and Visitors Association, "there is no room in Toronto for new hotels." The city now has 15,414 rooms downtown, and 32,030 Metro-wide, with a steadily declining average occupancy rate over the past three years—a glut, says Hamilton, caused by massive overbuilding in the 1980s.

Exhibit B is La Fabrica, the Barcelona home and office of architect Ricardo Bofill, his "freethinking lay convent, dedicated to work." The old cement factory on which Bofill and his colleagues performed their genuinely delightful magic, between 1973 and 1975, was a disused group of short silos and extensive underground passages and surface structures, set in a dry, rugged Mediterranean landscape begging for the oasislike gardens eventually planted there by the architect and his associates. Now, a highly inventive and extremely rich architectural partnership might be able to turn Canada Malting into a faintly similar fantasia—though the cold, flat lakeshore setting, the dank silos and oily waters of the lake, will never add up to Catalonia.

The city's 1993 call reminded the interested citizens of what could be put on the Canada Malting site under then-current zoning regulations, and urged them to think "community centre," "public playground," "elementary school," "day nursery," and other programming of a "cultural" or "artistic" nature—everything, that is, except a much-needed infusion of heavy, imaginative private capital. While artists in need of cheap studios and parents in need of day-care facilities will likely find these prospects exciting, the city's lack of interest in attracting serious investment to Bathurst Quay should alert Toronto taxpayers to the absurdity of encouraging idealistic folk to make outlandish proposals to a municipality already strapped for cash, for a general area already much damaged by piecemeal planning and short-sighted development.

At the time of this writing, no decision has been taken. But since large private investment is not likely to be forthcoming, I cast my vote with great reluctance for a possibly viable scheme that surfaced briefly during the 1992 think-session.

It would involve the takeover of the silos by the Archives of Ontario for use as the central storehouse for about 200,000 cubic feet of documents and historic materials now scattered among warehouses throughout Metro. The cost of converting plant to archive has been variously estimated by federal and provincial offices at between $80 million and $100 million, while a new building on some other site would come in at between $40 million and $80 million, plus land and site preparation costs. Whatever the exact figure might turn out to be, retrofitting would probably be more expensive at the end of the day—and, given Ontario's dim financial prospects, a go-ahead for a huge capital building project of this sort should not be given without the gravest consideration. At the present time, that consideration would almost certainly result in the nixing of the project.

But, were this interesting pipe dream to come true, at least a good use would have been found for the factory's thick, solid walls and the silos' adjacent office buildings. Architectural preservationists would get the industrial fabric intact, without windows punched in it and with few other rude external changes. The province would have its long-needed central storage facility. A forgotten place would again become a place that thinks, that recollects and provides room for recollection. And all of us would see the humane resolution of yet another bit of business left dangling after twenty years of our waterfront's thoughtless devastation and transformation by governments and private interests.

# *On the Land*

*Holiday Inn, Toronto West*

# THE SHAPE OF THE CITY

A couple of autumns ago, after Toronto caught its first snowfall of the season, I rang up Environment Canada's Ontario Climate Centre to find out what they could tell me about this debut.

The weatherfolk there seemed faintly perplexed by my call. After all, everybody who knows Toronto knows the annual rhythms of cold and snow, which determine so much of what we do, and how and when we do it. As climatologist Bryan Smith confirmed, the first serious snowfall had come that year around the same time as always, the middle of November. And, as usual, it was a trifle: just 63,000 litres of frozen water—which sounds like a lot of water to me, but, said Smith, was nothing to get excited over—descending on Metro's 632 square kilometres. The fall began before dawn, and had stopped nearly everywhere before noon.

Throughout the city that early morning, in Forest Hill palaces and Etobicoke ranch-styles and Scarborough bungalows, Metropolitan Toronto's millions enacted the first rites of winter. Among them: locating the car-window brush, and discovering you forgot to replace last year's broken one; and rummaging inside the hall closet for overshoes and the kids' boots, devoured by the darkness deep behind the coats on the last day of slush the spring before. And remembering how much longer than usual it will take to get to work or school.

These are not weighty matters. Winter in Toronto is not as dangerously cold and stormy as it is on the Canadian prairies, or as windy and wet as the Maritimes. It does not endure as long as winter in Montreal, nor is it, say lifelong residents, as long and severe in Toronto as it used to be. Nor do we get the very heavy accumulations of snow that regularly paralyze nearby Buffalo and Rochester. To dwellers in this city and climate, winter is merely an inevitable fact of life, like aging, to be got through as gracefully as possible.

Because it is neither especially mild nor particularly snowy, Toronto's winter is no source of joy, except to skiers. But to those of us who don't ski, and who grew up in warm climes where "snow" was a kind of toxic plastic fuzz sprayed from a can on Christmas trees, the first Toronto fall of the season brings an ineffable lift and delight, and a novelty most born-and-bred Canadians never know.

Of course, this enchantment will wear off halfway through the second snowstorm. By March, I'll be disliking the threatening skies and blowing snowflakes as much as anyone else who drives or walks around town. But throughout the first snowfall's early hours, the city seems to lie under a spell, everything transformed.

An air of great beauty—solemn, subtle, softly calm—graces the town's streets and structures. All the usual bright colours and sharp, tall shapes of the urban cityscape have been softened over night, as though wrapped in cloud. The top of the wooden fence outside the bedroom window, the angry brow of an ecclesiastical gargoyle I pass each morning, even the round lids of the wine barrels stored in my neighbour's backyard—so many dark, ordinary things we seldom notice—all seem strangely vivid, as though heightened by sweeping strokes and dense scrubbings of luminous silvery chalk.

Driving my daughter to school in this first wintry weather, I enjoy glimpses of the deep ravine that cuts south from St. Clair

Avenue West near Spadina Road. It's just a gloomy winter gulch lined with dry, sharp trees, rasping against each other in the autumn wind, until the snow comes. Then it becomes an abstract etching composed of ricocheting, criss-crossing black lines, the bare undersides of branches sketched on the greys, whites, silvers of snowy backdrops and shroudings.

Most Torontonians, I suppose, find snow a kind of lovely nuisance. If thought of at all, it's the only substance that can provide a delightful sport and, after pollution by salt-bearing humans, rot your car. I cannot say precisely when snow became more interesting to me than just that, though it seems to have been during a time of much reading about the underground art of our stone-age European ancestors. Those people who so splendidly decorated the famous caves of Spain and the south of France lived in a cold world only gradually returning to general plant and animal inhabitation after a glaciation of great expanse and devastating force. Prehistorians naturally give scant notice to the ice sheet, since nobody and no animal lived on it, or survived its crushing advance. But snow is wonderful and fearful, especially when it stops being the ephemeral thing Torontonians experience, and begins to add up and up—as it has done on this continent, every few thousand years, for a very long time—becoming a tool of almost unimaginably grand devastation and transformation. One can live happily forever in Toronto without giving mind to the glacier that once bore down upon this site. But nobody can understand the cityscape without acknowledging the vast powers which created it.

The landform over which Metro sprawls today was crossed by the Wisconsin glacier—the fourth to crush our territory in the last million years—and rendered lifeless by this advancing sheet of snow-driven ice more than 110,000 years ago. Then, about 13,000 years before the present, as the most recent glaciation was ending across North America, the layer of ice melted away in our neighbourhood, leaving the Great Lakes behind as a memento, and an unspeakable mess of frozen mud, rubble and clay. After the titanic weight of ice, the next principal instrument of landscape formation was the enormous volume of melt water released by the retreating glacier. We have this water to thank for the creation of Metro's treasured pattern of sharp, deep ravines, and the division of its site into two more or less distinct levels.

North of the steep drop-off running lengthwise across the city between St. Clair Ave. West and Davenport Road is a high, well-drained plateau, rising gently as it backs away from Lake Ontario, and much scarred by valleys and gulleys. The downtown skyscrapers and all other structures built south of Davenport stand, in contrast, on the low, swampy bed of postglacial Lake Iroquois, still a deep catch-basin for the glacial runoff less than 12,000 years ago. After the waters had fallen below the clay bluffs and rocky beaches of Lake Ontario, the great forest took root where it could, among the beaver ponds and marshes on the old lake-bottom. The early explorers who passed this way were struck by the thick stands of walnut, sycamore and chestnut edging Lake Ontario; de Lamothe Cadillac, in 1702, viewed these hardwood stands as "so temperate, so good and beautiful that one can justly call it the earthly paradise of North America." Cadillac knew nothing of the glaciers, of course, since their existence had not yet been discovered. The land, however, remembered the high, ancient lake on whose bottom the beautiful forests stood. Its steep, long shoreline is balefully familiar to anyone who's ever skidded in an icestorm down the abrupt decline of Avenue Road (or Yonge Street, or Dufferin) south of St. Clair.

To imagine the titanic and enduring force of those endless winters 18,000 years ago is to start recognizing what snow can do, which is infinitely more than send you into a fender-bending skid. Fortunately, life is short enough that no one now living has to think about the next ice age. For Bryan Smith, my informant at Environment Canada, the more immediate worry is global warming. If it continues, he warns, this gradual rise in world temperatures could loose the waters now frozen in the polar ice-caps, causing a rise in sea levels, and thus drowning Vancouver, New York, New Orleans. In sharp contradiction to griping Toronto snow-shovellers, Smith says that annual snowfall in Toronto has in fact been *decreasing* over the last several years.

But that there will eventually be another ice age, erasing all traces of our passage and again reconfiguring the face of the land, is virtually certain, and also worthy of contemplation, according to Canadian scientist E. C. Pielou, author of *After the Ice Age.*

Pielou is not a popularizer. Her book is a heavy-going technical study done for fellow specialists, not interested eavesdroppers like me. But you don't have to be a scientist to understand one well-argued observation in this book: that the current epoch of Canada's geological history is *glacial,* meaning that for most of the last million years massive ice sheets have lain over huge areas of the continent—though every now and again we get a brief melt-away, such as the present one. The interglacial warm spells are always short; and this one is due to end soon, Pielou believes, slowly allowing the return of winters that never cease.

The next glaciation will begin with an almost imperceptibly slow back-up of the date of each year's first snowfall. Symmetrically, the spring melt will begin later, and the winter's snow will run off slower.

Then, after a great many years, somewhere far to the north of Toronto, summer will gradually close down to a brief interval between snowfalls, then be extinguished altogether. The snows will never stop, and the white ground cover will never melt. And thus the glacial age will begin in earnest, with the inexorable compression of underlying snow by new snowfalls on top, locking up almost unimaginable volumes of water in a steadily growing ice sheet. Meanwhile, our more southerly summers will be disappearing, gardens will no longer grow, the beautiful hardwood forests of the Toronto region will die off as tundra conditions again come gradually to prevail.

Now few Torontonians will still be around by the time the enormous build-up of snow begins to push the ice sheet southward, crushing the low hills of Muskoka and Haliburton, bulldozing the abandoned towns and villages into oblivion. No one will be left to witness the approach of the grinding ice, wreathed in eternal, swirling snows, on the edge of our doomed northern suburbs. But if our distant descendants, hundreds of generations hence, will have found refuge in some warmer clime, the architectural trace we and our ancestors have made on this land will disappear forever.

I am not trying to ruin anybody's day with all this talk of disaster and disappearance. It's just that living fully and mindfully anyplace, I believe, involves giving thought to all the rhythms we move within—the personal ones, from birth to death, but also the historical ones, preserved and recalled by the artifacts of architecture and urban planning, art and writing and music. And the far grander cycles, as well, which leave their evidence inscribed in the clay and dirt, the topography and scenery, on which Torontonians have dwelt, worked, made love and brought forth children, gardened and worshipped and built for the first two centuries of our fragile urban prevailing.

## LIVING WITH WHAT IS

Given the remoteness of the next glaciation, it's enough for now to think about the land under our feet and weathers over our heads, and how these mutable facts shape even our intimate, simplest decisions. Like the time we leave the house for work, for example—later than usual on an icy day, so as to make sure the road-crews have salted the roads descending

*Near Bathurst Street, January*

down the old Lake Iroquois shoreline, where no up-and-down roads should ever have been built. Or the exact spot in the soil you plant your clematis. This glorious high-summer vine, by the way, likes Toronto's sunny summers; but it will never understand if you thrust it unceremoniously into the ground without first loosening and treating the tough, sticky glacial clay, everywhere just below our paper-thin topsoil. You must carefully make a place for any clematis you want to grow. You've got the last advance of the ice sheet to thank for that.

In fact, the way one gardens is perhaps the best indicator of how well he or she has accepted the great, but also the minutely specific, natural framework in which living and working are done here.

Until recently, I was not a gardener, and despite some study and practical learning, am still an ignorant one. Not so my grandmother and Aunt Vandalia, in whose rambling house and ample grounds I lived and played for a few childhood years. They gardened as ferociously as their unswerving Victorian commitment to a deathly pale complexion allowed. And with the help of a handyman to do the hard work, they kept the grounds of their comfortable Edwardian house ineffably beautiful with exquisite old roses, wisteria, common honeysuckle and other blooming things, aristocratic and common. It was perhaps these early memories—a curious mix of recollections about fragrances and colours at twilight, fireflies among the night-blooming blossoms, bee-stings and thorn-pricks, blue bottles of poisons in the shed, the scatter of petals on the grass after a storm—that left me with an enduring delight in idly leafing through gardening books, and a permanent belief that someday I would get my hands into dirt.

I eventually did so a few years ago, after settling into the reconstructed tool-and-die factory I call home. The only available open space for a garden was a large third-storey deck, which faces south and, on sunny days, is gloriously bright and warm. The dirt, hauled up the stairs bag by bag, was dumped into insulated wooden planters I designed and had built; and into the dirt went vines, small trees, shrubs and annuals. And shouldering up out of the ground or gushing from unpromising stalks and trunks came much beauty—not exactly what I'd hoped for, and nothing I dare take credit for, but a sobering lesson, as things turned out, in the variously shy, pushy, mischievous and pampered personalities of plants. Contrary to what the stern greenhouse people told me, by the way, the clematis variety Lady Betty Balfour loves its place aloft, and is not a bit snobbish about having to look at a toilet factory's backside and a laneway teeming, in summer, with muscle cars, boom boxes turned up to max.

My decision to create a garden came at almost the same time as the assignment to write a column about city sites; and, though I didn't realize it at first, my deck garden was to become a particularly subtle, intimate tool for learning Toronto, the weathers and winds, spectra of light and atmospheres specific to this place, and what it means to live, and live *here.* While I spend considerable time with my plant books, at least in winter, I am only interested in facts that help me refine the instrument of discovery my garden has become. To make a garden of salad greens in Toronto strikes me as time-wasting and even faintly strange, given the ready availability of locally grown, cheap greens at the grocers throughout the summer months. Nor do great formal gardens, with their immaculate lawns and intricately orchestrated plantings, have any appeal. Of the other sorts of stately European gardens—the rationalist Italian or English Romantic ones, for instance—I have read something, but apparently not enough to make me go out of my way to visit one.

My earliest model—indeed, the garden that got me started in earnest—lies just beyond the edge of Toronto's eastward reach, on the country property of gifted city friends who are together creating a garden very much attuned to our soil and bugs, breezes and droughts and downpours. It has been organized with a casually theatrical sense, but without ostentation. Turning off the town road into the driveway, the visitor in mid-June is immediately saluted by a line of rose bushes, their abundant blossoms bright and alert as an honour guard. Arriving at the house, one is greeted by an informal platoon of more frank, sociable blue and yellow flowers blooming by the door.

But it's in the garden proper—the array of flowers low and tall, noble as roses and ordinary as daisies, falling away from the conservatory window down a gentle, shaded slope—that the real enchantment lies. The uncareful observer would sense little evidence of the assiduous planning that came before the blooming—simply because the florals and non-flowering plants seem so much at home there. The ground cover of low plants ranging in colour from acrid green to a burnished silver, the taller flowers, those translucent dabs of white and yellow watercolour on a rough ground, cascades of roses on the garden wall, the gradual opening of the view through the trees towards the farmer's field beyond: it all appears effortless, without rigour.

Until you sit a while under those tall trees, considering the visual music of the garden's layout. Melodic transitions take place, from a wall of climbing roses which stop the eye with a barrier of matronal opulence, through an open conference of large golden blossoms nodding on tall stems, to the sunshine of that very different world of growing things, the field.

When I asked the lady of the garden to explain how it all worked, she gladly obliged. It's a planned and carefully tended project, she told me, but not so perfectly organized that it becomes an abstract exercise, or a kind of botanical travelogue of some other clime or place. It's deliberately not meant to transcend its site on the depleted soil of old Ontario farming country, with the trying, tiresomely unpredictable winters and abruptly hot summers. It's not supposed to turn into a fantasia of ye olde England, or anywhere else. Rather, this garden is to

be both beautiful and tough; a haven, to be sure, but also a
kind of vegetative architecture that never forgets what and
where it is.

Every garden embodies some kind of symbolism of human
dwelling, some suggestion of a strategy for living. To this
viewer, the garden of our friends is about survival and grace
under pressure. The pressure is great and unceasing, from crit-
ters of four to innumerable legs, from disease, from blustery
summer storms and snapping winter cold and blasting, intol-
erant sunshine year-round. The beauty here has been hard-
won; but, in good southern Ontario fashion, the flowers that
have survived adversity bear their triumph modestly, as though
nothing could have been easier.

Some day the bugs and blights may win, because our
friends will move along, and newcomers without any interest
in this green building will take up residence in the shaded
house. Until then, however, the present tenders expect to go
on minding their plot, as one aspect of the quietly defiant attitude towards life and work they share—though they do not
talk about gardening in so hifalutin a way. That manner
belongs to us Toronto-dwellers, out for the day, and out of the
usual urban power-game, involving mastery and defeat.

We do have such a hard time with things that will not
bend to our will. Rivers, for example, always seem to be in the
"wrong" place. Therefore, they must must be bridged, redi-
rected, dammed, or channelled through concrete pipes. Hills
must be amputated or swept aside altogether to make way for
roads. Swamps are almost always "wrong"; they must be filled.
And if a feature of the natural world is simply too big to "correct"—the Great Lakes, for example—it still must be subju-
gated to human use, as a power source, or merely a sump for
our poisons. The project of Western urbanism, which our
branch of the human family abruptly embarked upon eight
thousand years ago in the Middle East, has never been minded
just to let things be as they are. Our work has always been one

of eliminating the "wrongness" of Nature, and making it conform to our notion of "rightness."

Which is exactly why gardening under the unsteady weathers and in the bad soil of Ontario is instructive, and a good way to learn grace and patience where we really are. We cannot correct Nature; we can only change it a little, into the "Nature" which Aldo Rossi defines as "the artificial homeland which contains all the experiences of mankind." Yet it forcefully remains itself, neither Eden nor pure Culture. My friends' plot is certainly no Garden of Eden. It's just Ontario as it can be, given time and a certain devotion to tending and letting be, and knowing the difference between the two.

## DWELLING AND THE GROUP OF SEVEN

Beshorted in cabbage-green Bermudas picked up at Sears on the way out of town, equipped with a gym bag full of books that really ought to be ploughed through someday—say, the novels of Edith Wharton—and armed with a vat of bug-off, I joined the tense, sluggish flow of cars northward on the expressway one recent summer Friday. Three hours, two pit-stops for the kid, and one milk-shake spilled all over the back seat later, we'd reached Fairy Lake, to which a family friend had kindly invited us.

The lake is a sheet of water sheltered by low hills, near Huntsville. The cottage itself, which Anita has been renting for the summer since time out of mind, is a charming story-book house built in the 1930s, nestled among throngs of unattended blue and golden perennials planted long ago. I was bewitched by the hammock slung between tall pines on a broad lawn sloping down to the shore. Three days after touchdown, not one book had been opened, there was sand in my shoes, and cottage country had worked its spell, melting away city knots I didn't even know I had.

At Fairy Lake, there may be more to that spell than just warm sun and sparkling blue water. The lake was given its curious name by the first European settlers in the area, who had heard from the native people that spirits haunted the waters. Early lakeside dwellers reported strange voices in the night, and mysterious lights skittering over the surface. Whether or not the lake's magic is otherworldly, it surely touched the imagination of Canada's first important modern artists. Tom Thomson, the extraordinary Canadian landscape painter, dropped by on one of his sketching trips into Ontario's north woods. A result of that stop was an oil, done in 1912, called *Fairy Lake*. Both Arthur Lismer and A. Y. Jackson, later founding members of Canada's nationalistic Group of Seven landscape painters, visited Thomson at Fairy Lake, and may have sketched with him there.

As often happens when the art-minded venture into Ontario's near north, thoughts turn almost automatically to an interesting puzzle of Canadian culture. When we look out the cottage window at, say, a sunset smouldering over the sparkling waves, *exactly* what are we seeing? Is it Nature, redolent with raw, primordial beauty? Or are we seeing a scene so subtly colonized by our experience of landscape paintings, that we can't tell the difference any more? Is that really a glorious sunset? Or did we learn the meaning of *glorious* from a painting by some member of the Group of Seven?

After all, the visual education of Ontarians, and perhaps all Canadians, is saturated with Group pictures, whether in the real or in reproduction. Each year, some forty-five thousand school children are bussed down to the Art Gallery of Ontario to look at some of Canada's most famous landscape paintings. Those who grow up to become gallery-goers will certainly be seeing that art, in settings ranging from special exhibits to permanent displays, every year, probably forever. And even those who never set foot in a gallery after high-school graduation will never quite escape the calendars and posters, postcards and greeting cards, or the bottom-line fact that Group works are among the most highly valued Canadian artworks, predictably making auction-room news a couple of times each season.

There's no scientific way to tell how much of Fairy Lake is nature, and how much is art. But dozing on the dock through a Saturday afternoon, with my toes in the waters, I made certain common-sense observations that may have a bearing on the case.

The day was muggily hot, hazy and still, with a thin grey scrim covering the sky. The hills across the lake were dull olive-green. A tiny, rocky island between this side and the far shore was an angular blackish brown sherd against the gun-metal water.

By that time, I was no longer surprised to catch myself thinking: "It's just not a Group of Seven kind of day"—a day of stormy lights, of water lashed by summer storms or made irridescent by brilliant, failing light. What is odd is the way Fairy Lake, overcast and calm, tends to disappear, or become strangely remote. The lake doesn't look much different from Lake Ontario on a dog day afternoon.

In reality, a muggy day in Muskoka during August is not unusual. Despite the regional tourist hype, the stuffy weather farther south often creeps up north of Orillia, into the rocky lakes clawed open by the ice centuries ago. This condition may be disappointing to those who have fled Toronto for what they believe will be cooler climes—but definition, not disappointment, is what I'm talking about here. A hot, becalmed Fairy Lake seems to disappear from our mental atlas of "cottage country sites" at the precise moment it no longer evokes the nationalist, nativist, vitalistic mystique of Group painting. It comes back, however, as soon as the wind whips up, the clouds become ragged and the water begins to lash the boathouse.

There is nothing really peculiar about this common experience. The visual codes of painterly wildness, freedom, urgency, the primitive and such have become the basis of our visual doctrine about what's really cottage country and what isn't—supplying, that is, all that's missing from the *real* Muskoka spectacle of endless electrified, plumbered, septic-tanked little lakeside houses, each with its gas barbecue and each readily accessible by paved road. But our eyes forget things slowly, and the codes of popular art most slowly of all.

Even so, the staying power of the Group's ways of seeing the world is a remarkable fact. Notable recent attempts to re-vision the Ontario landscape have been made by a number of contemporary Canadian painters. But whatever their interest to art-world professionals—and the interest is often keen— these attempts to debunk or displace or revise the Group's visual myths haven't worked. At least not on the level of those forty-five thousand school children who are guided through the AGO each year, or for the millions for whom Canadian art *is* Group art, and Group art is the only true national art. It should come as no surprise that every weekend between Victoria Day and Thanksgiving, *Tout* Toronto hits the great road north, to see—actually *see*—a visual world constructed by a few magnificent and wonderfully memorable paintings done at the far side of the twentieth century.

But did the Group of Seven know both ethos and public *too* well, and address their nation a little *too* cannily? They were certainly in a professional position to do so, since almost all the future group artists earned their living as commercial artists in the Toronto studio of Grip Ltd., using its offices as a kind of clubhouse in the years leading up to their 1920 launch. The Grip touch is certainly to be found in many a slick, illustra-tional canvas and sketch by group members, early and late. Many a finished Group canvas seems more cartoonish than painterly, more akin to drawings in popular field-and-stream magazines than alert to the venerable traditions of landscape painting. And the work often seems dated by its lazy display of gimmicks and flourishes borrowed from popular design trends such as Art Nouveau or Art Deco; see, for example the streamlined styling affected by Lawren Harris when trying to be very inspirational to us all, and the stiff, furniture-like *Jugendstil* of Thomson at his least inspired.

But having said all that, we can still be impressed and moved by the most restless, thoughtful work of the Seven. Indeed, I suspect that we may yet have much to learn from the Group of Seven, despite the fame of these artists and the scholarly effort expended on their art over the past three decades. Perhaps the day has come for an exhibition that will chart the relation of Canada's best-known images in painting, not back to antecedents in high art, but out to the actual day-to-day operation of Toronto's Grip Ltd. and the industries of mass communications, advertising and north-country tourism in Canada during the first three decades of this century. By placing the group's work in the context of consumerism in the Edwardian and postwar Dominion, even the images of the North we know best might be coaxed into disclosing their origin in *Toronto's* urban understanding of itself, in the nostalgia that city-folk often develop for rural zones, the oppressions and bitter hardships of which they no longer have to endure.

# Binding and
# Loosing the Waters

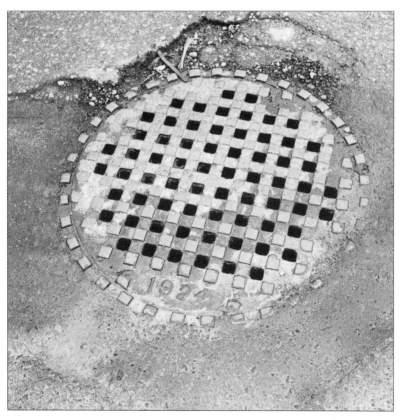

*Manhole, 1924*

# Lost Streams

If we think of vanished urban beauty, the ghosts of foolishly demolished buildings—remembrances of photographs, old drawings—are the first things that pass before our inner eye. We think less readily, for some reason, of the myriad ancient streams and brooks and little rivers, all but the largest of which—the Don River and the Humber—were beneath the concrete a century ago.

On a city map drawn up in 1884, we find that Mount Pleasant Creek, just at the northern edge of the urban advance, had already been pushed underground as it approached the Don River. Rosedale Brook was still running free through its deep ravine, and thence into the Don—though a little way upstream, it was already inside brick tunnels and under earth. This creek was open only north of Yorkville, a respectable suburban village in decline before its annexation by Toronto in 1883. By the turn of this century—like so many formerly clear downtown streams, providing delightful banks for picnics— Castle Frank Brook had become a sluggish, stinking ditch, and so was banished under Rosedale Valley Road where it still flows through its conduit. Indeed, a close look at the 1898 city map turns up very few streams still above ground anywhere south of Bloor Street, the venerable dividing line laid out by Toronto founder and governor John Graves Simcoe in the

1790s between Civilization and Beyond, and still our most famous cross-street. Russell Creek, which provided water for cows grazing below Bloor alongside dusty, rural Bathurst Street is gone, doomed to burial, along with the others, by the powerful surge of Toronto's population in late Victorian times.

Among the more lamentable of these disappearances is Taddle Creek, which rises from springs north of St. Clair Avenue and to this day feeds a pond under 250-year-old oaks in Wychwood Park, a secluded residential estate on the escarpment north of Davenport Road and west of Bathurst, then empties south under the bus barn of the Toronto Transit Commission. As recently as 1886, Taddle Creek sparkled in the meadows, shaded hillsides and tangled ravines of Queen's Park, future site of the Ontario Legislature. This much, we know from a charming painting of that year called *Barbara and Alice, Queen's Park,* at the Art Gallery of Ontario, a work of Marmaduke Matthews, who incidentally founded and planned Wychwood Park. In it two young ladies relax by the rivulet, now deep under the park. (The boring flatness of Queen's Park was inflicted during a revision of its original picturesque appearance, which had been created by landscape architect William Mundy in the 1850s.)

From Queen's Park, then part of the University of Toronto and still owned by it, Taddle Creek went underground, flowing through sewers or meandering through basements beneath "new" downtown, west of Yonge Street and far west of the old town of York—though at least the name of the stream has survived, if not the sight of it, in the name of a short, dead-end lane on the University of Toronto campus.

On this map of 1898, at least one remnant of the vast network of streams draining Toronto can still be detected: a short stretch of Garrison Creek, still wandering freely north of Bloor Street westward as far as Ossington Avenue. That twisting line, no wider than a silk thread on the large map, is all that remains to remind us of the creek that once supplied the Imperial

*Grape Spill, Emerson Alley*

legions stationed at Fort York with an easily defensible, navigable source of abundant fresh water—hence its name—and also supplied a good reason for centring the fortification there.

In the boom years before the First World War, Toronto did its best to erase the streams from the cityscape, for two reasons. The first, and more commendable, had to do with the stinking hazard so many of them had become. The second reason, and (from a modern perspective) less noble one, was the dogged tendency of these wandering waters to obstruct Toronto's historic insistent drive to remain what it had been at the very beginning, a city laid out on a Euclidean grid, every angle not a snitch less than ninety degrees, and topography be damned.

But the habitual walker has little difficulty finding and following the rainwater's old paths. No matter how urbanized, old landscapes have stubborn ways of remembering, and reminding, despite the encasing of their waters in cylinders of stone, brick and concrete. An otherwise inexplicable dip or bend in a street with no reason to dip or bend, for example. Or the damp chill breathed up from underground into a sunken, lawned park at dusk.

Sometimes very early in the morning, before the city fully awakens and long before the rush hour makes such hearing impossible, I walk to a sewer grate at the bottom of a ditch near my house, and listen to the whisperings of an old stream, now imprisoned deep under concrete and asphalt. I try to imagine what it might have been, to see it bearing away the cold melt under vaults of birch, oak, aspen and sycamore boughs, a thousand springs ago.

## THE DON RIVER FORGOTTEN

It's no pleasant stroll, whatever the weather, to hike the lower Don River, in its final stretch from Cabbagetown, southward to its ignominious ending in a port industrial ditch south of the Gardiner Expressway. The inhuman din of the Don Valley Parkway makes conversation softer than a shout impossible. A few ducks churning the turbid waters and the odd fish are just about the only wildlife left to remind us of what creatures roamed the valley in Toronto's earliest days—lynx, bear and fox—and the annual salmon runs that made the river famous. A few lovely willows and other trees are all that remain of the forests that graced the Don flood plain.

Virtually everything else one sees is the result of human handiwork, evidence of the human drive to control and organize—visually abrasive, surely, yet deeply expressive of the values that drove Toronto from village to metropolis. One is immediately struck by the linear geometry of it all. The gentle meander of the Don in its final approach to Lake Ontario was strictly straightened more than a century ago. Parallel to its present concrete channel runs a straight stretch of railroad, with bridges and hydroelectric wires spanning both river and railway crossing at right angles.

But for all the visual rigidity, a visit to the homely Don still has a certain pleasure—if only because, unlike the numerous lovely Toronto streams running, almost forgotten, under city streets, the Don was just too big to bury. One has to admire that about a river, even if it is today jailed in a grid of steel and concrete.

If a lively group of urban activists and Toronto city bureaucrats has its way, however, the Don might yet get a parole from its long imprisonment. Instead of being made to dump its waters into a port channel by Lake Ontario, the Don would once again be allowed to end serenely in a broad lakeside marsh busy with wetland wildlife. The portion immediately to the north of this marsh—the part straightened in Victorian times—would remain straight, the Don Valley expressway would remain intact, but the lower valley would be green again. Farther upriver, in the vicinity of Rosedale, the stream would once more be allowed to spread and puddle, nourishing marshes and the wildlife that lives in them.

Such were the recommendations of the city-sponsored Task Force To Bring Back the Don, outlined in its $80,000 report released in 1991. The nobility, practicality and visionary power of this document have been widely and justly hailed, and its recommendations were widely reported.

As the introduction explains, this proposal is "to start thinking of the lower Don Valley as a place in itself, not as a gap between places"—a place with memories of its own, and a peculiar monumentality. One could imagine few notions more foreign to Toronto's prevailing spirit of urban modernity, which strait-jacketed its principal river system in the first place. Three years after the report's release, not surprisingly, little movement has taken place on the political front towards letting the Don become the old river, and active city site it could be.

Yet the task force soldiers on, guiding would-be converts to the cause through the traffic noise, and the mud and garbage alongside the Canadian Pacific tracks parallel to the Don's final passage, and doing other good works of reminding. On a Sunday morning not long ago, for instance, I found them wiring up some two hundred black-painted plywood silhouettes to a rusty fence running along Bayview Avenue and the CP tracks, south from Rosedale Valley Road to just above Queen Street. Designed by artist, writer and task-force activist Marie Day, and fabricated with the help of a dozen or so kids recruited from the nearby Regent Park public-housing project, the cut-outs represent wild mammals, fish, fowl and assorted slinkers and creepers that once called the Don Valley home, and some of which, astonishingly, still do keep a claw-hold on this wasteland of rotting concrete, scraggly trees and incessant din.

The bears and moose and other big animals seen in outline on the fence lumbered away north almost two centuries

ago, when the millers and brick-makers took over the valley of
the thirty-eight-kilometre river for their factories. (The mammoth had vacated the premises some time before, though not
without leaving a skeleton or two behind. Salmon left the Don
in the middle of the last century, while the brook trout held
on until fifty years ago.)

Despite all the industrial waste and street mess dumped
into the river, however, great blue heron can still be seen
majestically lifting into the air from the valley's pools. Foxes,
too, have their holes in the clay embankment, and are said to
raid the chicken coops at the valleyside Riverdale Farm from
time to time. And not many months ago, writer Pat
Ohlendorf-Moffat reported in *The Globe and Mail* her dis-
coveries of "sunfish and perch...creek chub, white sucker,
blacknosed dace and longnosed dace" still negotiating the dirty
waters of the lower Don.

The task force's reason for putting up the silhouettes,
members told me, is to remind commuters, cyclists and others
passing through the valley of its past richness as a natural habi-
tat, and to summon up a vision of what the valley could be
again if restored to even a shadow of its former wildness and
beauty.

Nobody wiring up pieces of plywood by the Don thought
he or she was going to save the world, or even the river, by this
action alone. But doing that was at least something; and the
task force thereby served notice on the politicians that it is not
a group to be easily daunted, even though its options are now
limited to small gestures. Mark Wilson, computer consultant
and infectiously devoted chairman of the group, speaks fervently of the "reconnection of the people of the city and the
Don, the heart of the city," from which we have been barred
by fences, railway lines, the expressway. He foresees "a restored
natural landscape, a wilderness in the city"—no pipedream, in
his view, given the gradual abandonment of the river's edges
by the industries that once hemmed it in.

The decline in Toronto's industrialization—or, more accurately, the shift of the city's prime economic force from mechanized object-production to cybernetic information processing, electronic banking and publishing may in time allow the river to come back, and the citizenry to return to a refreshed valley. All that, of course, remains to be seen. But no one who witnessed the wiring-up of those fragile animal silhouettes would have come away unmoved by this small pledge to the waters, and to the renewal of our awareness of their healing powers.

## GARRISON CREEK

Garrison Creek can lay fair claim to being Toronto's most famous waterway never seen above ground, at least by anyone I've ever met except Roy Wood, of whom more presently.

Its system of forks, gathering rivulets and ravines, focusing around Bloor and Christie Streets to Fort York and finally emptying into Lake Ontario, had been turned by early Victorian farmers and workers into a stinking latrine and garbage dump long before the Old Queen died. Also, as Toronto's most conspicuous natural feature between Bay Street and High Park, Garrison was doomed to be a "problem" for city planners. The more or less organized westward urban sprawl reached the creek around 1850, building up rapidly after that, and leaving many a skew around this "obstacle," in the form of kinks, twists and wrinkles in street pattern. But the residential developers of the latter nineteenth century seemed happy enough to build on the soggy trash that had by then clogged whole sections of the creek, even though almost anyone with a scrap of engineering know-how could have predicted the outcome: a lot of nice Victorian and later brick houses today slowly tilting and listing and sinking into the sub-surface muck. The result can be seen in those streets, north of Bloor, that look like rows of crooked teeth.

Like many an ancient victim of urban modernity—the Don Valley is another example—Garrison Creek became much cherished by urban historians, naturalists, and community activists in the early 1990s. A residents' group in the neighbourhood of Trinity-Bellwoods Park, under which the creek's waters silently slide today, is writing its history, from the glory days as the strategically vital water-source for Fort York to its current ignominious state. The formation of a Garrison Creek Historical Society is under way, I understand, and tours of the area are conducted by John Harstone, a local historian.

In the spring of 1993, I got wind of perhaps the most ambitious and intriguing plan so far inspired by this invisible stream. It was called the Garrison Creek Community Project, and, if the modest resources being sought are soon found, will be carried out by Toronto landscape designer and horticulturist Terry McGlade, architects James Brown and Kim Storey, and ecological activist Whitney Smith. The Project's initial goal is simply to create public awareness of this topographical, ecological and historical fact, which links so many ethnically, culturally diverse communities along its path—to educate, in other words, and to animate. Longer-range objectives include architectural and natural-history studies, and, eventually, the unbinding and resurrection of at least part of Garrison Creek from its brick-lined grave.

I hope Roy Wood lives to see it.

Long ago retired from schoolteaching, Wood is the only person I've ever met who remembers Garrison Creek when it flowed freely above ground. One sunny, crisp autumn day in 1992, this bright, elderly gentleman took me on a guided tour of the old trace, where he played and splashed as a boy.

Travelling by car, we commenced our trip at St. Clair Avenue West just east of Oakwood, following the old track of the creek along steep, twisting streets. The brief descent took us down the precipitous shoreline of old Lake Iroquois, down to Davenport Road, at its foot. Once south of that thorough-fare, just before twisting over the site of the former sand quarry known as the Christie Pits, at Bloor Street West and Christie, Garrison Creek made a sharp bend, crossed Ossington Avenue under a wooden bridge demolished long ago, and flowed through the Wood family's rhubarb patch. (Like so much of the west end developed shortly after the beginning of this century, the area is now a zone of small-scale workers' housing.)

Making that short southbound trip, one could easily imag-ine the old creek, which slowly gathered its waters on the plain overlooking the dense forest on the Lake Iroquois lakebed. Then, abruptly hastening, it bore its wild waters down over the edge, carving the gullies remembered today in the twists of Mount Royal Road and other small, winding streets on the escarpment. At the bottom, it broadened and slowed, picking up more waters from forest tributaries, finally gaining the weight to gouge a broad, sandy trough that can still be traced in the densely populated urban landscape between the Christie Pits park and the lakeshore.

By the time Wood came along, the burying and shrinking of Toronto's streams was, of course, far advanced. He recalls that, when he was small and Garrison Creek flowed openly across the Woods' truck farm, it was only a skinny rivulet. Except, that is, during spring run-off, when it briefly remem-bered its ancient task of gathering melt water and early rains from atop the escarpment, and bringing the torrent tumbling and splashing down through the middle of the farm. You can't have that sort of wild thing happening on a good farm, on the north-west edge of a rapidly growing city. And so it was, in 1913, when Wood was about seven, that the last visible trace of the old creek was put away underground.

While enjoying Roy Wood's reminiscences, I could never quite push from my mind the unsettling thought that this was probably the only person I shall ever meet who actually *saw*

Garrison Creek—diminished, but still flowing under the sun, as it had since Toronto emerged from the cold waters to receive the returning forests.

Some time after my visit with Wood, I did see Garrison Creek, or what's left of it, the only safe way one can nowadays: suited in orange coveralls, rubber gloves and boots and a hard hat, trussed up in a web of straps resembling rock-climbing gear and outfitted with an emergency oxygen tank, and being lowered from the daylit world, through a small manhole, into the eternal darkness of the century-old sewer through which the creek flows today.

As I dropped down the hole, Salvatore Pasquale, an inspector for the city's public works department and our guide, was waiting for me at the bottom, lethal-gas detector at the ready. Coming down into the nether gloom after me, with his tape recorder, was Jeffrey Kofman, host of the CBC rush-hour radio show which had set up this descent, and Richard Stromberg, an archaeologist with the Toronto Historical Board. Each of us was equipped with a flashlight designed not to spark an explosion of undetected gas when switched on.

Seeping into the blackness from only five metres above us, the strong morning daylight swiftly dimmed, turning blue as it sank, becoming merely a ghostly pale glow at the bottom. Along with light, we had left behind all the sounds of the city. Down there, one could hear only the sounds of water: the loud, distant rush from a slaughterhouse down the line, the nearer trickling from small lines running into the main sewer, and the sloshing of our high boots through the shallow run-off, hardly higher than the steel-reinforced toes of our footgear. If the humidity was stifling and somehow insidious—I experienced an unfamiliar tightness of the lungs for two days afterward—there was no foul odour. Even the slaughterhouse effluent turned out to be clean water. I was disappointed to see no rats scampering away from us (or making ready for attack), nor evidence of any other living creatures, except some wispy strands of spider webs dangling inside the narrow pipes feeding into the main sewer.

In fact, there was nothing to see, except the lights of our flashlights on the sewer wall, and the structure itself: a perfectly round tube, eight feet in diameter, built of double-layered brick between 1885 and 1892.

The trickle under our feet was all that remained of Garrison Creek, once navigable by canoe, Richard Stromberg told us, as far north as Bloor Street West, which bridged the waterway. Increasingly fastidious about urban sanitation, Toronto's Victorian forefathers decided as early as 1884 that this "open sewer" and "absolute nuisance"—so-called by a Toronto mayor in his inaugural speech—had to go; and go it did, down into the dank, eerie tunnel through which we groped our way.

Many of the artifacts of civil engineering—bridges, dams, hydro lines, and so on—forcefully and eloquently express the Modern spirit, without meaning to be anything other than unassuming, workaday things. Garrison Sewer is a piece of such engineering, and deserving of special praise, even if its beauty was unintended.

The Victorian immigrant masons who laid the bricks of this tubular fabric did so with the care for detail and precise pointing one might expect to find on the façade of a Rosedale mansion, and hardly in a place of utter darkness where the round walls are meant only to serve, not to be seen.

Deep under our city—a city of bricks, since Toronto's earliest urban builders did not have the stone so readily available in other parts of the country—there is a masterwork of Toronto Victorian brickwork, too handsome to ignore, far too dangerous to visit under any but the strictest supervision, too historic to forget, yet destined to be forever unseen under the city's skin of concrete and asphalt.

## THE DON REMEMBERING

In the late spring of 1992, plans for the huge, troubled Ataratiri mixed-use project, slated to rise on thirty-two hectares of polluted, expropriated industrial land east of downtown Toronto, finally died on the drawing board.

As it happened, the death blow to this visionary complex of houses, schools and community facilities was administered by the Ontario government. But for some time, several powerful forces had been mortally threatening to knock the pins from underneath the dream structure. Two of them had origins in the doings of humans: the steep slide of Toronto real-estate prices in the early 1990s, and the soaring costs of rinsing the poisons from the soil.

A third had to do with the lay of the land, and the fact that the site picked for Ataratiri—a roughly pie-shaped wedge broadening eastward from the crossing of Front and Parliament streets, and showing its flat side to the Don River—lies on the Don's ancient flood plain, at the edge of Lake Ontario. What had not been foreseen was the near-impossibility of keeping the river from soaking the soil each spring, flooding basements and underground parking garages, and standing above ground in puddles everywhere. Although corseted in concrete, its final meander towards Lake Ontario straightened out and banked up long ago, the Don, we find, is still wild enough to wreck the dreams of idealistic folk whose plans did not pay it proper respect and take it into proper account.

As I walked the rubble-strewn vacant lots and demolition sites of this district on a blustery cold spring day shortly after the end of Ataratiri, pacing its long, straight and nearly deserted streets, the term "flood plain" took on new, faintly menacing meaning for me. There was no sign here of the rises and ravines and the gulleys of ancient streams that give the old lakeshore topography of Toronto much of its character. The marshy, muddy ground is nearly flat, remorselessly smoothed and scoured by brimming melt water from the ten thousand spring thaws that have come since the glaciers withdrew.

If factories and warehouses and industrial enterprises of various sorts were once thick on the ground here, many had gone, leaving only ghostly oblong shadows of brick dust on boggy fields. Other buildings remained. Some of these survivors stood abruptly isolated—the empty, ponderously pillared warehouse, for one, now a pedestal for an enormous Toshiba sign, beaming its message at the Don Valley Parkway's inbound commuter traffic. Some stood together in the interestingly impure architectural ensembles typical of industrial zones—finely detailed Victorian red brickwork, dumb postwar cinder-block fabrication in the barracks manner, an office building from the 1930s, all tumbled together as the enterprises on the streetscape artlessly multiplied.

Bought up by the province and vacated some time ago, almost all were dark, quiet and ominous, like skulls. About the only living structure in the district is the red-brick building at the corner of Front and Cherry streets, deep in Ataratiri country. The earliest part of this romantic architectural fabric was stacked up in 1859 to house a public school. When the residential area it served was displaced by industry, the old school was turned into an tasteful, small hotel for business travellers known as the Eastern Star. Today, it is home to some small businesses, and to the Canary Restaurant.

Driven off the bleak mud and cracked sidewalks by damp wind, I found a good cup of coffee and a place to warm up in the Canary. But I could not get the eerie music of the spring breeze out of my ears, or stop thinking about the patient surrounding flat-lands, which had soaked up so much public money and defeated so many well-meant plans, and were now waiting under the leaden skies of late winter for the rains and run-off that were due in Toronto, in not so many days.

Humans certainly had played a role in this desolation— but it is easy to dream, while sipping coffee at the Canary, that the wreckers had really been the secret agents of the river, which once owned the land and now was taking back its own. Nor was it hard to imagine what the Ataratiri site would look and be like, were both province and local idealists to surrender, and let the Don get it all. Instead of the present wasteland of rubble and dead buildings—which surely has its own quiet and poignant beauty—we would have a deep, damp forest just touching the eastern edge of downtown. It would be flooded in the spring, and city folk would be driven from its paths. But the little stands of poplars, sycamores and other lowland trees would be annually renewed and invigorated, and begin to spread, gradually embracing the ruined buildings, while healing the wounds inflicted on the ground by the factories. As we were reminded by the Ataratiri cancellation, the river will let us use its ancient flood plain, but on its own terms. Perhaps it is time to accept this reality, and give the land back forever to our silent, powerful partner.

# Tales of the Pioneers

*The Pavillion, Allan Gardens*

# UNROMANCING FORT YORK

In full swing during the spring and summer of 1993, Toronto 200—as the city's official bicentennial jubilee called itself—was mostly an embarrassment and a bore. Such "heritage" extravaganzas always are. Across the town, we got the usual dull unveilings of plaques. In April, around the anniversary of the 1813 American sack of Toronto—or York, as it was known then—costumed and bewigged actors representing the British 8th Regiment celebrated this defeat by drilling, marching and blowing off muskets. I can't tell you why this disgrace was thought to need a commemoration, though I am certain it didn't. And in August, lest we forget the 200th anniversary of the arrival by founding grandees John and Elizabeth Simcoe, along with some colonial poobahs and a musical band of oom-pa-pahing Queen's Rangers, we got a pageant at the harbour featuring a sailing ship and, in the odd words of a press release, "costumed reenactment troops."

What never occurs to the bureaucrats who plan such tourist carry-ons is that history is more interesting than costume. A brush with the real history of a Toronto site, its special wrinkles and local textures and how they came to be that way, might actually pique new curiosity in otherwise indifferent folk among the Metro area's 4.2-million inhabitants. Among the better opportunities to do so is "Historic Fort

York," the lakeside military installation Governor Simcoe came in 1793 to carve from the wilderness.

Thanks to the Toronto Historical Board, which runs it mainly as a tourist attraction, Fort York is a veritable Santa's workshop of the "heritage industry," with blunderbusses booming, cookies in the oven, the works. But beyond the marketing of the Fort, there is a military and architectural history of high interest. Inside its earthen enclosure—the foundation of long-vanished log palisades—is a scatter of eight buildings. None date from the very earliest days of the fortress, an outcome partly intentional since Governor Simcoe meant what he called "comfortable Barracks of log work" to last no more than seven years. The survivors, however, all hold considerable architectural and historical interest. Included in this ensemble are two handsomely ponderous blockhouses built in 1813, instances of expert log construction on the uneasy British-American frontier, three one-storey brick barracks raised in 1815, and a thick-walled stone powder magazine from the same year, skilfully ventilated and furnished with spark-proof copper and brass fittings. Taken together, the Fort York structures provide an excellent early vignette of colonial military architecture, and are notable for that reason alone.

Why they exist where they do, and why they should be visited, may seem a mystery nowadays. The shoreline lies little less than a mile south—pushed there by landfill over the last one hundred years—and the little fortification itself, once on a low headland overlooking the lake—is virtually invisible behind the immense concrete colonnade bearing the Gardiner Expressway, smokestacks and a dusty cement-block factory, and billboards meant to catch the eye of high-speed commuters with ads for TV sets. The stone wall running round the site is a make-work project of Depression-era vintage. Its abrasive industrial context seems to heighten its character as a fantasy-redoubt of staunch Englishry, perfumed with memories of red-jacketed Christian soldiers living the hard, chaste and loyal life in defence of British North America.

Tourists have become visibly upset upon learning that red-jacketed Jews served along with stalwart Anglicans at Fort York, and that the wives of officers occasionally lived and kept house within the fortification. (Married officers more commonly lived in the nearby town of York.) These tiny facts are arresting in a way mulled cider and cookies fresh from the oven, staged bayonet attacks, cannons booming and so forth never are. But if such fact is what's wanted, there is no better resource than *Historic Fort York 1793–1993,* a readable and profitably illustrated book by Carl Benn, Fort York's curator of military and marine history, and one of the few serious memorials to remain after the bicentennial hoopla had come and gone.

Credit for the founding of Toronto, we learn from Benn, should go to the Americans, indirectly at least. By 1793, the revolutionaries to the south had again become restive about not having grabbed *all* British North America when they had the chance. Whereupon Colonel John Graves Simcoe, lieutenant-governor of the British colony of Upper Canada, fearing attack by U.S. troops on his more or less indefensible forts at Detroit, Niagara and Kingston, decided to build a battle station and administrative centre far up the wild north shore of Lake Ontario. The desolate spot later to become Toronto was an easy choice. It featured a defensible harbour, with only one entrance in those days, a good strategic water supply in Garrison Creek, and a healthy distance across open water between itself and the United States. Simcoe quickly threw up some log bunkers at the entrance to the harbour—the site of present Fort York—and ordered the first plans for a civilian town and port to be constructed about a mile east, in the relative safety of the enclosed bay. On August 17, 1793, Simcoe christened his tiny settlement York, since he believed in giving his foundations names resounding of England.

The colonial administration of British North America turned a deaf ear to Simcoe's pleas for a heavy military build-up of Fort York—meaning that there was only a tiny force here and a tiny town in 1796, when John and Elizabeth Simcoe departed York forever. Only 241 souls lived here. In 1810, there was a single brick house in the town.

If it hadn't been for the ongoing belligerence of the Yankee rebels against the Lord and His Anointed King—my revolutionary ancestors, that is—one of Simcoe's successors might well have abandoned the boggy frontier outpost at York, and moved the capital of Upper Canada to a more civilized spot, Niagara or Kingston, say, or—Simcoe's preference—London. Abandoned by its legion, Fort York and its attached town would then have surely vanished, and millions of people would not now be living in bungalows and apartment blocks on land once covered by dense forests, and later large farms. There would be no commuting, no high-rises, no SkyDome. Just to mark the spot, perhaps, some government might have put up a little theme park, of the "ye olde" sort the heritage people love. (Chicago got lucky, too. The muddy location of the Americans' Fort Dearborn after 1804, Chicago didn't amount to much until the later nineteenth century, when it took off for the same reason Toronto did: the continental railways.)

But as it happened, the Americans did remain feisty, and greedy for Canada; President James Madison was particularly keen on establishing a trade monopoly covering all North America's fantastically abundant natural resources. Such idealism had no room in it for a European outpost, so, on June 18, 1812, Washington declared war on Great Britain. Not that the officers, civilians, colonial bureaucrats and military planners at York could do much else than stay huddled in the mud; the official shorting of York's defensive capacities had seen to that. When the Americans got around to attacking York, in April, 1813, they had little trouble taking the town, which they looted and terrorized before taking their leave in May. In retaliation, British troops burned Washington to the ground in August, 1814. John Strachan, Toronto's first bishop, later told

Thomas Jefferson that the United States capital got just what it deserved. Shortly after the catastrophe, the British began strengthening Fort York—the earliest extant buildings date from this time—which, by 1814, were imposing enough to make an American naval unit think twice about attacking, then back off.

Although Fort York is advertised as a relic of the War of 1812, its most heavy use as a military base came in the later nineteenth century. It was abandoned as an official military fortress in the 1930s. By that time, the only action its troops had seen were in skirmishes against other Canadians. The first was in 1837, when the garrison defended Toronto's Anglican colonial élite against republican-minded Upper Canadian merchants, industrialists and farmers, trouncing them. The 1837 rebels were suppressed, banished or executed, and then transformed into figures of textbook myth. (For some reason, Canada has a tradition of turning its traitors into heroes.) The second engagement took place in 1906, with violent Hamilton streetcar operators on strike.

After the War of 1812, the United States would never again try to finish its incomplete seizure of all British North America. But military strategists in London and in Canada did not know that, and could not count on the eternal international peace Canadians now take for granted. As recently as the 1860s, defence planners considered using the Toronto fort to help save this country should the huge armies of the Republic and the Confederacy decide to stop fighting each other and join forces against Canada. But by the 1890s, Fort York had become militarily obsolete, and so played no part in the last known plans laid, just before the First World War, to counter an American invasion. (The idea was to have Australian and Indian troops attack California if the U.S. launched an aggressive action against Canada.)

What remains of Fort York isn't much to look at, which is why Carl Benn's book should be carried along on every visit.

The sober, thorough text is supplemented by nineteen maps and seventy-seven reproduced photographs, drawings and paintings, enabling any visitor to envision this volatile site, with its built forms rising and changing and disappearing—walls destroyed in 1916 to make way for streetcar tracks, an encroaching slaughterhouse, barracks quickly constructed and quickly demolished, obsolete eighteenth-century cannon put into service as fencing, the gunboats and frigates now utterly gone. Too, these pictures can kindle in the imagination moving pictures of the men and women who lived, served and died here, and laid the tiny foundations of what would become, by a curious historical irony, not a mere memory but a megalopolis.

## B LACK   C REEK   P IONEER   V ILLAGE

Black Creek Pioneer Village is a theme park nestled behind hedges and artificial hillocks meant to mask the fast surburban traffic in its crime-ridden environs on Metro's north-west fringe.

A self-described simulation of a "typical nineteenth-century crossroads settlement in southern Ontario," Black Creek comprises forty-odd houses, stores, barns, utility buildings and other edifices, most rescued from ruin elsewhere in Ontario, trucked in and set down along dirt streets winding picturesquely through a fifty-six-acre landscaped tract. Among the oldest structures at Black Creek, and the only ones standing where they were built, are the 1816 log cabin of farmer Daniel Stong, his piggery and grain barn, both built in 1825, and the more comfortable house Stong put up for his family in 1832.

Roblin's flour mill, the most imposing industrial structure in the "village," and complemented by a charming pond and mill-race, is a fake, built to resemble an 1842 facility in Prince

Edward County and to house its internal machinery. Many of the other buildings, however, are genuine artifacts, giving Black Creek the potential of being a useful architectural set-piece. There's the Emporium, built in 1856 at Laskay, Ontario, and the circa-1860 blacksmith shop from Nobleton, all looking, we are supposed to believe, as they did when put up.

No book can be found among the doodads in the sprawling gift shop to supply a sense of these dislodged structures' social and cultural contexts. But it would appear that few buildings here, apart from the Stong piggery and such, had much to do with pioneers or pioneering. The Emporium probably did sell local produce; but its very existence, and what was supplied by it—imported wines, molasses, and tropical fruits such as oranges—suggests the existence of a widespread, efficient system for distributing both basic and luxury goods throughout Upper Canada by the 1850s.

It follows that numerous other features of Victorian industrial culture—pornography and prostitution, popular magazines and penny dreadfuls, pervasive religious doubt, mass-produced consumer goods of every sort, the dream of upward mobility—were also rapidly making their way into the Ontario outback. There's no sign of any of that here. What we have at Black Creek, instead, is neither a "pioneer village" nor a reproduction of a rural Canadian community, but a picturesque heap of fakes and architectural relics of Ontario's continuing commercial and industrial modernization.

Such matters seem to be of little interest to the Metropolitan Toronto bureaucrats who created and operate Black Creek Pioneer Village. The idea appears to have been to make, not a place where our understanding can be quickened, but a benign opium den of escapism into "the way we were," and really weren't. As visitors pass through the toll gate, says the glossy guidebook, "they are at once entering a different world…another age…reminiscent of a time when life was harder and simpler but rewarding."

If that's not bad enough, the prose gets even more queasy-making. "From the first step onto the wooden boardwalk," we read, "time changes. The smell of cooking, the sound of the blacksmith hammering at his anvil, the feel of soft fleece, the taste of fresh whole wheat bread and the sight of crinolined skirts swaying along the pathways, all help to erase the modern world for a short while." As a young female guide in long skirt and bonnet cheerily asked me, as I tried to keep from getting knocked from the plank sidewalk into the mud by a mob of adolescents being herded my way by their exasperated teacher: "It's so peaceful and quiet here, isn't it?"

The answer is *no*. Everything about Black Creek is annoying, from the musty museological atmosphere of the "village" itself to the junk-crammed boutique and fries-and-burger outlet masked by sentimental, schmoozy exaltation. But Black Creek can be a delight for the connoisseur of ironies and human folly. The buildings so diligently hauled to Toronto and carefully put here to evoke nostalgia for a "harder, simpler" time, for instance, were abandoned precisely because the society they served was much harder, and made obsolete by Ontario's swift industrial modernization between late Victorian times and the end of the Second World War. They were left to rot where they stood, because most people with good sense got out of those cruelly isolated "pioneer villages" as soon as they could, and moved into Ontario's industrial towns, for a crack at the jobs being multiplied astonishingly by new industries and enterprises.

The 1890s saw the first dramatic moves of Ontario farm folk to the towns and cities; by 1911, the urbanized population had surpassed the number of people still living in the country. In 1921, 58 per cent of Ontario's 2.9 million people were city-dwellers; and, by 1961—a year after Black Creek opened to the public—a mere 8 per cent still lived on farms. The people who streamed into the cities did so to join the industrialized, mass-political life the curators at Black Creek

Pioneer Village want to help us escape.

Every year, almost a third of a million people heed the call, and come to the "village" to recollect a sanitized, sentimentalized, utterly pleasant version of the wretchedness their ancestors left behind. This is a common human foible, and is not uncommon even among those of us who have undergone the traumatic leave-taking of the country and the embrace of the city, and should know better than to be nostalgic. Every year, untold millions of North Americans pay to "go back in time" to another architectural or archaeological fiction of the same sort—some "native encampment" or "frontier town." Nobody needs a survey to prove that this kind of fantastical tourism is hugely popular with urbanized mass populations.

I am sure of two things in this regard. First, that the Victorians who answered the siren song of urbanity, and forsook the miseries of farm work or the deadly constrictions of small-town life—indeed, everything Black Creek tries to make seem appealing—cannot be blamed for leaving. (Why don't these nostalgia factories ever include touches of real rural Victorian life? A child dying of typhoid or cholera, for instance, with a doctor and mother looking on helplessly?) Second, that Black Creek Pioneer Village and places like it are only helping the urbanized population avoid the consequences, rewards and complex moral questions involved in embracing urban modernity without reservation. One is not born a city person, after all. Urban sophistication, devotion to city liberty, are things that must be learned, patiently and carefully.

This learning is unquestionably difficult. Evidence: the thousands upon thousands of people fleeing the city via expressway every weekend, bound for the carefully regulated "hardness" and "simplicities" of cottage, chalet, anywhere but here; and the hundreds of thousands who each year visit Black Creek Pioneer Village, and perhaps believe that this self-induced amnesia is in fact a kind of recollection of paradise lost.

WESTON

At first, the property manager of the Weston apartment tower thought I had dropped by to write something about the bodies.

The corpses of two people, dead in an apparent murder-suicide, had been found the afternoon before in her high-rise building, a block or so east of Weston Road, and the place was busy with the comings and goings of investigators. She wasn't talking to reporters. It took a few moments to convince the lady that I had little interest in the bodies, which I had not even heard of, and considerable interest in her flat-topped metal and concrete block, towering improbably over the low-rise, rambling mumble of beautiful old houses, a church, seedy stores and weedy empty lots just north-west of what was once the town centre of Weston, when it was a town.

That once-upon-a-time, by the way, wasn't very long ago. Weston surrendered its official civic identity only in 1967, when it joined the Borough (later City) of York, itself a visually indistinguishable zone in Metro Toronto's westward expanse. As usually happens to villages overwhelmed by expanding large cities, the little one, Weston in this case, becomes a romantic victim, and the subject of myth and legend. The older citizenry of such towns seem particularly susceptible to the idealization of the past, and the twisting or more subtle editing of the facts to fit memories, real or wished-for. Those who live there invariably use prejudicial words like "gobbled up" or "buried" to describe what has happened to places like Weston.

Towns that have utterly vanished are, of course, not likely objects for such poignancy, simply because no architectural traces remain for the preservationists to draw their wagons round and fight for. Weston, in contrast, is still adorned with distinctive sites built in better times, excellent old houses, variously rustic, august and quaint, on deliciously secretive dead-end roads and fine maple-shaded residential streets, as gracious as any in rural Victorian Ontario. Too, Weston can boast Metro's most noble local library in the Romanesque Revival style, graced with gleaming mosaics around its stained-glass windows—a work of 1914 built with largesse donated by U.S. philanthropist Andrew Carnegie—and a history going back to the earliest British enterprise in this region.

Quite enough of old Weston remains intact, that is, to keep the local history and preservation industry busy, and quietly militant. Examples of this polite defiance includes the local historical society's *Pictorial History of Weston,* launched in 1981 on the occasion of the centenary of the ex-town, and the six mimeographed reports of The Town Project, a group of students pledged "to preserve the flavour of the village in 1882." In none of these publications do we find references to the Modernist slab high-rises so typical of Weston Road's streetscape today, or the large assembly-line operations that gave Weston economic cohesion during its final days of independence. The concern is, as always, with that intangible thing, "community spirit." "With the inflow of newcomers to the town, and the growth of apartment complexes," says a Town Project flyer, "the community spirit may be forgotten in the rush of development."

For a taste of what's meant by "community spirit," we have the archival photos gathered into the *Pictorial History.* This refined and busy Weston of myth and half-memory is captured in an 1869 snap of Prince Arthur, son of Victoria, turning the sod for the new railroad line; in a 1907 team portrait made when the Weston Lacrosse Club bagged a trophy; in a 1911 tableau, showing the Presbyterian congregation parading staunchly through the snow, like good soldiers of the Lord, preceded by billowing flags, to open its new Sunday school. We are supposed to be moved by the recollection, from 1924, when the village turned out to watch Miss Fisher, the school principal, march her charges to the fairgrounds down by the Humber River.

In the pre-metropolitan tale sketched out in such texts and compilations of images, Weston of old was a simple community of good folk of solid British stock, ever marching shoulder-to-shoulder, whether for Christ, a new railroad, the Orange Lodge, the Crown, the advancement of lawn bowling, or abstinence from liquor. It was certainly not the kind of place in which people were found murdered in twenty-eighth-floor apartments, or spoke foreign languages in the Jumbo Save, or worshipped strange gods which Victorian Westonians would have only known about from savage boys' books, or Kiplingesque hero-stories of the Raj.

What I find interesting in pseudo-historical publications such as these—works as numerous in North America as the declining small towns whose citizens produce them—is the pervasive assumption that some terrible gulf has opened between a happily stable, civic-minded past, illustrated therein, and a speedy, restless, incomprehensible present, unworthy of attention and certainly of preservation. Only indirectly or euphemistically—as "the inflow of newcomers" or "the growth of apartment complexes"—can the displacement and disintegration of the village's old Great British establishment be named. "Community spirit" is always another name for power, especially after it has been irretrievably dispersed, or seized by others.

I should quickly make it clear that I have no wish to lay blame on anyone here. Nor do I intend to portray Weston's preservationists as exceptional examples of what is, after all, an ancient and well-nigh universal imaginative tendency. Again and again, in narratives as old as Mesopotamian creation epics and the Bible and the earliest Greek poets, we find history's beginning in a lost, paradisical *illud tempus,* from which we have fallen into the baleful, alienated *hoc tempus,* our prison and destiny and present.

Surely, things have changed in Weston, but not as drastically as all that. The town, it appears from a close reading of

*Sports Bar, Weston*

the photos in *A Pictorial History,* has always been open to the
tumults of modernization, from its beginnings as an lumber
milling centre in 1792 until the present—revising itself architecturally and socially, refacing and gutting old buildings that
lent themselves to such recycling, ripping down the rest. The
mid-nineteenth-century improvement of Weston Road (a key
link between burgeoning Toronto and the agricultural communities lying north-west of the city), the building of important bridges across the Humber River and especially the
coming of the national Canadian railways in 1856 and 1869,
sharply accelerated Weston's population growth and prosperity,
and the cultural wrenching that comes in the wake of such
change. Unlike other small towns besieged and occupied—if
not yet actually annexed—during Toronto's extraordinary
nineteenth-century expansion, Weston has always been reli-
giously and ethnically heterogeneous. The process has merely
continued: a 1986 provincial study showed that almost half of
Weston's inhabitants at that time had a mother-tongue other
than English.

Even before it joined the list of Toronto's self-abolished villages and small towns, Weston had lost its innocence of dis-
tinctively big-city traits. Metropolitan Toronto's 1960 aerial
portrait of this minute region indeed shows the fancily
porched Eagle House Hotel, built in 1870, still occupying the
best corner of Lawrence Avenue West and Weston Road, the
traditional hub of the village. But it also discloses the long
shadows of high-rise apartment blocks along the western side
of Weston Road, on narrow lots dropping off into the
Humber River valley. Aerial atlases of the late 1970s reveal the
non-town of Weston still moving right along that path
towards full modern urbanism, with ever more conspicuous
apartment blocks going up here and there. The Eagle House
was gone by this time, its site filled by a cloddish cement mall
and apartment superstructure.

And a less lofty survey of the same area, conducted by this

observer in sneakers in the autumn of 1992, tells the same story, but with details aerial photos do not offer. On Weston Road north and south of Lawrence Avenue, we find the hubbub of architectural styles, spread along a tawdry commercial strip, common to all arterial throughways which have remained in active, increasing use. What appears to have been a large Victorian family house on Weston Road, has had a billboard for wristwatches dropped in front of its second storey, and at street level, a pizza parlour installed in what was probably, well, the parlour. A low store-front with Depression Modern touches has been inserted between a tall façade of wackily fancy nineteenth-century brickwork and a squalid building of utterly indeterminate age. And a simple gabled house of the last century has been recently engulfed by a one-storey box sheltering a florist and a "men's shop," leaving only the old house's peaked roof and second-storey windows visible above its modern girdle. Had Weston actually been frozen in place at some point in its history—as its fans seem to wish—its older, distinguished buildings would never have had such interesting, quirky and always instructive perversions visited upon them. Yet these are bits of evidence for a history of demolitions and replacements, of urbanization itself, that remains unwritten, clearly because it is unloved.

To return to the murder building—or King Square, to give the block its proper name—this thirty-two-storey structure was built in 1975, said the manager. Its shadow is the most striking one I saw in the post-1975 atlases, due to the abruptness of the building's full-blown appearance, and its size, grotesquely outscaling the humbler buildings around it. King Square seems to be a monstrous intrusion into an otherwise largely unchanging town plan, however, only when viewed from afar, or from the air, or, lazily, over the rooftops of the much lower commercial buildings along Weston Road. Seen against the actual historical development of Weston, the apartment block is just an especially conspicuous instance of the casually chaotic modernizing that's been going on for what seems like forever.

Granted, you couldn't always browse in a sex-toy shop on Weston's main street, as you can now. Considered as an expressive architectural ensemble, Weston is, in its small way, as rich in the perverse, eclectic, confused spirit of contemporary urbanism as the immense city that took it over after the railways had gone belly-up and the town had fallen on hard times, making it the gobbled instead of the gobbler, and spawning many a devotee to the good old days which, if they did exist, weren't *that* good.

## ABOUT WILLIAM GILPIN

This is partly the story of a cottage on Broadview Avenue, but mostly the tale of William Gilpin, who is a curious man. It is also a reminder of the mysteries that gather round every house with the passage of years, waiting for a curious person to come along and patiently untie the knots of history and unhood the shrouds of time.

Speeding down Broadview south from Danforth Avenue, with its panoramic views towards the radiant Toronto skyline across the Don Valley, you don't tend to notice the little old cottage, painted white with green trim. It is set well back from the avenue behind a front garden only gradually being recovered from dilapidation and decades of neglect, and crowded in between two big, muscle-bound Edwardians. If it hadn't been pointed out to me, I might never have appreciated this charming reminder of earlier Toronto, its symmetrical façade still prim, its hipped roof and external chimneys on either side still straight.

Despite the house's demure manner—or, rather, because of it—Gilpin had delighted in it for more than a decade, from the vantage-point of his Cabbagetown apartment opposite, across the Don. He has always loved old things, old stories and romantic songs, he told me over a cup of espresso in his inexpensively antiqued front parlour, and he had been "an archaeologist by inclination" since childhood. He and the cottage were meant for each other—such had been his belief for years—when, in 1992, this tattered survivor of better days went up for sale.

Gilpin clearly had, and has, the urban pioneering sensibility—an acquired trait, by the way—required to repair and live in such a place. A sensibility, that is, disinclined to clear and conquer, and much inclined to save and spare. He cherishes furnishings and ornaments and out-of-date architectural "improvements" that more speedy, self-consciously progressive people would throw out. He is enchanted by traces, however scanty or fragmentary, of the past—which he imagines, with forgiveable incorrectness, to be more elegant and leisurely than the present—and is devoted to preserving each trace, like a talisman enabling communion with the long-dead souls who left it.

But Gilpin, now in his thirties, has also been a rolling stone all his life—working just long enough to save up money for the next wander around the world, odd-jobbing and living gracefully on little—and so did not have a nickel to put down on the house. Nor did he have much time: the lot size was perfect for a duplex, and the asking price was only $218,000, a Toronto developer's dream in the slow housing market of the early 1990s.

But with the good fortune that often shadows gentle fans and aficionados, and with remarkable generosity on the vendor's part, Gilpin managed to piece together the necessary financing, beat out the developers who would have handily knocked down the house in a day, moved in, and got down to work.

The most immediate job was the physical redemption of the cottage from the gradual ruin visited upon it during decades as a rental property. I would not be writing this, however, were Gilpin just your basic Toronto white-painter and fixer-upper, buying cheap this year in order to sell dear three years down the line. What makes his story interesting is his commitment to stay put—not something Torontonians are inclined to do—and patiently reconstruct his house's entire history from the fragments, hints and concealed systems in the shelter itself, and from what pictures, genealogies, deeds and any other documents he can find.

In the kitchen, Gilpin showed me a frayed but still radiant expanse of deep violet printed wallpaper in a flourishing Arts and Crafts pattern, pasted up perhaps in late Victorian times on the wood wall by someone with high style, and perhaps a bit of highfalutin attitude. He discovered it under a stratum of cheap tile. In his cozily fusty dining room, Gilpin takes down an anonymous junktique-store portrait from its hook and handily rips aside a section of modern hardware-store panelling, to reveal a swatch of fine mass-produced wallpaper, circa the Roaring Twenties. Every scrap of wallcovering Gilpin finds, by the way, he carefully preserves and catalogues and researches, in hopes of someday reproducing the patterns, or perhaps even finding long-forgotten bolts of the original stuff stacked in a dusty warehouse.

With the removal of each patch of beaverboard or parquet flooring, another level of the cottage's history, and the tale of the people who lived there, has been revealed. And under each level is another clue on the route backward in time, farther down the rabbit hole which this unimposing cottage has become for the inquiring imagination of William Gilpin.

Of all the clues the owner has uncovered, surely the most intriguing and puzzling is to be found in the main-floor bathroom. There, after pulling away later wall facings, he found a rough wall of square-hewn logs. Gilpin had never believed his cottage was as late as its quaint Victorian front porch suggested—in the 1880s, that is, when the east side of the Don

Valley was annexed by the City of Toronto. His guess, based on a study of early Ontario architecture of the same type, was that the house could have gone up as early as the 1840s.

But finding the log house wrapped inside the later architectural fabric could, Gilpin believes, put the house back to a very early date—perhaps as long ago as the mid-1790s, when European settlement and first construction took place in this part of the world. Peculiarities about its construction, and records and pictures Gilpin has dredged out of public archives, suggest the cabin may have been moved from another location to its present site after 1815, with a mind to using it as the architectural basis for the larger house that was, in fact, built around it. (Part of the cabin's original roof can be seen in the attic of the expanded house.)

The siting was done with "a degree of pretension," in Gilpin's opinion, who makes his point with a sweeping gesture towards the landscape beyond the front window and Broadview Avenue. Indeed, one could hardly have chosen a more propitious spot on the east side of the Don, if what was wanted was a peculiarly Victorian Sublime view of the valley and town beyond. He then heaps the parlour table high with documents, maps, reproductions of old watercolours and photographs, abstracts and wills, branching and twigging genealogies of families who lived here or owned the land, all gleaned from myriad city and provincial sources; then begins going through the stack with exacting concern.

I do not intend to evaluate this evidence here, or further describe it. Perhaps the curious man who owns it does indeed live in the oldest house in Toronto, as he fervently wants to believe. But even if it were possible to pinpoint the cottage's origin and numerous transformations—obviously a matter of considerable interest to local historians and architectural buffs—I would find all that less interesting than the discovery of William Gilpin himself. While I have met only a handful, there may well be hundreds of people like him across

Metropolitan Toronto, who share his sheer joy in the legends and mysteries and odd clues already unmasked in house and home, and the quiet thrill about the many others waiting, behind baseboards and plaster and flooring, to be discovered. I would like to hope there are thousands—if only because each of us needs at least one charmed guide to get us started on this safari of intellect and soul into the hidden heart of where we are.

# Pleasures in Places

*Fall Yard, St. Clarens Avenue*

# CHRISTMAS AT COLBORNE LODGE

In an effort to brighten an especially dreary December morning, I dropped by the country house of John and Jemima Howard, known as Colborne Lodge.

The Howards were out. In fact, they've been out now for upwards of 120 years. Nor is Colborne Lodge in the country any more. This eccentric, asymmetric house, begun in 1837 and believed by its proprietors to be one of the oldest examples of the picturesque "cottage ornée" in North America, now stands atop a hill at the south end of High Park, once the Howard farm and now in deep city. The house's bluff-top situation once commanded a fine, panoramic view of nearby Lake Ontario, and it still does—though in between edifice and water now lie a broad hem of landfill and noisy torrents of road and rail traffic which never stop.

Once inside the front door of Colborne Lodge, however, the city and cars seem very far away, as indeed the Toronto Historical Board, which operates it, intends. Hot spiced cider and fresh-baked molasses cookies perfume the air. Candles on the dining-room mantel illuminate a table laden with tarts and cakes, petits fours and puddings. The pleasantly stodgy nineteenth-century decor of the downstairs rooms—all polished dark oak, floral wallpaper, heavy swags, embroidery, patriotic prints—is festive with boughs of pine and red ribbon and festoons of cranberry and popcorn. The Christmas tree stands at military attention in the parlour, bright with quilled snowflakes, beaded eggs and little presents.

Taken together, the Howards' Yuletide decorations are a museum display of what Christmas was for Toronto's middle class, and has almost completely ceased to be. Merry, but not gaudy. Sparing, but never plain; an adult occasion, but without a certain officiousness. Jubilant, but without a whiff of High Toronto ostentation. The word I want to use for the atmosphere in Colborne Lodge is *jovial*—though nowadays this term has lost most of its old associations with King Jove, and fine royal joy, and celebrations high and serious without being in the least stuffy or solemn.

Colborne Lodge is the carefully preserved setting of a fiction created by Sandra Molyneaux, an anthropologist by training and senior curatorial assistant at the Lodge. So how did Molyneaux know what a Toronto Christmas, circa 1870, was supposed to look like?

Some of the sources come from mass-produced images of the period—those popular portrayals of happy hearthsides and Christmas customs that reached their zenith of appeal and jollity during the 1870s in the work of U.S. illustrator Thomas Nast. Then there are the literary descriptions, notably one written in 1850 by Charles Dickens about a contemporary Christmas tree—still a novelty in England at that time, since Prince Albert had imported the idea from his native Germany, and set up the Anglophone world's first Christmas tree at Windsor Castle in 1841. Gorging at Christmas was well established in Toronto—in 1860, *The Globe* ran a seasonal food column hymning the sweets, lobsters, sardines, oysters, wild fowl, grapes and ciders for purchase from a King Street purveyor—though taking the day off to enjoy the feast became official in Canada only in 1867. (William Lyon Mackenzie, editor and rebel and muckraker, docked a copy boy sixty-six cents for taking off Christmas Day in 1839.)

Nobody's stockings have been hung by the Howards' chimney with care, because Canadians did not do that sort of thing in 1870. Christmas cards, too, were new; they had been invented in England in 1846, but would not come into common use in Canada until almost fifty years later. Giving presents to teachers, bosses or anyone outside one's immediate family and most intimate circle of friends, and the paper-wasting business of wrapping gifts, are even more recent "traditions."

What's on view at Colborne Lodge can be looked at merely in a tiresomely grown-up way, as an illustration of seasonal interior-decorating practices in old Ontario. But get as swept up in the anthropology as you will, the decor at Colborne Lodge keeps whispering a question that all the file-cards and scholarly books in the world probably can't answer satisfactorily: What makes this seasonal carry-on work so well, and so durably?

The answer isn't in the strength of something called "tradition," since, we are reminded at the Lodge, the "traditional" Victorian Christmas was itself a pastiche of novelties. Yet at some time around or just after the era represented at Colborne Lodge, the whole heap of stuff known as "Christmas decoration" or "Christmas custom" came together and froze into place exactly as we have it now. Nothing else at Colborne Lodge has worn so well as this instant so-called tradition of holly, wreaths and all the rest. Of course, the taste for the Lodge's kind of Victorian furniture and furnishings comes and goes, but the taste for the Victorian Yuletide ensemble of mistletoe, mincemeat tarts, evergreen and presents and so on is as strong today as at any time in the century since it was all invented.

Despite this novelty, however, the traditions of Christmas have proven astonishingly resistant to the various modern movements in design and architecture, which have profoundly reshaped virtually everything around us and utterly demoted most other instances of Victorian fussiness from their previous ascendancy. Mistletoe is now hung from steel girders in high-tech urban lofts or freshly installed light fixtures, instead of from glittering chandeliers—but it does continue to be hung. Instead of the cut-glass punch cups of yore, neatly laid out on a linen tablecloth, one can now find plastic glasses arrayed on a blond ovoid table of Scandinavian design, or smoked crystal tumblers gleaming atop glass-and-steel wet bars—but what goes into these vessels year after year is still the same old Victorian cider, accompanied by the same old fruit-cake and shortbreads.

I am inclined to think that the importance of these dear symbols—which it would feel like a kind of blasphemy to omit—resides in the specious and imaginary link they provide with some vague land of "what came before." This is not a link I otherwise do much to preserve, and have done much to break. Nevertheless, this Christmas as at every Christmas, the wreath of pine boughs and red ribbons will hang on the steel and industrial glass door of the reclaimed and renovated furniture factory I call home. I can do without a front or back garden, I can live with exposed industrial girders, and am happy to have a kitchen fitted out with modern appliances, and a fridge capable of holding a prodigious amount of heat-and-eat. But, without that guilty wreath, it just wouldn't be Christmas.

## Unknown Gardens

Elsewhere, this book is an appeal to curiosity—to the natural intellectual desire, often dulled by the routines of city living, to know just where we stand, and find out what sort of place it is. Elsewhere, that is; but not here.

My topic at this point is the vein-like net of railway corridors. Visiting them is not legally forbidden. Due to an apparent oversight, the federal Parliament left out penalties against trespassing in its most recent legislation regulating the railways.

But this network *is* private property, after all, and peculiarly dangerous property as well.

The most deadly threat is posed, of course, by the rolling stock. Despite their huge size, and the mechanical ruckus they kick up as they move, trains are stealthy. Anyone who has walked railway tracks, as I have, all my life, knows that a train can be almost on top of you before you know it's coming. One has to have an uncommon attentiveness to what's happening on and around the tracks, an habitual resistance to distraction, to keep from getting hit. Then, on the right-of-way, there is many an uncovered pit to break a leg in, and numerous old track ties and iron oddments hidden in the weeds to fall over. Warning signs are, of course, almost non-existent. You are not supposed to be there. And I would urge anyone not already accustomed to them already to stay off railway tracks forever.

That said, I would nevertheless urge everyone to be more alert to these remarkable, much-disregarded facts of urban architecture, which lie everywhere in the city—behind rickety wooden fences at the end of dingy streets of auto-body shops and decaying houses, at the rear of important houses in Rosedale, in the cleft of ravines and on high stone bridges, concealed by street-long factories.

One safe, informative vantage point is from the window of a GO commuter train. Another, good for studying the one-dimensional architecture of railway corridors is any footbridge. My favourite is the old steel Junction footbridge in Toronto's west end, a sturdy little work of utilitarian building from Toronto's late industrial age providing safe passage for pedestrians over the north-south Canadian Pacific tracks, from Wallace Avenue to Dundas Street West. (The newer fashion in avoiding level pedestrian crossings, incidentally, is to run the footpath under the tracks, thereby creating dank, menacing, repulsive concrete burrows.) From the breezy overlook afforded by the Wallace Avenue footbridge, a certain irony of the corridor is apparent at once.

In both directions run the thin parallel threads of gleaming steel, opening prospects as staunchly rational and uncompromisingly naked to the sun as an alley at Versailles. Here, indeed, is a sublime, if unintentionally sublime, expression of one of the nineteenth century's most radically new architectures of transport. Here is the endless metal form that in a generation displaced the river and lake systems' age-old rule over North American trade and travel, and instantly became its era's monument to the new age of mechanized speed.

But if rivers have been routinely honoured by rows of costly houses with picture windows and scenic parks with belvederes, railways see only the city's interesting technical backside. The factories show the railway passage their tubes and tanks, chutes of cascading rubble and racks of shiny car bumpers, tangles and bundles of wires, steam-belching pipes, flapping building exhausts, snappish guard-dogs, junked transformers, the rusting guts of dead trucks. Walkers in the ditch beside the tracks at a certain west-end location see what the street side of a tall brick façade is supposed to conceal: a conclave of skeletal steel titans festooned with wires, all part of a complex and majestic hydroelectric installation its makers apparently thought ugly enough to merit camouflage. So, too, the residents think nobody's noticing—but a hiker alongside the tracks knows of their attachment to clothes-lines, the elegance of their tree-houses, their forbidden backyard businesses (keeping chickens, curing meat in smoke-houses), their past taste in broadloom and sofas, discarded over the fence to decline into soggy pulp.

As an unintended result of its danger and the unpopularity, the urban rail corridor, otherwise so eerily splendid a piece of modern calculation, is also the largest of the city's wild, raw places. In it every sort of garden flower and blooming shrub gone AWOL finds refuge among their feral cousins, the lovely weeds and wildflowers, untamed vines and fruit trees, all come from distant regions into the city's heart with little meddling by any people other than the railway folk.

And people like me. From early spring to the first snow-storm, our dining-room table and desks are rarely without branches of cherry and fragrant blossoms, bunches of wild grapes, cattails and thistles, fragile blue and yellow blossoms cut from broad spills down embankments, and, after freeze-up, selections from the gaunt, rattling skeletons of summer flowers.

The railway officials, quite properly, do their best to keep this botanical invasion at bay, hacking the weeds and striplings and creeping vines back away from the tracks. But some things manage to survive, by luck or just because they're tough. In early spring, the first patches of pushy green can be seen coming up and shouldering aside the dead stalks and grasses along the Canadian Pacific track in my neighbourhood, while nearby lawns are still moribund. The gnarled vines sprawling crazily across the cinder-block backsides of factories are still grey, though scrubby clumps of trees, clumsy thickets and shrubs crowded against fences and walls are thick with plump buds. And before very long, this unfussiest of Toronto land-scapes again is graced with our brief spring's wildflowers, dis-playing their colours under a sky kept wide and open—not for them, of course, but for the trains that have unintentionally created Toronto's sunniest, most savage garden.

## ST. JAMES' CEMETERY

The gilded afternoons of October are surely the year's best for rediscovering the special peace and pleasure of city cemeteries. The long days and abundant flourishing of summer are past; the iron-grey skies of winter are yet to come. Yet in this inter-val between, the stone monuments seem to find their perfect backdrop, against the yellow and red blaze of tree and shrub, and green lawns crossed by skipping scatters of flame-coloured leaves.

There are a number of old Toronto burial grounds to stroll through, and one should take them all in. Gradually, one finds favourites; among mine is St. James' Cemetery, just south of Bloor Street East, on a stretch of rather level ground between Parliament Street and the steep drop-off to Rosedale Valley Road.

A simple explanation for the enjoyment such places provide, beyond their scenic beauty, is the sense of unbreakable kinship with the dead they offer, and the gratitude they solicit for those buried there. Now I know St. James' reputation as Toronto's toniest resting place. It is "the Four Seasons of Toronto cemeteries," a reader of this manuscript jotted in the margin. "You pretty much have to be a member of the Social Register to get in." It is true that many of the city's high and mighty await the Last Judgment in this ground, and will doubtless (like the rest of us) have much to answer for.

Like most of those buried in St. James, I belong to the Anglican tradition of Christian practice; the dead here are my kinsmen and kinswomen in faith, to be honoured in death for reasons of loyalty alone. Moreover, if some of the oldest burials are members of the Family Compact—figures of almost demonic wickedness in nationalist Canadian mythology—this colonial ruling group of soldiers and entrepreneurs, presided over by the Anglican prelate John Strachan, has always struck me as a remarkable bunch, courageously establishing British institutions and cultural ideals in a bleak, muddy no-place at the edge of the Empire, because they believed it their duty to do so. Toronto owes a great deal, including its very existence, to the first creators and sustainers of urban civilization on this hostile shore, and to their early successors—men and women buried here, with such names as Jarvis and Gooderham, Ridout and Osler, Baldwin and Austin and Gzowski.

Whether or not another visitor could summon up such an attitude towards the dead of St. James, anyone interested in cities and urban change will be intrigued by the architecture of death here, and its visible symbolism of the great mental change in our thinking about death that occurred in Victorian times.

The surveying and layout of a new cemetery was undertaken by John Howard in 1842 on behalf of the Church (later Cathedral) of St. James, after it had become clear that the downtown burying ground adjoining the church was no longer big enough for the clientele. The bodies which had gone in the ground since the burial site was established, in 1797, were reverently dug up and moved uptown in 1844 to the new cemetery, established in what was then undeveloped countryside, north-east of the built-up town.

Viewed as a moment in the nineteenth-century transformation of cemetery design, St. James is poised almost exactly in the middle. It was laid out by our prolific first city engineer, John Howard, whose work, it should be noted, began after the inauguration of the modish "new" North American graveyard style, featuring ponds, surprising views, shrubbery, Arcadian hills and dells, pioneered by the Boston Horticultural Society's Mount Auburn Cemetery, a Cambridge establishment of 1831. By the standards of such "advanced" cemetery design, St. James was old-fashioned at the time Howard made it. (By 1849, Philadelphia had almost twenty new-style cemeteries, and an issue of *The Horticulturalist* in that year could proclaim that there was virtually no American city of note "that did not have its rural cemetery.")

At St. James, we certainly find no romantic landscape of tiny secret valleys, streets of Greek tombs, few twisting paths, little sorrowing yew or dripping willow—and precious little else to "elevate the mourner's feelings, reduce his sorrow, promote religious meditations and foster a sweet melancholy," as a recent architectural study has described the effects desirable in a rural cemetery. Instead, St. James is characterized by unscholarly plantings of sturdy Ontario shade trees, a generally unmodified flatness of its terrain (at least in its earliest sections), and many more or less unimposing monuments set on a plain grid.

Architectural fashion appears to have held little interest for the planner of St. James, who was merely trying to replicate, on a large scale, the ordinary grid of the English parish churchyard as it had existed from the early Middle Ages through the nineteenth century—though without a church in the midst. In 1861, as the Gothic Revival was gaining ground in all areas of North American design, this unsophisticated English-churchyard look was suddenly reinforced by the construction of the Chapel of St. James-the-Less. Its interior, clearly a one-stop affair, is invariably disappointing. But on its exterior the outstanding Toronto partnership of Frederick Cumberland and William George Storm expended all their romantic love of twilights and shades, and delight in the antique. (Cumberland, after all, knew John Ruskin; and he had only recently returned from England, ravished by a new-found love of the British Middle Ages.)

The result is a perfection of Gothic Revival mortuary building, antiquarian and mindful, and Toronto's most exquisite and sensitively realized instance of Victorian medievalizing. The addition of this chapel, however, does not alter the fact that St. James is *not* a parish churchyard—and that's where lies the interest in the place for the fan of urban transformations. In 1844, when the original graveyard was full, old Christian practice would have dictated that the churchwardens just dig up the old bones, heap them up in storage sheds somewhere on the property—back in England, the church attic had always been a favourite place—and start dropping more bodies into the ground.

This ancient practice is undergirded by an idea that may seem odd to secular urbanites, who do not sense the novelty of a Christian cemetery separate from a place of worship. In a revolutionary departure from the near-universal practice of ancient Mediterranean peoples, who looked upon corpses as unclean and spiritually contaminating, early European Christians cherished their dead, and expressed their belief in the defeat of death's power to break the unity of the Church by keeping the Christian dead as near as possible to living believers. From at least the fifth century, dead Christians were buried in places of worship—under the floor or in the walls— or at least immediately nearby: hence, the evolution of the English churchyard into perhaps the most sociable and delightful meeting-place of living and dead ever created.

The custom continues almost nowhere today. By the middle of the eighteenth century Enlightenment, the old pagan idea of burial outside the gates was making a strong comeback in European thought, under the guise of a "scientific" worry about sanitation. In France first, later in England and in its colonies, the ancient Roman standard of burying the dead beyond the city gates returned, creating—as an architectural historian has noted with a smile—the first modern suburbs. The full-blown expressions of this notion, part of a far more general secularizing and repaganizing of modern thought, are the churchless, romantically rural picturesque cemeteries of the Mount Auburn type, which were only later engulfed by the cities outside which they were originally constructed. St. James is an example of a "modern" burial ground—laid just outside the mid-century bounds of the fledgling city of Toronto—but largely innocent of Rural Cemetery Movement influence.

It did, of course, get a token parish-style church two decades after its inauguration. This fact may cause archaeologists of the distant future, digging up the site of St. James' Cemetery, to scratch their heads over this Christian burial site of the late second millenium. It will look something like other parish churchyards, though the church on the grounds—the little chapel of St. James-the-Less—will seem unusually tiny when compared to the great number of burials around it. Even more puzzling, perhaps, will be the crematorium in the basement of the chapel.

These researchers will almost certainly know that, for most

of the first two thousand years of Christian history, believers strictly avoided cremation, just as they tended not to bury their dead outside the city gates. So how did it happen that Anglicans started cremating? For the sake of posterity, and supposing this book survives longer than its author, here's the answer.

After cremation, like exurban burial, was revived and popularized in the late eighteenth century, thoughtful Anglicans, like other thoughtful Christians, began to worry about this issue. They were pulled back and forth by formidably old, deep customs concerning the disposal of the dead nearby, and by the new, persuasive and plausible theories of sanitation then making the popular rounds. The argument continued until 1944, when the dying William Temple, Archbishop of Canterbury and one of the Church of England's great minds in our century, decided to settle the matter once and for all. He did so in a peculiarly Anglican way—not by issuing a decree with all the august authority of his ecclesiastical office behind it, but by simply ordering that his body, once the spirit had taken flight, be cremated; which it was. The crematorium at St. James-the-Less was installed in 1947.

## MOUNT PLEASANT

Mount Pleasant Cemetery is the stylish modern burying ground that makes St. James seem stolid and bluestocking today. It is located on a 206-acre tract north of St. Clair Avenue. Were I not resigned to take my final rest in consecrated ground, I can think of few more tranquil places to await the Great Getting-Up Morning than non-sectarian Mount Pleasant, which opened for burials in 1876.

Nor does Toronto offer a better place to start collecting ideas for interesting markers, crypts and such—inventive markers being one legacy of the Garden Cemetery Movement.

In Mount Pleasant's secret glades and on its sunny hillsides, one can find excellent evidence of virtually every sort of taste in monuments, ranging from the post-Christian and melancholic (exampled by those shroud-draped urns and broken columns beloved by sceptical Victorian mourners) to the defiant (the soaring obelisks and serviceable benches of rationalists, the tall, stately crosses put up by Christians) to the efficiently informative (name and dates only).

Some of the best ideas (and also those to be most carefully avoided) are embodied in the grander monuments. Among the noteworthy mausoleums of old is the Massey family's stout, sturdy Romanesque fantasia, created in 1891 by Toronto architect Edward James Lennox, who also gave us Old City Hall, Casa Loma and other studious memorials to grand-manner styles of the past.

Then there's the imperiously pagan Classical temple wherein the remains of the Eatons, of department store fame and Protestant affiliation, lie forever guarded by bronze lions; and, near it, the smaller, exquisitely proportioned Greek study erected in 1905 for himself by financier George Albertus Cox. (The Cox mausoleum, incidentally, has perhaps the most beautiful pictorial stained glass in Mount Pleasant: a faintly decadent *fin-de-siècle* portrayal of the Risen Christ, floating in opalescent, mystic light.)

It has been a long time of course, since any but the very rich have been able to afford the imaginative design and craftsmanship that went into such masterpieces of funereal architecture as the Massey and Cox mausoleums. Anyway, funeral memorials meant to aggrandize the dead and insist upon their splendour are now out of style, even in bad taste; yet the reaction against this former inclination has not, by and large, been a happy one. The long-term design trend suggested by what's in this burial ground is from monumental towards puny, from ornate towards spare, from exuberantly hand-crafted towards routine, mechanical, trite.

*Mount Pleasant Cemetery*

Like other cemeteries in which people are still being buried, the area of Mount Pleasant in most recent use is altogether too cluttered by squat, small grey-granite markers with curving crowns and straight sides, all looking more or less alike—"serp-tops," so called, with faint contempt, by monument designers on account of the serpent-like curve characteristic of their crests.

But even if you have decided to settle for a serp-top, there are still a number of lessons to be learned from Mount Pleasant's wealth of monuments. The first, and perhaps most important: make your gravestone as free of lofty words and pious expressions as possible. The older monuments of Mount Pleasant are mercifully short on vaguely spiritual drivel, though as one moves towards the present the twaddle does seem to increase. We are treated to many a dreary bit of Edwardian uplift, along the lines of "the progress of mankind onward and upward forever," or a school-days tag from Shakespeare plucked out of context.

Most people will want to have at least their names put on the rock. But the rule here, again, is: the less said, the better. Few people, I suspect, will want to go as far in the direction of muteness as Toronto art collector and financier Christopher Horne, whose Mount Pleasant monument, by Ontario sculptor John Noestheden, is simply an unimproved boulder poised atop an open bronze frame—just a plain Ontario rock, and no words or names on the plinth. If an unusual statement, the Horne marker is nevertheless a useful corrective, and a reminder of what's good about the best gravestones, old and new, in this "modern" graveyard: their insistence on the heft, density and solemnity of stone, ideal in this picturesque green setting, and a corresponding reluctance to yap on about the dear departed.

Mount Pleasant is, of course, a romantic (if exceptionally large) modern cemetery, intended to rob death of its grimness and give it a touch of the dramatic—an intention its older sections admirably fulfil. The statues and inscriptions, the heroic sighs and pluck made visible in stone, the reminders of all the murders, sinkings, crashes, heart attacks, shenanigans and quiet, noble passings that brought the current inhabitants of Mount Pleasant to their graves among the ravines, hollows and hills seem all to be neutralized by the exuberant land-scaping. It should come as no surprise that, unlike St. James, Mount Pleasant has become a favourite place to jog or stroll—bringing the recent history of cemeteries around full circle. Towards the end of the eighteenth century, the dead were banished from the dwelling-places of the living; at the end of our century, urban life would hardly be complete without a gracious downtown cemetery to repair to, to work out in, or merely to enjoy. The picturesqueness of the cemetery has drained proximity to the dead of morbidity and fearful-ness—an effect I'm not sure a cemetery *should* have. There is surely health and good sense in being reminded from time to time that we are but dust, and to dust we shall return.

## THE EX

Every August, usually on the stickiest, hottest day of the summer, the main gate swings open to the latest Canadian National Exhibition, the modern world's oldest annual agri-cultural and fun fair, and just about the most gaudy, raucous, sweaty, and low-down-dirty thing we tasteful Torontonians do on a regular basis, in public anyway.

But whatever may go on behind it, the principal entrance of Exhibition Place, known as the Princes' Gates, represents Toronto's most lofty attempt to produce a local item of the "City Beautiful" architectural confectionery popularized by the 1893 World's Columbian Exposition in Chicago. For the North American inventors of our century's best build-ing—plain, businesslike, structurally clear—the fair had been a disaster, and chief designer Daniel Burnham's panoply of white neoclassical fantasy buildings set among artificial lagoons, the source of visual plague. As Louis Sullivan remarked: "The damage wrought by the World's Fair will last a half a century from its date, if not longer."

His judgment would have seemed just to the most forward-looking architects of his time, but to many a builder, I suspect, it would have been absurd. A generation of ambitious American and Canadian architects rushed home from Chicago, their heads busy with plans to put Beauty—the ornamental and grandiose and historic—at the service of civic Boosterism. Thomas H. Mawson swept across the Canadian prairies, laying plans in 1912 for a Saskatchewan Lieutenant-Governor's palace of czarist dimensions, and in the same year envisioning a civic centre for Calgary featuring blocks of enormous white classical office buildings set on a titanic plaza beside an artificial lake.

While these projects in the west came to nothing, Toronto did get its most self-consciously noble piece of city decoration. The Princes' Gates is materially pedestrian, unadventurous in design, and distinctly lacking suitably aristocratic context. It is nevertheless our most wonderfully attractive bit of colonial pomp, show-off and would-be grandeur.

Designed by Toronto architect Alfred Chapman and engineer Morrow Oxley, the "Gates" is actually a single ceremonial gateway, done more or less in the manner of a bewinged Roman arch, but rather more dainty than the heavy old Romans would have abided. The occasion of its building was Confederation's diamond jubilee, in 1927. Its ostensible purpose was to pay patriotic and loyal tribute to the work and know-how that had made Canada a prosperous land.

The gateway is crowned with a flamboyant winged Victory—or, to be precise, a plastic copy of the original, which quickly deteriorated—who stands proudly at the prow of her onrushing ship, a laurel wreath held high for Canada's farmers, industrialists and workers, the true heroes of the nation's modern age. From either side of the gateway stretch complementary colonnades of nine unfluted Doric columns each, tributes to the Canadian provinces that existed in 1927. Both colonnades end in a sort of short curving tower topped by a flourish of Canadian and loyal British heraldry, and fitted out with a lion's-mouth fountain, which occasionally operates.

Unlike a Roman triumphal arch, however, the Princes' Gates is visually most effective when glimpsed from afar and at high speed, like any roadside architecture (such as billboards)—out your car window, that is, while negotiating the broad curve of Lake Shore Boulevard around Exhibition Place.

Stop and examine the structure close up, and the surface grandeur of its styling is quickly deflated. First, there's the matter of the building material, which is not marble but just poured concrete in a couple of complementary tones, one eggshell white, the other gritty beige. And then there's the fact that all the ornamental drama is at the top, to the neglect of what happens down below.

But up along the defining horizontal line of this confection, things are very theatrical indeed. The entablature above the Corinthian columns of the gateway is crisply dramatic in effect and academic in detail. To temper this vigour at the top, Chapman and Oxley fashioned the next level down as a stage for a suite of four pensive allegorical figures, bearing cornucopias and beehives, traditional emblems of plenty and industry. A proper Beaux-Arts monumental fabrication would then have brought the viewer's eye down from this exalted mythological platform, along the serene verticals of the columns, to a dignified horizontal base in the here-and-now world, and, finally, out to the formal garden or promenade which the arch was designed to frame and introduce.

But it's towards the bottom that everything about the Princes' Gates goes wrong. The capitals of the Doric columns representing the provinces, for instance, have been cast correctly and carefully, according to the fashionable textbooks of the day—Chapman learned well his conventional Beaux-Arts architectural flourishes in Paris and New York—but the feet of these columns are merely ugly barrels or cylinders of concrete, without dignity or finesse.

But the real wretchedness starts beyond these pseudo-bases. The Gates fronts directly, with virtually no decent interval, on a busy street feeding cars onto Lake Shore Boulevard. Lying immediately on the inner side of the Gates, on the grounds of Exhibition Place, is a straight avenue which was, until the 1960s, a grand entry-way flanked by trees and fine buildings. All the pavilions of this promenade are gone, along with the trees, save for the beautiful Automotive Building, standing in Art Deco dignity just south-west of the gateway. It is today the only tribute left to Labour and Industry announced by the portal itself. (The handsome Electrical and Engineering Building, on the north side, was demolished and replaced by a parking lot.

The gateway was inaugurated, promisingly, not by an opening-day's crowd of curious visitors, but, as a plaque affixed to the structure tells us, by "a veterans' parade under the auspices of the Canadian Legion & the British Empire Service League for review by H.R.H. The Prince of Wales."

All else in the region is commercial squalour: a jumble of ticket booths and signage, and, worse still, vast deserts of asphalt beyond which rise the tacky façades of the Midway attractions.

Despite the fact that its vision of the nobility of labour in a stately, important architectural ensemble at the east end of Exhibition Place has been lost, the Princes' Gates is surely the most affecting memorial to an honourable aspect of the old Ex that contemporary fair-goers are likely to forget, if they ever knew about it.

Not that the CNE was ever all that serious and honourable. There were weird animal acts and lurid sex shows on the Midway, and all the icky pink cotton-candy you could eat, back in 1927, when Edward, Prince of Wales, and his brother George officially opened the Princes' Gates, and gave the monument its name. The amusements you can buy your way into nowadays are, in fact, distinctly tamer than the really vulgar ones that used to get Toronto's Calvinistic knickers in a proper knot once a year.

But even as the little booths of horrors and tents of wicked pleasures have slowly disappeared from the Ex, so has the fair's role as Canada's grandest annual celebration of its industrial and agricultural progress, and the nation's rootedness in Victorian ideals of loyalty to the Crown and commitment to technological advance declined into insignificance. Only the Princes' Gates remains, to recall this venerable dimension of the Exhibition's long history as a tribute to Empire and excellence, and its role—the role of such fairs in general—in heralding the onset of technological and architectural modernity.

In 1882, the dim night-time alleys between tents and pavillions were turned to day, as Exhibition Place became the first in the world to be lit by the genii of electric lights. The world's first automobile shows were held there, and the first demonstrations of phonograph recordings. Even as recently as the early war years, crowds of CNE visitors were among North America's first people to witness the transfiguration of the human image into electronic signs, as Jack Dempsey and chanteuse Jessica Dragonette faced crude television cameras.

With the electrified fair of 1882, the Exhibition also presented the first instance of the new industrial empire's typical entertainment—not mass warfare, but mass spectacle mimicking the organization of battle-groups. The premiere event was called *The Battle of Alexandria,* and featured bombardments, fireworks, immense painted sets, fiery dragons hovering in the sky and a cast of many hundreds. The spectacles in subsequent years included *The Siege of Peking, The Burning of Moscow, The Last Days of Pompeii*—historical pageants speaking in their content of the empires of this world, but in their form of the coming empire of organization promised by capitalism, catalogues of battles transformed into entertainments, crisis transmogrified into the sustained dazzle of the sign. In *The Burning of Rome,* sheets of fire blazed up, hundreds of actors thronged the market-place before the palace where Nero strummed—then, with abandon, a fight broke out between a coastal fort and an airship, and a collision between a fire engine and an automobile. Already, we find, the spectacle has begun to dissolve historical fact, creating the perverse sidewise slide of signs that characterizes all modern culture, and its sites.

For, indeed, the perverse and the monstrous is the other side of the modern, its demon brother—the subversive side of modern culture that is only discovered, it seems, once the glory of modernist emancipation has been accepted. For the same visitors who came to the CNE to marvel at the revelations of science and technology also came to pay a nickel to peek into the sleazy little tents off the Midway, where JoJo the Dog-Faced Boy displayed his deformity nakedly, the Geeks tore live chickens to pieces and ate them, and the Pinheads, pathetic microcephalic freaks dressed in Mother Hubbards, darted about, chattering imbecilically.

They came for the lurid sex shows, of course, but also for the wonders of primitive movies with titles like *The Laboratory of Mephistopheles*—for tastes of the industrialized empire's promised honky-tonk glitter, allure and horror, sex and the occult, transports of fancy and modern invention at its most wonderful and daring.

Thus for a couple of weeks each year, on the site of the outpost of an older empire, rose this palisaded outpost of the new, in all the optimism, perversity and delight in spectacle of industrialism's infancy.

For me, that delight was always summed up and symbolized best by the Flyer. The 1992 decision by the Canadian National Exhibition to tear down the roller coaster kicked up no fuss. Even the Toronto Historical Board, our town's official worrier about "architectural heritage," did not get involved in one of its usual campaigns of compromise. Nor was anybody else likely to take to the barricades over this issue. The CNE's official reason for dismantling Toronto's only permanent roller coaster was that it just wasn't thrilling any more, or at least not as thrilling as the real stomach-churners being put up at new theme parks such as Canada's Wonderland, just north of Metropolitan Toronto. Only the most fanatical roller coaster aficionado—let alone a less committed pleasure seeker such as this writer, who has ridden the Flyer innumerable times just for the heck of it—would disagree with the CNE's decision to kill off a sure money-loser.

The destruction took place swiftly. By the time the 1992 CNE opened at Exhibition Place, the fusty old coaster was just so many splinters of pressure-treated British Columbia fir—the stuff from which it was constructed, back in 1953—and about a half-mile of crumpled steel track, on which we Flyer veterans experienced so many moments of helplessness, terror and exaltation.

While I never planned to lobby to save the doomed coaster, I did take an early-morning drive down to Exhibition Place after I got the news, just to get a last good look at the Flyer before the wreckers got down to work.

During Ex time, of course, the asphalt wasteland around the Flyer site is thick with the deafening shows of the Midway and crammed with sweaty fun-seekers. The Flyer itself—long ago upstaged by Doppel Looping, the German-built, ideal ride for zero-gravity freaks—was always festooned with glittering lights, like a luxury ocean liner in port, and noisy with the clattering cars and the shrieks of passengers. Late evening was the ideal time to take a ride, since the whip-turns and plunges of the Flyer made the garish carnival lights of the Ex seem passionate, spinning, phantasmagorical.

But in the light of a Toronto spring morning the week the

news came, the Flyer seemed anything but wild and menacing. The waving, soaring lines of its wooden structure rose from the vast flat expanse of deserted asphalt like a voluptuous sculpture, its delicate fabric of bolted, white-painted wood catching the early sun. A roller coaster, I was reminded in that quiet moment, is architecture, not machinery; it had beauty, but the rigorous, new beauty of intelligent, functional form that modern architecture created, and has taught us to appreciate. A roller coaster must be strong but subtly flexible, and precisely, predictably responsive to the extreme physical forces it must contain, channel, withstand. Such principles are expressed in every line of the Flyer, with economical eloquence and entire seriousness.

The poetry of the roller coaster can be experienced, then, in two ways, each quite different from the other. One is a lonely dawn visit, such as the one I just described. The other is by doing the coaster itself.

The projects of all architecture are to define space, and to provide a choreography for moving through it. The roller coaster is an architecture like that of an expressway or an airport runway, intended to abolish limitation, free us from the staid forces of gravity and the facts of natural obstruction. But unlike an expressway, which has no real beginning or end, every coaster creates a precisely predetermined narrative for the traveller, much as a maze does.

The Flyer, for instance, first assured you with a long, slow, seemingly harmless turn. Only gradually did the ground begin to recede, and the fear began to mount, as you were dragged upward by powerful mechanical forces. Then came the first, largest fall—a grand, fast, free descent, more exhilarating than terrorizing—followed by a swooping left turn, a series of quick rises and falls, and a final, especially harrowing whip-turn and sudden stop. The repeat visitor quickly learned the sequence of experiences, though going back again and again never diminished the pleasure. A favourite short story is no less fun to reread, just because you know what happens. Coaster riding is among the few architectural experiences with a precise parallel kinship to reading.

The Flyer never was a great roller coaster. It was more like a tale one loves at thirty and has less time for at fifty. But, all the same, I will miss it—especially the vision of its light, sensuous and architecturally sensible lines drawn, as if by a white pencil, against the grey sky of a Toronto dawn.

*Modern*

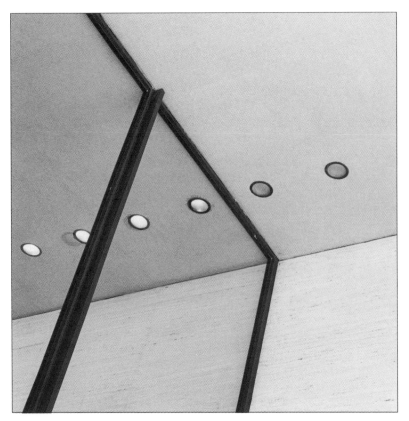

*Curtain Wall, Toronto-Dominion Centre*

# THE CRYSTAL CITY OF HUGH FERRISS

The psalms raised to Toronto journalist and urban activist Jane Jacobs in 1991, the thirtieth anniversary of her famous book *The Death and Life of Great American Cities,* dwelt at length on her opposition to what used to be called "urban renewal," and to her role as North America's most famous officially indignant opponent of urban expressways, the abandonment of the streets and other outcomes of the great postwar love affair with our cars. The crusading tone of *Death and Life* is endearing, and is struck on the first page. "This book is an attack on current city planning and rebuilding," she announces in the introduction. "My attack is not based on quibbles about rebuilding methods or hair-splitting about fashions in design. It is an attack, rather, on the principles and aims that have shaped modern, orthodox city planning and rebuilding."

The enemy was (or at least seemed) clear: the radical idealist megavision in city planning, shaped and popularized among emerging architects and planners in Europe and the United States in the 1920s, eclipsed by the Depression, then brought back into the spotlight and crowned Prom Queen immediately after the Second World War, and given bulldozers to carry her to victory over city messiness. Her quarry, according to Jacobs, was the "organic," makeshift city of scruffy neighbourhoods and casual street life, where presumably workable solutions to urban problems were invented by the folks who actually lived with the problems. In retrospect, the scenario could have been written by Tolkien: real-folk anarchists and small freeholders, facing with courage the robotlike advance of the wicked Prom Queen, and the utopian social engineers in her service.

Nobody nowadays would argue that, by 1961, the record of idealistic planning in North America's cities had become a decidedly mixed business, compounded of magnificent new tall office blocks and of mediocre housing developments, some poorly planned expressways, some superbly planned and executed. Jacobs's portrayal of this complicated scene is caricature, not portraiture. It harped much upon the undeniable ruthlessness of comprehensive city planning, while wilfully shrugging aside the serious philosophical motives in the vision she opposed, and the fervent, even desperate hopes of the young planners and architects riding the bulldozers.

These hopes were rooted in an historic critique of the squalid, crowded industrial city, which had hitherto seemed impermeable, irremediable. The crowded city of the nineteenth century had been breeding grounds for terrible diseases; the great cities of this century, jammed with a poorly urbanized industrial proletariat of new immigrants had been breeding grounds for the even more deadly viruses of revolution and nationalism. To save us from ourselves, in architectural historian Spiro Kostof's words, the great architectural visionaries at our century's dawn wanted to replace all that by "a communitarian utopia beyond regional or national parochialisms," a crystalline, centrally organized "environment consonant with a world free of conflict."

This is not the place to chart the historical trajectory of such visionary megaschemes from their brave beginnings in the drawings of Bruno Taut and Le Corbusier and the young Mies van der Rohe down to the present; and there is hardly a need to dismantle Jacobs's arguments point by point. The successes of Modernist urban planning and architecture that dot and inform Toronto's urban fabric have done that job for me. Yet one Jacobean misrepresentation does deserve debunking: the suggestion that this idealism was an élitist plot, without grounds in concrete historical experience, to smash mindlessly the chummy streets and cozy neighbourhoods of the helpless little folk, huddled in their rabbit warrens within the traditional city (whatever *that* is). Look into the mass culture of the United States or Canada during the 1920s and especially the 1930s, and everywhere—in Buck Rogers cartoons, popular sci-fi movies, futuristic pulp novels—one finds yearning for a clean, monumental, big-city future, and for escape from the limitations of neighbourhood culture. A particularly interesting expression of this street-level longing came my way recently, when a colleague passed along a 1929 book by the popular American architectural illustrator Hugh Ferriss, entitled *The Metropolis of Tomorrow*. Ferriss was no intellectual; but he did understand the international yen for order that had arisen after the First World War, and gave it marvellous visual embodiment in texts, and in his thrillingly evocative charcoal drawings.

His book opens with a description, in word and image, of the spires and masses of the great contemporary metropolis emerging from the mists of dawn. The transfixed writer is plunged into reflection, and imagines himself to be witnessing "some gigantic spectacle, some cyclopean drama of forms..."

Within this architectural spectacle, souls are being formed, lives are being shaped. But how can good souls be formed, he wonders, when so much in the urban environment is still ugly, untidy, dishonest?

Ferriss is appalled by the "thin coating of architectural confectionery," the meretricious "disguises" that line the streets. He is appalled by the jumble of styles, the crowded streets and clumped buildings. "Do we not traverse, in our daily walks, districts which are stupid and miscellaneous rather than logical and serene—and move, day long, through an absence of viewpoint, vista, axis, relation or plan?"

Yet even in the midst of the unkempt contemporary city, Ferriss finds "a hope [which] may begin to define itself in our minds," and he prophesies the arising of a new generation of architects and planners dedicated to bringing this hope to fruition.

The seedlings of Ferriss's hope are, as you might imagine, the first great American skyscrapers. The artist's illustrations of such buildings are reverential and fantastic, not straightforwardly narrative. The Chicago Tribune Building, the Fisher Building in Detroit, the Los Angeles Municipal Tower, the Chrysler Building in New York (here depicted in unfinished form)—these and other buildings, in Ferriss's hands, become titanic, radiant with mystical power and promise. They surge heavenward, dwarfing the streets, and, floodlit, stand out against the gloom of night sky like huge gods adored by the million dwellers of Metropolis.

They are icons of the future city, the scattered hope of things to come. But to what promised land will they take us? Hugh Ferriss whisks us into the modern, mechanical city which he believes must succeed the clumsy, organic one of his own day.

All will be an honest, stern play of materials—concrete, steel and glass—devoid of plaster frills and the ornaments beloved by the academic, historicizing architects. In this truthfulness to materials surrounding us, we city-dwellers shall learn the meaning of truth, and freedom from artifice, contrivance, deceit. Instead of decentralization—a planning goal which "must be dismissed as a mere dream"—the city must be radically centralized, rationalized, transformed into an integrated, compact appliance. (In this celebration of the tight centre, Ferriss is following the lead of the European architectural optimists, from Bruno Taut onward.) To contain and support this intense concentration, the buildings must soar upward from huge bases, becoming objects of geologic scale, like mountains. Through the valleys of this mountain range will surge rivers of expressways, affording free, high-speed movement for all the free citizens of the city's huge population.

Then, in a rather charming touch that betrays Ferriss's typically eclectic American background, the artist pulls back from the European intellectuals' fierce proscription of all historical references, and allows architectural history a literally lofty role. On the highest terraces of Ferriss's gigantic pedestals, Greek Revival temples and neo-Gothic churches rise into the bright, clear air, like shrines on lofty Alpine peaks. But the only deity worshipped therein will be the new Holy Trinity of the future: concrete, steel and glass.

We may smile at the extravagant impracticality of Ferriss's vision, but few people now, I imagine, would find it horrifying. I, for one, find it enthralling. The artist's prophecies are entirely serious, and they are affecting in their urgency and their devotion to showing a way towards a more stable, supportive urban environment. Despite Jane Jacobs's nay-saying, the dreams worked out in Ferriss's head, and the immensely sophisticated mega-urban projects being developed by European thinkers, *were* works of conscience, not drivel, as she has always portrayed them. It is the imaginative richness of this conscience which gave Modernist architectural cosmopolitanism and idealism its early force and popularity, and sustained its European proponents through the tremendous revival of the vicious parochialisms and reactionary politics they despised, through exile, through a second, even more terrible world war. Is it any wonder that such long-frustrated planners and architects felt, after VE Day, that their chance to change urban life and perhaps save us from another such war had finally come—and took it?

## THE TORONTO-DOMINION CENTRE

In 1992 the Toronto-Dominion Centre passed its twenty-fifth birthday. By any measure, this was an important date in the history of Toronto urbanism. The original group of buildings was the largest and last commercial real-estate development Ludwig Mies van der Rohe oversaw in his lifetime. It was the anniversary of Toronto's first architectural scandal, remembered as a time of much shock and pall and aghastness amongst the citizenry, who'd never before seen buildings like these in Toronto. The Centre is today, despite a great deal of later development in the same spirit, the most august stamp of the Modernist idea on Toronto's cityscape.

The anniversary was apparently all a big bother to the Toronto-based Cadillac Fairview Corporation, which manages and partly owns the six-building complex, and whose property managers wished I would stop calling them up to ask their plans. For months, they stalled, hemmed and hawed. Finally, in the spring of 1992, a Cadillac Fairview person rang me up to say they'd decided to throw a little public party that June, "with hot dogs and birthday cake and all that kind of stuff" on the plaza defined by the centre's four original structures. The tone of the affair was to be decidedly low-key. In the shaky commercial real-estate market of the early 1990s, I was told, "you don't want to be too lavish. We want to celebrate, but we don't want to throw big bucks at it."

It never happened. The only thing Cadillac Fairview did— and certainly a more useful thing, at that—was kick in support for a city-sponsored scholarly symposium on Mies van der Rohe, which included such distinguished architectural panellists as Phyllis Lambert, George Baird and Detlef Mertins. Even if the management had thrown a party, I suspect few Torontonians would have danced in the streets. By and large, we have always despised the Centre, though, after the first shock, without passion. Mies's magisterial towers of black steel and glass were immediately dubbed "the coffins" by suburban gawkers and downtown enemies. Not that they were the first office buildings in the International Style Toronto had ever seen. Peter Dickinson's Prudential Building, at King and Yonge, had gone up in 1958, John Parkin's Sun Life Building at 196 University Avenue was done in 1961; and there were others. But the Toronto-Dominion Centre offended as others had not, becoming a lightning rod for those wanting to blame *something* for the death of the cozy, low-profile city centre of yesteryear, and the batallions of hackneyed glass boxes that have been marching into our downtown, just behind the bulldozers, ever since.

Indeed, Toronto did lose a considerable amount of charm when the towers went up, and has never forgiven the loss. Gone is Millstone Lane, and it is missed, if only for its charming name. Gone, also, is a Beaux-Arts, columned bank building which Toronto's tribal memory still cherishes as magnificent and noble. Scraps of graceful ornament, tall and well-turned columns, large fragments of façade from these and other structures swept away by Toronto's surge of downtown development do exist, saved by entrepreneur Spencer Clarke, who set them on lawns of his lakeside Guild Inn, in the suburb of Scarborough. Without them, we would have very little material evidence of what was taken away to make way for Mies's buildings.

If unloved by many from the start, the Toronto-Dominion Centre did at least try to be something other than a misliked curiosity. The city's highest restaurant and observation deck and the first underground movie theatre were all intended by developers to make the site a tourist attraction. This new sophistication was quickly made old-hat by the rise of towers yet taller, and the proliferation of submerged downtown cinema buildings; yet, through the early 1970s, the Centre continued to exercise a peculiar fascination, at least over city-desk editors. As late as 1970, two years after the first towers were occupied, reporters were regularly dispatched to the Centre to report on a broken fire sprinkler, the sighting of a racoon on the roof of the Banking Pavilion, and the anxious utterances of naturalists about the mass crash-deaths of migrating birds.

The 1971 blow-out of a glass window from a high floor of a black tower even prompted a high-profile city safety investigation. There were hints of forthcoming revelations from T-D Centre employees about more glass about to blow. But whether no more windows fell out, or nobody ever came forward with the promised horror stories, or the newspapers just lost interest, I do not know. By the early seventies, in any case, the Centre was well down its slide into the state of taken-for-grantedness it was to enjoy at least until the summer of 1993, when a thirty-nine-year-old corporate lawyer employed in the Toronto-Dominion Tower jumped playfully against a floor-to-ceiling glass panel to see what would happen, and was rewarded with a twenty-four-storey fall to his death.

Like most stories about the Centre in the last two decades, the reporting on this unfortunate incident was routine. We had perhaps gotten used to the towers. In contrast, the early newspaper stories—hoots of scorn or ridicule, and tales of things breaking or going wrong—appear in retrospect to have been attempts to come to terms, somehow, with these immense, solemn and strange buildings: some, by dismissing them as brusquely as they seemed to dismiss us; others, by showing that, because they break and get racoons, these menacing blocks of machined steel and gleaming glass are, well, sort of human.

When the original towers were new and not yet overshadowed by the taller Bay Street skyscrapers to come, their purity and severity may well have seemed overbearing, ostentatious, even menacing. At least some also believed them to be a slap in the face to the stuffily comfortable Edwardianism typical of city culture in the past. The towers seemed to be saying: Toronto the Good—church-going, God-fearing Toronto, the

*Column, Royal Trust Tower*

city of steeples—is no more. If the metropolis needs symbols of its new status, we're the ones: tall, black steel, godless boxes, with nary a whiff of the Victorian spire about us.

Nobody gets exercised about such matters any more, largely, I imagine, because Toronto has accepted the image of itself it glimpses in the mirror of the T-D Centre—an image that is too American for some tastes, and far too imperious and imperial for many Canadians elsewhere. But, by the late 1960s, Toronto had in fact joined the élite fraternity of international centres of finance, industry, investment and development; and it had eclipsed its ancient rival, Montreal, in the race to national economic and urban supremacy. If the exhiliration felt by some about this rapid attainment was called into sharp question during Toronto's anti-development fights of the early 1970s—notably, the campaign to save majestic Union Station from demolition, and the crusade against the Spadina Expressway—the four original structures at the Centre have remained our finest monuments to the sense of civic attainment. They are also intellectually and esthetically compelling, in ways that very few Toronto buildings put up in the Corporate Power Style of the postwar period can match.

For the record, these earliest buildings one sees sited with great precision on the south-west corner of King and Bay streets are: the Toronto-Dominion Bank Tower (fifty-six storeys, officially opened 1967); the flat, single-storied Banking Pavilion (1968); the Royal Trust Tower (forty-six storeys, 1969); and the Commercial Union Tower (thirty-two storeys, 1974), all set on a spacious stone platform elevated above street level.

Walking around them, you sense immediately what early critics loved to hate about these structures: the vast indifference of the project to human scale, however defined; the unrelenting impersonality of the soaring walls of glass and blackened steel; the dramatically vacant intervals among the buildings; the celebration of open space and shunning of cozy nooks; the nearly comfortless stone-lined, glass-walled lobbies (now unfortunately compromised by mediocre fabric wall-hangings). I suspect only the most dogmatic anti-Modernist could fail to find a classic, ancient beauty in the rhythm and consummate grace of the slender square steel pillars holding aloft the roof over the Banking Pavilion, or the rigorous, perfect poetry of black metal, glass and warm beige stone in the ground-level areas of the three original towers. This powerful architecture is also as beautiful at night as during the day, and in this detail the Centre is most radical. No Hollywood-like spotlighting is needed to save it from disappearing after dark—as the designers of futuristic skyscrapers in the interwar years apparently feared—since the walls of glass enable the interior lights of the Centre to become the night sun of the plaza.

Now that Toronto is less cocky than it used to be, the original T-D Centre continues to project immense dignity and intellectual seriousness in the midst of much frivolity and architectural ostentation. It has also been looking faintly run-down of late. One notes with sinking heart, for example, the indifference of the managers, who too often don't bother to change burnt-out bulbs in the magnificent grid of light in the ceiling of the Banking Pavilion, thereby spoiling one of the most sheerly beautiful rooms in Toronto.

If the rigour and purity of the high Modernist building style embodied in the Toronto-Dominion Centre were once daunting, the tastelessness of the designers who have given us the two new towers built into the ensemble since the early 1970s makes such lofty virtues seem downright endearing. In the IBM Tower (1985), we see the transformation of Mies's clear, open entry floor into a boutique-like diversion, with a mezzanine, obfuscating barricades of stone, and shiny stainless-steel staircases.

The most spectacular travesty of Mies's stringent idealism on the site, however, is the Ernst & Young Tower, on Bay

Street just east of the Toronto-Dominion Bank Tower. At ground level, this newest addition to the T-D Centre features the old beige limestone home of the Toronto Stock Exchange (1934), wrapped up in pseudo-Miesian black steel corsetry mixed with references to deluxe Art Deco architecture. This visual gobbledegook goes on for the first several metres of the thirty-one-storey building's rise, whereupon the style abruptly and unaccountably lapses back into the routine Miesian rhymes of black-painted steel and glass the rest of the way up.

This attempt to grind together two great and incompatible agendas of twentieth-century architecture—the radical-utopian and the conservationist—is understandable, if not forgivable, given the avid, eclectic waywardness of corporate architecture nowadays. The Ernst & Young Tower will have done a positively good thing, if it prompts critics to go back and appreciate anew the integrity and beauty of the original three towers and the Banking Pavilion.

Returning to the older buildings, we are reminded that, to Mies's way of thinking, the plain structural elements of steel, stone and glass are not ornaments or images excerpted from the history of building types, and infinitely open to whatever free, witty, imaginative combinations the designer can think up. These very deliberate buildings express no arid logic or functionalism, but rather recall, with splendid clarity, the rational, human mobilizations involved in the making of such tall structures. The industries of mining and steel milling, for instance; the assembly and deployment of workers, the coordination of financing, design, many technologies, and, above all, precise information of every sort. The towers give visual expression to the energies and abilities that have given us the modern world.

Architectural post-Modernism has attempted to bring back into building the wit, inspiration and expression of traditional Western architecture. In the rational-utopian Modernism embodied in the Toronto-Dominion Centre, wit is excluded;

but so is imagination itself, that most durable idea we have inherited from Romanticism.

In this revolutionary view of building, Technology takes the laurel wreath that, for so many centuries, crowned Imagination. That doesn't mean a Miesian building is a simple machine. It does mean that the imagery of such building—the openly architectonic, systematic, non-ornamental ways materials are used and combined, the aloof indifference of the building to context—are grounded in an experience of how modern machines and mechanized social forces look and work, instead of springing from some mysterious play of fancy in the mind of the architect.

I find it interesting to note how unquestioned the idea of Imagination is nowadays, as a way to explain the creative process of building. Many people, who are not inclined to invoke divine inspiration in a discussion of creativity, would be quite speechless if you took the equally mysterious doctrine of Imagination away from them. Yet Imagination is neither a particularly old nor eternal notion. Miesian architecture would have us leave this theoretical novelty behind, and move to a post-religious, post-Romantic philosophy of making things. One is tempted even to call it an architectural spirituality: though its terms would include neither God nor Imagination, the idea of Modern supplies radical and transcendental values for negotiating our position in the world, and for guiding our construction of dwelling.

The towers on the south-west corner of Bay and King are serviceable office buildings; but they are also evangelical statements of a profound idea of our moment in time and history. They call us to resign ourselves to our situation in the wholly technological, post-human yet endlessly interesting world our machines have given us—to leave nostalgia and the sumptuous self-centredness of humanism behind, and embrace the unromantic, creatively alienated present which industrial capitalism has created for us.

No wonder people were upset when these uncompromis-
ing edifices in downtown Toronto went up. Yet we would do
well to attend carefully to the severe doctrine of creative and
spiritual life embodied in them, if only to understand why we
are inclined to answer the summons of these buildings with
the single, emphatic word *no.*


## LESSER MODERN

"If you are ever driving on I-91 through Connecticut, don't
miss the Colt Firearms Building on your way to New England
diversions."

So begins Ada Louise Huxtable's *Architecture, Anyone?*, a
1986 gathering of reviews done during her long, distinguished
stint as architecture critic for *The New York Times*. Not that
the nineteenth-century brick Colt building is blessed with any
particular magnificence, or historic importance. It's just been
the landmark that, for many years, has been telling the author
she's gotten to Hartford.

"I find, when I think of it," Huxtable continues, "that I
have a set of such landmarks—personal, transient, and indelible—that mark the stages of my journeys and the stages of my
life. I wait for these particular places on trips year after year;
they are all old friends." I was delighted to discover that
Huxtable and I share one of these old friends: the streamlined
Bulova watch factory near La Guardia Airport, that, for
decades, has been letting me know I've again hit the Big Apple.

Think about it, and you'll probably find that what's true
on the long-haul car or plane trip is also true on the short hop
across town, or around the block to office or supermarket or
mall—though you may not even become aware of your personal landmark until it has disappeared.

Here's an example. Almost every school-day since my tot
was marched into junior kindergarten, some seven years ago, I

have driven home from the morning drop-off the same way. Though I don't remember consciously having picked it for this reason, the route ensured that I would always pass a small, blockish brick and concrete storage building of some kind, completely ordinary except for a few discs and flutings on its plain façade, and a certain dignity—broad-shouldered, utilitarian—about the relations of flat roofline, door and strip windows. No engineer had thoughtlessly thrown up this building to shelter something. It had been designed by some corporate or municipal wage-slave who could nevertheless draw well, who had a taste for high style, if tiny scope to project his taste into the stuff of architecture.

Then, one afternoon, this unimportant little structure vanished. Until my first pass by its rubble-strewn site the next morning, I'd never realized how much the sight of it each morning had meant to me, or even that it had meant anything at all. The building was always just there, morning after morning: a station on the *via dolorosa* of the cross-town traffic crawl, a signal that I was exactly a minute away from home and peace.

This little loss disconcerted me, and set me to thinking of other personal urban landmarks that I've noted for years, with similar absent-minded appreciation, and without a thought of how quickly they can disappear.

The list is not long. But towards the top of it is surely the derelict steel-framed glass work occupying a narrow triangular property bounded, on the north, by the grim old wall of the Queen Street Mental Health Centre, and unpopulated Sudbury Street, slanting sharply sidewise down to King Street.

On countless trips between home and office, I have driven past this long glass edifice—or sequence of boxy glass structures, apparently added on to one another over time—but hardly ever without experiencing a certain delight. This delight is akin to the exaltation we know in the presence of serious, thoughtful architecture, but is tinged with the regret we often feel about fine, perfectly serviceable buildings that have been allowed to fall into disuse, and slip into decay.

Now the glass shed on Sudbury Street is not supposed to be taken seriously as architecture. It's engineering—built, it appears, just after the Second World War to meet the needs of the mighty Massey-Ferguson farm machinery company, which employed up to eleven thousand workers, and is yet another Toronto industrial titan to have passed recently over the Styx. But even if it's not architecture, the building is, or was, a glittering folk reminiscence of the International Style at its most transparent, utilitarian, explicit. The severe linearity of the glass curtain walls, the crisp right-angle meeting of flat roof and glass wall, the geometric clarity of design, and absence of jerry-building—such are among the beauties we find in the best Modernist factory construction, and also in this obscure, utterly unprepossessing ensemble of glass boxes. Trendy architectural historians hardly miss a chance to scoff at Modernism's claim to have discovered a genuinely timeless, styleless style, a manner of building devoid of ornament yet beautiful, lovely in its response to the basic forces of gravity, light, space and use. Quite often, when passing my dilapidated glass building, I have wondered whether the Modernists had not in fact recovered the great classic architectural truth of the ages.

This landmark on the personal map of Toronto I carry around in my head should not pass into oblivion without at least a notice, and a few words of historical description. Jotting about any such building is never easy, given the general poverty of documentation on industrial construction, and the rapidity and frequency with which they are swept away, *sans* plans or a trace of written history behind. But as near as I can make out, the reinforced concrete edifice at the corner of Shaw and King Street West, from the west side of which springs the glass structure, is a building of turn-of-the-century vintage, and of Chicago warehouse inspiration. It has pillars notched to make them look like masonry, and a cornice that runs all round, presumably to give the façade a touch of class. Neither it nor the glass annex stretching westward appear in any city directory until 1948. In the Toronto fire-insurance atlas updated to 1964, this set of two buildings is called the "north combine plant," and is included as part of the "Massey-Harris-Ferguson" plant site.

Beyond these meagre facts, I have been able to discover nothing. (Not that I have tried very hard to do so. Certain buildings spark curiosity, others, especially derelict ones, ask to be left enshrouded in obscurity; the north combine plant belongs to the latter sort.) But before it was allowed to slide into its present dinginess and dilapidation, this transparent composition of neatly, resolutely joined glass volumes must have gleamed brilliantly in the morning sunshine. And even in its current shabby condition—the structure is doomed, along with the other housings of the defunct Massey-Harris empire, once headquartered on King Street West—its purity and lucidity recalls a recurring dream in Western architecture. That dream, at least as old as the great European cathedrals, is to lighten walls and roof, minimizing the roof-supports, and opening previously dark, cavernous exteriors to sunshine and sky. Perhaps no drive in the project of Western architecture has been more durable. It has often suffered reversals, most recently in the religiose gloom and heaviness favoured by the American Romanesque revivalist Henry Hobson Richardson and his myriad clients and disciples, and in the opaque, lightly decorated wall and indirect or filtered light popular during the *rappel à l'ordre* of Depression-era building.

If, by the early 1990s, cladding whole buildings in glass had become the most boring stutter in the vocabulary of urban architecture, it was not always so. Before the end of the Second World War, it was do-able, even though rarely thinkable. Then, in 1948 or so, the Massey-Harris company decided to construct its north turbine plant, and the style picked, probably for its cheapness and utility alone, was that of

*117*

sturdy glass set in light steel frames, and covered with a flat roof. But even if nobody noticed, and if not many people will ever care, a dream almost as old as Western architecture itself unobtrusively came true on Sudbury Street, and endured, and was still there the last time I drove by it.

## CONFEDERATION LIFE

Upon completion late in the summer of 1992, the Confederation Life Insurance Company's national head office, located just below Bloor Street East, became an Instant Landmark.

As opposed to an *historical* Landmark, that is—a red brick mansion or venerable civic building through which schoolkids are herded while being lectured about grizzle-chinned Victorians whose names and accomplishments they forget at once. To become a shrine of *that* sort is easy. All an old building has to do is survive the tsunamis of urban renewal which sweep over old parts of every city from time to time.

To qualify as an Instant Landmark, however, a building has to be, like Confederation Life, a show-off and a likeable bully. It must poke fun at tiresome tastefulness, be impudent, outlandish. It helps, too, if it can be put in a stylish architectural "context." (Sceptics should be aware that neo-Gothic has definitely been in at least since 1987, when Philip Johnson and Raj Ahuaja's medievaloid, spired and piered IBM Tower opened in Atlanta.) It must come flirtatiously close to insulting its hometown's most venerated architectural monuments, thus imprinting itself on the maps in our heads as a downtown edifice we love to hate, or hate to love.

But love it or hate it—and we should definitely view it cautiously—there's nothing in Toronto quite like the eighteen-storey Confederation Life by architect Eberhard Zeidler, Toronto's best producer of comfort-controlled paradises for the era of Late High Consumerism. (Among Zeidler's former projects: the mammoth heaven of consumption known as Toronto Eaton Centre; the provincial government's water playground, Ontario Place; and the sprinkling of fairy dust that changed a dingy cement warehouse at Harbourfront into a glittering shopping mall.) From its enormous footprint—or dinosauric stomp—south of Bloor East's ceremonious strip of insurance companies, the glass-and-marble citadel punches towards heaven, with an occasional dodge-back here, and there, gleaming metal ornaments reminiscent of details from the Batman movie sets, and whimsical slants and angles everywhere. It's a game with eccentric building types, from medieval representations of the Tower of Babel to Buck Rogers, via the pyramidal Romanesque fancy at the Abbey of Fontevrault, France, known as Evraud's Tower.

The tower at Fontevrault, by the way, is remembered in local story as the lair of a robber. Its beaconlike shape was designed to lure lost travellers from the forest, into a place where they could be conveniently mugged. If that's not exactly a savoury association for the head office of an insurance company, who cares? The building is all dance and play. Anyway, serious architectural thinkers I pay attention to had already brushed off this architectural Carmen Miranda before it was finished. So passionate was the feeling that, after my *Globe and Mail* column about Confederation Life appeared, I got a number of anxious letters and phone-calls from professors and builders, who appeared to think my having just mentioned the structure in print was to bless it. Now while I did not then, and will not now, bless the building—everyone can relax—I confess it did set off a train of thinking in my head about how Toronto got flattened, and why we take this condition completely for granted.

For in addition to its gaming with historical forms, Zeidler's snappily eye-snagging structure did give Toronto's knocked-off Modern buildings and the flat skyline they've created a nice comeuppance, with a crown of up-jutting marble fangs and dormer windows, and a high green tower tapering upward to culminate in a voluminously steaming chimney, like the top of Dorothy's pal the Tin Man.

Of course, pitches, dormers, gables and other swell roof details have never disappeared from the single-family house; in Toronto, as elsewhere, the sleek glass-and-steel box-houses built in North America since the 1930s by Richard Neutra, Walter Gropius, Marcel Breuer and others, however exciting they look in picture books, never caught on with residential clients or builders. Nor, before 1945, had there been a great deal of interest in challenging the pieties of traditional historicist building. Toronto's townscape resembled that of any small, staid midwestern American city, with slender steeples punctuating the sky, acres of low Depression-era shanties and slums near industrial areas—and a few cautiously untraditional skyscrapers and monumental public buildings. Toronto was still quite literally pedestrian in 1945—designed, that is, to be viewed at walking, shopping, browsing or church-going speed. Hence, the prevalence of low skyline, and the continued tradition of crowning, hatting, cornicing and otherwise beautifying the façades above the first storey.

Emerging from the Depression and the Second World War with a boom-town in the making, and with attitude and ambition to match, Toronto and its developers lost little time in transforming the Toronto skyline from Victorian steeple-spiked to stylishly Modernist flat. Confederation Life cutely reminds us of this historical fact, simply by upstaging the Modernist drudge-work in its neighbourhood with much uppity, expensive festivity. (From what benumbed, T-squared architectural brain, one wonders, sprang the squat, ugly national headquarters of the Anglican Church of Canada, across Jarvis Street from Zeidler's pistachio sundae?)

In the first decades of the Cold War, the Western cities were ready for the flat roof and geometric outline, for reasons too easily forgotten or ignored. To draw a plain horizontal roofline across the top of an office building could be read—only then, and perhaps never again—as capitalist democracy's reply to several uglinesses. The neo-Gothic monstrosities going up in Stalin's Moscow, for example, and the Nazi romance with old-fashioned pitched roofs and other presumably *volk-ish* architectural recipes. The ideological motive was strong, in ways we find difficult to feel at this distance—so strong, in fact, that it overrode the ancient architectural truth that a flat roof is the worst kind imaginable.

Browsing in an architecture library recently, I came across a recent publication of the British government called *Flat Roofs Technical Guide.* This complicated engineering manual begins with this warning in bold-face type: "Flat roofs should only be considered when the ruse of a sloping or pitched roof is impracticable." (I don't understand why a sloping roof is a "ruse," but never mind.) The manual then follows up this stern advice with myriad illustrations of everything that can, and almost certainly will, go wrong with a horizontal roof—leaking, collapse, warping.

None of this practicality seems to have counted with, and may not have dawned upon, the postwar architectural avant-garde. They, and their ambitious clients, were ready to draw a line in the dirt between themselves and all that had gone before; and the level roofline seemed like something worth fighting for, against the mummery of roofs pitched, gabled, towered or domed. Thus was the traditional roof never even considered for inclusion in the lexicon of styles being developed by the designers of our new apartment blocks and institutional and office towers.

Some sensitive observers recollect Toronto's postwar epidemic of high and low flat-topped construction with horror, especially when the epic scale of demolition is factored in. As far as I can tell, this transformation left us with a cityscape visually more healthy, not sicklier; and more interesting than it had ever been before.

The story of the city's revision has been excellently sketched in the Bureau of Architecture and Urbanism's *Toronto Modern: Architecture 1945–1965*, which accompanied an exhibition held at City Hall in 1987. In their introduction, the producers of this show recall the *annus mirabilis* 1948: the year not only of *refus global*, Quebec's famous declaration of cultural independence from past, piety and parochialism, but also the year in which Modernist evangelist Siegfried Giedion's militantly titled *Mechanization Takes Command* appeared, and, by a nice coincidence, the Mechanical Building at the University of Toronto was built. If the book heralded the ascendence of Modernist urbanism and Euro-American avant-gardism in the built world, Allward and Gouinlock's academic pavilion—with its formal rhyming of horizontal volumes, its reinforced concrete and steel bones, its terrazzo floors and stainless steel railing—announced that the idealism of the Modern had arrived in Toronto.

From 1948 through the early 1970s, the Modernist reconstruction of Toronto continued—unrushed, with the deliberate, carefully plotted pacing typical of every project this city undertakes—leaving in its wake a great many forgettable steel and cement cereal boxes, a few masterpieces, and a cityscape and urban imagination transformed.

The catalogue of *Toronto Modern* lists and lauds a number of the great works. Among them: the remarkable new town of Don Mills (begun in 1953), where John B. Parkin, James Murray and other decisive figures in local architecture learned their craft, and the short, eccentric and brightly coloured Anglo Canada Insurance Co. at 76 St. Clair Avenue West (1954)—a controversial choice, to put it mildly. Then there is Parkin's serene, authoritative Ortho Pharmaceutical office building and plant (1955), Peter Dickinson's Benvenuto Place Apartments (1955)—still a paradigm of sophisticated city dwelling—the Toronto-Dominion Centre (begun 1963), of course, and Viljo Revell's daringly different Toronto City Hall (1965).

These are the monuments; the stand-outs from the crowd. The exhibit quietly omitted the embarrassments. But whatever one's discontents with this or that Modernist construction, or reservations about the process as a whole (which included expressways, superblock subdivisions and shopping malls, along with masterworks like Benvenuto Place), Toronto will never again be the place it was before 1945. The change in the city's mind has been wrought, and cannot be undone. As *Toronto Modern* states, "integrated and efficient public transportation, elegant open spaces, and monumental public, corporate and educational buildings are hallmarks of Toronto's ascendency as an international metropolis." The editors could have mentioned the rise of splendid bookshops, commercial galleries dealing in advanced contemporary art, a theatre and experimental music scene, vast record stores, a culture of high fashion—all elements in the economy of sophisticated desire, sexuality and knowledge that matured along with Toronto's measured, pervasive experiment in architectural Modernity.

While we need the occasional reminder of how good Toronto life is, we do not need many more funnily exotic buildings like Confederation Life. But huzzah! for Eberhard Zeidler and his curious beacon anyway, just for inspiring us to ignore Modernism's misbegotten cubes and domino stacks, and cherish Toronto's leap to Modernity, the immediate heritage of us all.

# Shopping

*Parking Lot, Galleria Mall*

# PARKDALE

It takes a good reason to get a Torontonian who doesn't live there down to Parkdale's smelly, rundown Queen Street strip. And it takes a strong stomach to stick around long enough to discover the higher cultural pleasures of this ill-famed neighbourhood west of downtown.

I know. I have spent more than one afternoon walking and photographing Queen West between Dufferin and Jameson, all the while avoiding meaningful eye-contact with the prostitutes in hot pants, dodging oblivious mental out-patients weaving along the sidewalks, almost tripping a couple of times over addicts slumped in doorways, and witnessing more human wreckage per metre of street than I've seen anywhere this side of lower Manhattan. But explorers can ill afford to be prim. And no one curious about how Toronto's important Victorian street looked and worked should skip a visit to the Parkdale strip.

As a whole, Queen—from its eastern termination at the R. C. Harris Filtration Plant, a Depression Modern masterpiece of civic architecture, to its less gracious west end just short of High Park—is a retail street unhonoured in Toronto, and even less admired than honoured. It is nevertheless a treasury of neglected architectural and cultural artifacts, displaying remnants of every fashion in commercial architecture to sweep

Toronto from early Victorian times to the late-Modern present and the post-Modern beyond. Apart from the Parkdale stretch of Queen—for reasons I'll get to presently—no nineteenth-century commercial streetscape of comparable uninterrupted length, architectural hauteur or aesthetic variety has survived Toronto's past one hundred years of ceaseless speculative destruction and replacement. Looking along the north side of Queen from the edge of Parkdale closest to downtown—where the eastbound Queen streetcar rumbles down into the stone tunnel under the railway tracks—one sees block after block of sophisticated and often sumptuously turned-out tall buildings from the 1880s, Parkdale's final decade as an independent political entity, and the early 1890s, its first years as a Toronto neighbourhood.

The street level of almost every tall, narrow retail establishment built during this consumer heyday featured a large-windowed shop with a prominent entrance, through which Parkdale's variously heeled citizenry passed in search of fine millinery and humble bonnets, bread and carriage fittings and fresh beef, the latest international fashion as well as heavy-duty clothes suitable for the working man. Retail outlets still face the street, though they are now places like The Wildside bar, countless Vietnamese video rental and doughnut shops, and one discount outlet after another.

Above each shop would typically have been a suite of offices, or a spacious two-storey flat for the store's proprietor, with parlour and large window on the second level, often showing a face of handsome Romanesque Revival brick and stone detail to the street, and with sleeping quarters on the third. Throughout this zone, the street architecture of Queen is self-conscious, ornamented, slow—built and adorned, that is, to be seen and savoured at pedestrian shopping speed, or at most, the speed of a horse.

But the automobile, which created an entirely new way to see the city: namely, as rumps—those of cars up ahead, and of sexually interesting pedestrians—and as a horizontal band of flashy store-front signs, sealed the fate of those fancy finials, upsweeps, knops and other ornaments that once crowned every respectable business establishment worth the name.

Mr. Small, the butcher, knew nothing of automobiles, but did intuit the relation between speed and awareness. So it was that he coiffed his abattoir at 1372 Queen W. with a tall, flourishing cornice, and installed good terracotta heads of cow and sheep on either side of its high bay windows to advertise his trade, and his own importance, and that of street and town. And when, in 1892, the builders of the music school at 1482–1486 Queen West put graceful towers atop a window-fabric of fluid Gothic tracery, they clearly expected their decoration to be a sign of prosperity, high culture and aspiration. Thus architecture, as always, matches civic ambition. Newspapers of the day reflected Parkdale's hype when they wrote of it as "floral suburb" of Toronto, a delicious refuge for those seeking "a refreshing coolness that is lacking in the close and sultry city."

Queen Street played a particularly important civic role in this Parkdale of affluence and ex-urban resort. It was then the principal entranceway for vehicular traffic approaching Toronto from the west—hence its double role, as eclectic shopping promenade serving a local clientele ranging from wealthy to working-class, and a ceremonial, auspicious entrance to the great Victorian city adjoining it on the east. As befitted such a street, Toronto's mainstream architects had a hand in creating the streetscape we see today. "Parkdale was no quaint village," Alec Keefer said as we strolled along Queen together last week. "It always knew itself to be part of the big city."

Though long an admirer of Parkdale, at least at a safe distance, I have Keefer to thank for unveiling the historical and architectural facts undergirding its visual patterns and pleasures. A resident of the neighbourhood, a passionate architectural conservationist and local historian, Keefer has developed every urban connoisseur's knack of simply ignoring the decay, and openly exulting in what's left of imaginative cultural form—in Parkdale's case, "an urban form dictated by this fact: the merchants had to cater to a complete society. They had to provide straw hats, as well as Paris originals."

He singles out two low, connected buildings a casual observer would easily overlook, and hails them as perhaps the earliest remaining structures on this strip of Queen West, dating from the 1860s. He delightedly relates that a broad and gracious palazzo-like fabric of shops and flats was constructed in 1898 as an investment property by the Anglican Church of Quebec, dabbling in real estate at the time. (We assume this origin has nothing to do with the sign reading "Jesus, I Trust You," that hangs from the imposing little Ionic belvedere high on the façade.) He proudly points out a multi-colour brick façade which he and fellow activists discovered and, after a campaign to remove the hateful metal siding which had long concealed it, uncovered.

This remarkable strip of commercial architecture, like many another precious urban survival, owes its enduring presence in our imagination to enthusiasts of Keefer's stripe. Its continuing physical existence, however, is largely due to calamities that turned out to be blessings after all.

The more important of these mishaps was the dethronement of Parkdale from triumphal entry into a dead corner of Toronto by the diversion of heavy, high-speed traffic from Queen onto the lakeshore traffic corridor. Like Weston and numerous other communities on Toronto's spreading fringe, Parkdale had already begun its decline in private riches and urban status before its wholesale engulfment by Toronto. In Weston, however, the continuing usefulness of its principal thoroughfare ensured an afterlife for it, however baleful and fitful; and it supplied a reason to continue demolition and renovation. In contrast, the final shunting of all traffic inbound from Niagara and the United States from Queen—along with the postwar move of shoppers away from street-front specialty stores to malls and chains—deprived shop-owners of any incentive to improve their store-fronts. Both ideological and economic motives for keeping Queen showily up-to-date had thus vanished. So it happened that virtually the whole north side of the strip—the finest commercial row, put on the north side to catch the sun—was left more or less alone as they were at the turn of the century. Less even than Spadina Avenue, a great old retail esplanade always much more proletarian in spirit, the essential architecture of Queen Street has remained largely undisfigured by garish neon lighting, shouting paint colours and metal siding.

Another calamity, this one unalloyed, was Toronto's indifference—at least this is the way Keefer weighs up the history—when it came to keeping Parkdale stocked with public amenities in top architectural styles following the municipality's annexation in 1889. The present public library, for instance, is a low, mean block of bricks, "sucking the life out of the street," says Keefer, and expressing nothing of learning's joy and richness. Among the very few noteworthy newer buildings on the strip is the streamlined police station—now an emergency shelter—put at 1313 Queen in the early 1930s by City of Toronto architect J.J. Woolnough, the same gifted stylist who gave us the magnificent Horse Palace at Exhibition Place.

Then descended the Great Depression, and the subsequent conversion of many of Parkdale's ample, upper-middle-class homes into cheap, crowded flop-houses. Later, after the Second World War, came the destruction of whole streetscapes to make way for high-rises packed with low-renters. More recently Parkdale has suffered the takeover of virtually all remaining detached houses south of Queen by absentee landlords, further contributing to the squalor into which much of the neighbourhood has sunk so deep.

But at the top of this commentary, you will recall, I said urban explorers cannot afford to be prim. I'm ending it with another admonition. Urban explorers cannot afford to ignore Parkdale and the many other high-style Toronto beauties that, through no fault of their own, have slid into urban eclipse and neglect during Toronto's two centuries of radical capitalist development and transformation.

## THE GOLDEN MILE

I went looking for the Golden Mile because of its lilting high-Modern name, and because it was one of those fabled places Toronto people pushing middle age mention with reverence. In the 1950s, what would become The Mile—then flat countryside beyond Toronto's north-east edge—had been sold to big manufacturers and their employees as "an oasis of industrial opportunity and harmony. Its booming factories fueled images of limitless wealth." This peppy quote, from a final memoir published by the union local at General Motors' Scarborough Van Plant. Almost three thousand members put in their last shift there in early 1993, and left the once-magnificent engine of local Progress and Prosperity an empty hulk, clean, flat and dead, set back from the broad stretch of Eglinton Avenue East bisecting The Mile's superblock.

The rolling carpets of lawn along Eglinton have gone shabby, and random shacking and shedding and putting up fast-food outlets have ruined the once-dramatic stripes of green and strong lines of horizontal factories paralleling the street. The Canadian General Electric plant still boldly faces Eglinton, though the grand building is an empty shell. Philips Electronics long ago moved its manufacturing of black-and-white TV sets to Taiwan. And no trace remains of developer Avie Bennett's tremendously popular and successful strip plaza that anchored The Mile's western end. It was the essence of The Mile's newness and flash, erected right after West Vancouver's Park Royal, the first shopping plaza in Canada, when the idea of shopping strips surrounded by acres of asphalt parking spots was the hot continental vogue in consumption. By the 1970s, the enclosed mall was leaching the vitality from such strips; and today, where Golden Mile Plaza once stood is a metal shed, sheltering bulk food stores, a discount grocery, cheap clothing stores, boom-box and heavy-metal record outlets, and all the other suppliers of a proletarian clientele on the slide.

When I went, I had in mind the writing of a hymn of praise to this jubilant, instantly famous act of Modernist planning. What I saw made me flip shut my notebook, and forget about ever writing up what I had seen. Until, that is, I happened upon a 1986 column about the site by John Sewell, former mayor of Toronto and sometime *Globe* columnist. It was a happy discovery.

Written on the occasion of the dilapidated Golden Mile Plaza's rip-down, Sewell's story is largely a tribute to the politicians, land developers and industrialists who made The Mile arise and flourish. If The Mile is a ruin today, Sewell reminds us, it is one with a proud, clever past. More district than strip—though strip is what its name makes it sound like—The Mile is the most memorable commercial and industrial superdevelopment to pop out of the serene countryside ringing Toronto immediately after the Second World War. Its creation also marks Toronto's first experience of instant industrial and commercial development as radical therapy for an ailing local economy. The malady of postwar Scarborough township, like many another urban ill, was brought on by loveliness, and a rolling landscape that seemed suffused with infinite opportunity. The green and subtle hills, peaceful farms and deep, shaded ravines made this patch of southern Ontario one of the most lovely places on earth. Indeed, for newlywed veterans and their families, and for waves of newcomers from across Canada and the world, the idea of living in the pre-sprawl expanses of Scarborough, quiet and rural under a cloudless summer sky, must have seemed like a storybook dream.

*Eglinton Avenue East*

This widespread perception was not lost, of course, on residential developers. Within weeks of VE Day, bulldozers were wrecking Scarborough's barns and farmhouses, and shaving the ground down to a flat plane suitable for the immense housing subdivisions then on the drawing boards. Over the next few months and years, the formerly pastoral township would be carpeted by low-cost bungalows and "starter homes" which, as it happened, became last stops for many, leaving the huge area the visually monotonous, slowly dilapidating scene it is today.

The high-rolling municipality had no crystal ball—and even if the councillors had possessed one, they probably would have ignored the dismal pictures of the future which lurked in its depths. All Scarborough could see were tax-coffers stuffed with gold, plucked from the pockets of the new homeowners riding the tide of economic hope into the subdivisions. But the town's rulers were quickly to learn the fiscal truth that no political entity can thrive, or even survive, on residential taxes alone. So it was, in 1948, that the town government snapped up 225 acres of land at the intersection of Victoria Park and Eglinton Avenue East, and began aggressively courting industrialists to set up shop there. It worked. Soon, fridge and toaster makers, car-part stampers, cosmetics and plastics manufacturers and other big corporate taxpayers had occupied the greensward along "Canada's Golden Mile of Industry," as the tax collector's golden goose had been dubbed. The huge human influx provided the labour power necessary to operate the plants, and generate both profits and taxes. Scarborough was saved.

It was in 1953 that the zone came into its fullest glory, when the first of the forty-two stores in Golden Mile Plaza opened for business. The unroofed strip mall, a revolutionary development in its day, was a hit with the parents of the baby-boomers from the start, and a trumpet-call to all that Toronto had made the grand switch from cozy British high-street shopping to American-style suburban consumerism. Many

Scarborough folk, I am sure, can fondly recall the day in 1959 when the Queen was brought to Golden Mile Plaza, to bless with her regal presence this newest of wonders, strip shopping.

We do not know what, if anything, Her Majesty thought about the Golden Mile. But we do have the musings of John Sewell, who did not forget the thrill of this early episode in Toronto's abrupt jump-up to urban Modernity. His memorial suggests more than mere admiration; indeed, it reveals a real soft spot for the Mile in its heyday: "The Fifties," crooned Sewell "when my generation drank milkshakes at the Honeymoon, and listened to Elvis Presley. We didn't share much with our parents, except perhaps the dream of the Golden Mile on the outskirts of Toronto. Now, in the eighties, dreams could never glitter in the same way."

It was something I did not expect from Toronto's only mayor ever to ride a bicycle to work, to fight the developers like a bobcat before, during and after his term of office in the early 1970s, and serve Toronto's anti-development neighbour-hoodniks as exemplary political advocate and hero. So what do we find in Sewell's nostalgia for "the dream of the Golden Mile," other than that the former mayor is made of the same stuff as us all?

Civic convictions, including the anti-development ones for which Sewell has been so eloquent and principled a spokesman, are formed in the crucible of maturity, urban experience, bad knocks, and revulsion against the damage the selfish and powerful can wreak on the city fabric. But if grown-up experience should lead a man to opinions more measured than those of his impulsive adolescence, he can never afford to forget the music and magazines, the soda shops and back seats, and places like Golden Mile Plaza in which he awoke to sexuality, his soul and adult body and its longings, and discovered the civic stage on which will and desire would be tested against reality. Much of life is spent overcoming the mistakes we made in such cultural environs, and learning from the successes.

So here's to His Former Worship, for reminding us to treasure the sites of our openings to the world, even after we've decided to write out of our political agenda much of what we learned there.


## MALL ENDURANCE

Here is your assignment.

You are to drive to one of North America's 2,500 regional malls—defined by retail analysts as a covered shopping centre featuring at least two department stores and one hundred shops, and attracting customers from within a twenty-mile radius—then lock and leave your car on the skirt of asphalt always surrounding such sites.

You are then to stay inside the building exactly three hours—the current average period of a mall visit in North America—and *hate* every single minute of it. Just being bored doesn't count, by the way. You really do have to hate it, from the first to the last minute you are there.

Now that may well be a problem. While pre-testing this assignment at two immense Toronto-area malls—Yorkdale, in North York, and Mississauga's Square One—I found myself becoming crashingly bored long before I could work up a decent hate for these dreamlands of consumerism. That's perhaps because my frequent visits to megamalls are almost always dominated by two specific needs—for the thing I want and for getting my business done as quickly as possible.

Not that I have anything against malls. Indeed, I have much to be grateful for. I am certainly old enough to remember being dragged by my mother from store to store along the blisteringly hot or miserably cold streets of the pre-mall world, and am therefore not keen on seeing this fate visited on any other child. For this reason alone, the abundance and variety, the easy access and quick exit summed up in the phrase "one-stop shopping," which I first heard and witnessed in the 1950s, has never lost its charm for me.

But unlike many other first-generation initiates into this postwar mode of consumer activity and architecture, I never took the common next step for some reason, becoming a browser or grazer. Nor did I ever become a mall layabout. Such persons did not exist during my growing-up years, since, in the 1950s, going to a mall was still a dress-up affair. I do not window-shop, and have never done so. And only rarely, while dashing around a mall on shopping errands, have I experienced what marketing analysts call "the Gruen Transfer." Named after architect Victor Gruen, it's what urbanist Margaret Crawford has described as "the moment a 'destination buyer'...is transformed into an impulse shopper, a crucial point immediately visible in the shift from a determined stride to an erratic and meandering gait." If you are committed, as I am, to picking up your case of cat food, two Jockey Classic briefs and a tube of Polyfilla in the shortest time possible, then the three hours in a mall I've assigned you will be well-nigh maddening.

For Margaret Crawford, those hours would be very hateful indeed. Or so one imagines after reading her essay "The World in a Shopping Mall," which opens Michael Sorkin's recent collection of outcries called *Variations on a Theme Park.*

Crawford is West Coast: an architectural historian and theorist at the Southern California Institute of Architecture. Sorkin is East Coast: an architect, former architecture critic of *The Village Voice,* and now a professor at Yale and New York's Cooper Union. Most contributors to this book, in fact, reside on one coast or the other. From their academic towers beside America's littered, polluted eastern and western shores, these observers gaze out upon a continent blighted by insidious homogeneity, gentrification and rigid social stratification, whole cities of streets empty of once-happy social tumult, and other nightmares embedded in the minds of the current generation of urbanists by Jane Jacobs and her fellow apocalyptarians, when younger and still on the professional rise. And, as is the fashion in academic tracts on North American cities nowadays, the critics' contempt for what they see is cast in the form of anarchist jeremiad, intended to bump us out of our (presumed) complacency and mobilize us into the struggle to save our continent's cities from Baskin-Robbins, Disneyland and the West Edmonton Mall.

The 5.2-million-square-foot West Edmonton Mall—WEM, as Crawford calls it—is her prime exhibit of the hell of simulation and false need about to overtake us all. She is aghast at WEM's eight hundred shops, its twenty movie theatres and thirteen nightclubs, and an artificial lagoon "where real submarines move through...imported coral and plastic seaweed inhabited by live penguins and electronically controlled rubber sharks." She also worries about the malign architectural tactics meant to produce the Gruen Transfer, forcing us to bend the knee to Mammon before we know what we're doing. She is concerned about what's to become of the buoyant intimacy, haggling, personal confrontation and other elements of village-market behaviour being liquidated by the anti-haggling, fixed-price system of merchandising of which the mall is the culmination.

But along with much fretting over the gross manipulation she finds (or thinks she finds) in mall culture, Crawford provides a concise survey of the history of the mall itself, from its rise out of the department-store consumerism launched in Paris around 1850, to its spectacular postwar apotheosis in the suburban American shopping plaza. She also offers a good analysis of the unique combination of applied sociology, marketing know-how, creative financing flexibility that has made the mall the most stunning financial success, per square foot, in the history of building for retail sales. What really makes her essay sparkle, however, is the outrage ever seething just below the surface of the sophisticated historical and cultural summary.

While Crawford's facts are provocative and her condemnations plausible, her essay nevertheless leaves me as incapable and unwilling as ever to work up even a theoretical hate for the big malls I often visit and often use. First, because they seem no more malignant or bewitching than Mr. Wong's corner milk store, the local hardware outlet or any other building designed to shelter the necessary acts of consumption and exchange. The Gruen Transfer can happen in little shops as easily as in great malls, though it need not happen at all, if you keep your mind on what you are doing. And as for getting distracted by all the goodies in the stores, which Crawford finds awful: gimme a break. Getting seduced by alluring things, being lured onto unexpected paths, entangled by unpredicted passions are all parts, if potentially dangerous parts, of being incarnate and alive.

My second reason for not hating malls has to do with a certain hesitation about stern moralizing against anything so successful with the public at large. At bottom, Crawford's attack is snobbish, and driven by an élite nostalgia for a kind of hectic working-class street culture which nearly all urbanized North Americans disliked before Margaret Crawford or I were born, and which most have happily abandoned since then.

My last reason springs from the almost certain doom of malls and mall culture. What's the point, after all, in getting worked up about an architectural type that, some fifteen years ago, had attained numerical saturation of its market, and may now be enjoying the Indian summer of its short life?

No urban architectural formations are as liable to sudden change as those shaped by desire, consumption, longing and satisfaction. As street shopping lost its appeal for the middle classes, and strip shopping died after that, so the department store—the indispensible key to the success of every regional mall, and consumer retailing itself for more than a century—appears set to follow suit. For every $100 spent by Canadians in stores a decade ago, $9.53 went into department stores tills; nowadays, the figure is around $6.60, and headed down. Doing the damage are the chain-linked specialty monster houses, such as Toys 'R' Us, Business Depot, Aikenhead's hardware, each standing vast and stuffed with things on its own parking lot.

If department stores are crucial to malls, and department stores are vanishing, then what architectural mode will desire-supply take next? Is the titanic warehouse-outlet the next stage in the history of consumption, or, like the strip plaza, a short-lived glitch? I do not have the answer, though such are the questions ambitious young architects should certainly be asking themselves. And learned urbanists of the sort represented in Sorkin's interesting anthology might more profitably spend their time dreaming up new civic and suburban configurations for the more chaste, pennywise shopping of the 1990s and beyond, rather than beating the expiring horse of mall culture.

## EATON CENTRE

Once, while strolling through Toronto Eaton Centre's multi-level galleries of shops, I caught a glimpse of myself in a shirt-store mirror, and beheld the enemy.

The suburbanites are causing one sort of blight. But it's downtown-dwellers like *that*, I thought of the middle-aged visage in the mirror, whom many a critic believes responsible for everything that's wrong with the urban core.

We have forsaken the street. We avoid festive collisions with persons from other socio-economic groups.

We urban traitors do most of our consuming in the city's bright, climate-controlled, constantly policed shopping tunnels and multilevel city-core malls. While benighted suburbanites may be forgiven for their mall addiction, educated urbanites will never be acquitted of the crime of abandoning the corner store, and flinging themselves into the ecstatic gleam of Eaton Centre. We take refuge inside burglar-alarmed, camouflaged, anti-street-oriented "stealth houses" (as a hostile architectural critic has called them)—homes deliberately concealed from the attention, and even knowledge, of our neighbours.

I confess. I live in a stealth house. I shop in downtown malls. I walk between the tall buildings through pedestrian tunnels and bridges, even when the weather is nice. I am one of the enemies of the people who, in the view of Trevor Boddy, is deforming the contemporary city from "a zone of coexistence, of dialogue, of friction" into an ugly, self-absorbed network of "monoclass, monoform, and decidedly monotonous hermetic architectural archipelagos," i.e. malls and enclosed shopping corridors.

In Boddy's fact-rich contribution to *Variations on a Theme Park,* the Ottawa architectural historian and theorist delivers the ominous news that "under the guise of convenience, we are imposing a middle-class tyranny on...downtown streets." He ends by calling upon us to "resist the temptation to fancy ourselves the new Medici, with our continuous sealed walker's highways to art gallery, shopping centre, health club and other splendid palaces of refuge...We must quit the splendid surroundings of our new bridges and return to the streets, with all their hectoring danger, their swirling confusion, and their muddled vitality."

Specifically, "we" would-be Florentine plutocrats must abandon Eaton Centre, Boddy's Toronto example of these hateful "palaces of refuge."

Curiously, the author seems unaware that the genesis of the downtown enclosed mall is no novelty, but merely the latest move in a century-old trend to intensify and focus city-centre pedestrian movement and consumption. Be that as it may, however, "we" aren't about to give up Eaton Centre, because "we" like it very much. Each year, some 42 million people wander among the Centre's 1.6-million square feet of enclosed retail areas—that's a crowd about ten times the size of the Metropolitan Toronto region's total population—because (1) they are crazed or (2), as I believe, they like what they see for sale there. The 14.5-acre site, extending along Yonge Street the entire distance between the cross-town thoroughfares of Dundas Street West and Queen Street West, is middle-brow and middle-class, with mid-priced items for every middle-range lifestyle. That is, it's got no low-down, dirty video stores or bargain warehouses; nor does it sport a Holt Renfrew outlet in which the ostentiously affluent can flaunt their affluence. It's got Roots and Gap Kids and Shopper's Drug Mart and Birks and Tip Top Tailors, and a self-proclaimed "classical" record store featuring Franz Schubert and Barbara Streisand side by side. For a megamall that's middle-aged—sixteen years old is getting up there, as such palaces of refuge go—the vast building is as spiffy, clean and neat as a north Toronto *en suite* bathroom.

Quite apart from its enduring vogue, and despite the hostile, slit-eyed glances it gets from Trevor Boddy and other self-appointed defenders of "downtown vitality," Eaton Centre should be cherished for its peculiar architectural importance.

That's not saying we have to love it. Most of us don't. But the behemoth is Toronto's grandest commercial real-estate statement of the styling called, with attractive frankness, Brutalism. In its twilight during the decade of the Centre's design and construction (by Toronto's Bregman & Hamann, and the Zeidler Roberts Partnership), this thuggish Anglo-American architectural manner marshalled exposed ductwork and elevator machinery, obvious structural steel and showoffishly pre-fab surface coverings and massive poured concrete, all to one end: the celebration of mass democracy's victory over ideological scruples, right or left, and its stylish embrace of godless materialistic consumerism. Now think what you will of the Brutalist gospel—it has always seemed pedantic and exhaustingly optimistic to me—Toronto Eaton Centre still constitutes an unforgettably forceful expression of its final, faded popularity.

Perhaps because I find shopping there practical, and the galleria's apocalyptic architectural message interesting, I am not able to view the Centre through Boddy's jaundiced eyes, as an instrument of anti-urban evil. And while agreeing with many of his useful factual observations, I cannot share his horror about mall-and-tunnel architecture's transformation of my hometown's population into what he calls "a wholly disaggregated series of social, racial, class and sexual subtypes, without the possibility of contact, divided by occupation, bylaw, habit, or default." As it happens, I downright like the separations and distances and alienations which all metropolitan life and building increasingly, generously afford, and which Toronto offers more amply than perhaps any other Canadian city. (Really, Trevor Boddy should get out of Canada's tidy, officious, inflation-proof capital more often, fly down to Toronto, and get a stomach-full of real big-town street life—*then* tell us how thrilling it is.)

Anyway, if mingling with the motley throng is what the Eaton Centre shopper wants to do, it's available right at the north-east door. Twenty-four hours a day, that corner of Yonge and Dundas has more hectoring danger, swirling confusion and muddled vitality than any other intersection in Toronto. It's a constant, colourful near-riot of punks, grunges, passed-out addicts, teen dropouts waiting to score some dope or sell their bodies for a fix, evangelists noisily attempting to win souls for Jesus with conundrums and gimmicky magic tricks, faux-poor suburban boys and girls in "Rock Against Fur" T-shirts skipping school and looking for sins to commit, Salvadoran street bands and boom-boxes blasting out Stompin' Tom to lure gaudily track-suited American tourists to the cheap mirrored-sunglasses pushcart.

Handed the prospect of being plunged day after day into that or any other kind of hectic Boddyesque mixing, I'd take permanent confinement to my stealth house in a second.

## SCENES FROM THE UNDERWORLD

Most city folk know the labyrinth beneath the city, or at least short stretches of its twelve-odd kilometres of connected pathways, forking and winding through the spacious lobbies and food courts, and basements of tall buildings between Front Street West and Dundas Street West, and connecting an estimated fifty office towers, six hotels, five subway stations, our principal commuter and inter-city rail station, and more than a thousand shops, restaurants and other amenities.

For those who do not know it, and want to know how strange reality can be, here's my favourite route. The outing begins with a descent from street level at the network's north-westerly end, the recently spiffed-up thirties-style lobby of the old Gray Coach terminal on Bay Street. From there, the track continues eastbound through the shops of The Atrium on Bay. After the Dundas subway station, one goes south across the bottom levels of the Eaton Centre—a realm of blue jeans and cookies, and a huge waterfall cascading over an escarpment of stone—then under Queen Street, through an opulent grocery store deep beneath The Bay (formerly Simpson's), west under the Thomson Building, then generally south again below the tall bank towers at King and Bay to Union Station, and the end.

Now you will soon find this trek is not as reassuringly straightforward as I've made it sound. There has been a recent proliferation of directional helps, the so-called *PATH* markers designed by the Toronto firm of Gottschalk & Ash. But signage in the underworld remains confusing, and, despite improvement, the maps available at variety stores are still hard to follow. Toronto's underground, like some other places in the world—Venice comes to mind—may require living in, or at least a thousand walk-throughs, to understand thoroughly. Anyway, if you're like most urban wanderers, you enjoy getting lost, just to see what happens, and where it gets you.

To be sure, tracing this system of subterranean trails, with their shops and banks and even law offices and dental clinics, is to be bored by the gleaming sameness of it all, made uncomfortable by the humid atmosphere, certainly overloaded by the incessant, enveloping consumerism. Yet such vagabondage is fascinating, if only because it reveals how completely this new urban architecture overturns the connotations tunnels have had in Western culture until quite recent times.

Until this century, most underground structures—tombs, cellars, mines—have been the most fearful of places, connoting death and dire straits and hell. They were unnatural: tyrants maintained secret tunnels to escape through, concentration-camp inmates dug illegal burrows for the same reason. No one went willingly into an underground place, unless engaged in work, or in some dark, secret mission or conspiracy, or to escape catastrophe, such as bombing or tornado. The underworld was a place of death and the dead, of pirates and gangsters and monsters. The only terrifying place on the grounds of my otherwise unfearful childhood home was the storm cellar—a dark, dank haunt of spiders and unspeakable crawlers reserved for our use in case of violent storms. (The Roman catacombs may have been hallowed by their use as refuges by persecuted Christians, but this has not made them a place you want to stay in long.)

The modern, more benign architectural history of the submerged passageway was heralded some five hundred years ago by Leonardo da Vinci, who sketched out an imaginary city under which vehicular corridors would run. But like the airplane and other schemes by this Renaissance genius, the underground city was destined to remain unrealized until modern technology made it possible. London's Inner Circle

*Museum Station*

steam railway, put into operation in 1863, appears to have been the first subsurface transport system, and the sixty-two-mile network of freight tunnels burrowed under Chicago, licensed in 1899 and opened in 1909, may be the first true underground passages for individually operated and propelled vehicles. And throughout this century, architects and theorists—Le Corbusier, the Swiss engineer Max du Blois, the Italian visionary Sant'Elia and many lesser figures—have dreamed of dissolving the traffic jam by channelling the vehicular flow along ramps under or over habitation levels.

None of these precedents or notions, however, seems to be a direct ancestor of the contemporary subsurface *pedestrian* passageway. This structure, I'm inclined to think, is a rather straightforward result of the desire by postwar developers of tall buildings to maximize the commercial value of their deep foundation structures. Skyscrapers rise, after all, from posts sunk into the earth, not from platforms on it. So you open the otherwise unused intervals among the under-earth pylons, making the space bright and various and accessible, fill it with shops, make what short links as may prove necessary between your basement and adjoining ones, and market this network as escape from cruel and insufferable weather, which nobody had ever before thought cruel and insufferable. In any case, it is certain that Toronto's first underground shopping concourses came into being in the mid-1960s, along with the first Modernist office towers; and the former has spread at the same pace the latter have risen towards the sky.

The largely uninterrupted flow of Toronto's passageway—from tower lobby, down escalators, into retail zones, back up to food fair, back into office complex, and so on—was not, however, a feature of the system at the beginning. Behind that change stands the ambition of Toronto's Reichmann brothers, Paul, Ralph and Albert, for a while the most successful private real-estate developers in world history. And behind the Reichmanns' innovation is a story worth telling.

It all began around 1970, when the brothers decided to put up the world's tallest bank tower and a new home for the Toronto Stock Exchange on a seven-acre site at Bay and King Street West. The complex was to be known as First Canadian Place. No sooner had they embarked on their project, however, than they found themselves, plans in hand, frowning over a table at a squad of young, reform-minded and equally hard-headed City of Toronto planners and architects, pledged to the preservation of downtown breathing room and open corridors for public movement and amenities in Toronto's core.

"We wanted First Canadian Place to be a place where people would want to be," Ron Soskolne, then a planner sitting on the city's side, told me. "What we got was five acres of public space, and a new spaciousness in the lobby. It marked a change from the formal purity of the office tower to mixed use in a large development." If today the towers of the Toronto-Dominion Centre, rising from their low pedestal just across King Street, remain Toronto's finest instance of purist commercial real estate, the entry areas and the shopping mall of First Canadian Place—despite the monotony of all the white marble slapped up on every surface—have the expansiveness and readily available services which would characterize all the best Reichmann projects thereafter.

The Reichmanns got a winning formula from the guys across the table, and Soskolne, fellow planner Michael Dennis, city housing commissioner in the 1970s, and Toronto chief planner Tony Coombes eventually got top jobs in the Reichmann's Olympia & York Developments Ltd. For Soskolne—now with Reichmann International, successor to bankrupt O&Y—his switch-over to his former opponents was a natural development, not treason. "I was inherently a promoter, not a regulator," said Soskolne. "I much more enjoy making things happen instead of keeping them from happening." As for the urban values he upheld when working for the city, "they have changed hardly at all. Any of the projects we've done have those characteristics. I have learned a lot about development from the feasibility side, but the essential values are still valid."

These values can be summed up in the overworked phrase "public space," and the overworked word "access."

Access is guaranteed for those targeted to benefit from it. Sophisticated city executives and workers who want the on-site fashion and sports shops you find at First Canadian Place, the tailors and *chocolatiers,* dry cleaners and dentists and deluxe toyshops, situated along bright boulevards, both above and below ground. People who want quick access, without a trip through the slop and chill of a Toronto winter, to luxuriously appointed restaurants for serious lunches, to fast-food joints that are just fine without saying so, and to coffee nooks in pools of quiet, outside the stream's main current. People for whom the good life is a matter of proximity to subway and record stores, to ticket outlets and art exhibitions—all the things available in First Canadian Place's 500,000-square-foot shopping mall, or in nearby tunnels and basements.

The ambiguous nexus of overground and underground at First Canadian Place is as good an example of "access" as Toronto can offer. One recent morning, after the riptide of inbound commuters had slowed to a trickle and the traffic in the white and beige expanses of the shopping concourse had slowed to a grazing pace, I found a table and a coffee in a fast-food place overlooking the Bay Street entrance to the complex. My high vantage-point, on a level above the entry level, provided an impressive view of the corridor below, and the large glass-encased Bank of Montreal branch beyond it. Instead of being hidden underground in a catacomb sharply separated from the official entries of the building—like the shopping precinct beneath the slightly earlier Toronto-Dominion Centre, across the street—the restaurants and stores of First Canadian Place have been comfortably knit into the very fabric of the towers' multilevel public areas. The flow of space and joining of interior volumes are smooth, continuous, integrated with dignity—eloquently communicating the late-Modernist idea of erasing the formerly rigid boundaries between public and private, work and pleasure, production and consumption.

But just how public *is* public? Certainly, anyone could walk in through the doors, at least when the doors are open, which isn't all the time. But would just anyone do so?

The omnipresent Carrara marble, the swank decor of the shops and grand curtains of glass, the luxurious (if now dated) lobby light fixtures and other interior appointments, along with a dozen other not-so-subtle signals, say *keep out* to the homeless, the jobless, the penniless urban wanderer. This absorption of more and more "public" spaces and retail amenities into office towers and their underground components has recently come under heavy fire from urbanists and architects, for a number of reasons. One has to do with the presumably undesirable establishment of ever-larger exclusionary zones in the city's heart—exclusionary, that is, to the poor, homeless, derelict. Another criticism, closely allied to the first, has to do with the creation of similarly disagreeable territories of homogeneity, where people only see mirror images of themselves, and are spared the sight of the unlike.

Though ruefully, I find such a critique wanting, because it hangs on a feeble scaffolding of *non sequiturs* and wishful thinking, not the girders of urban fact. Poverty will not be eliminated by putting difficult distances between sophisticated city people and their pleasures and recreations. Nor will most of us willingly go very far out of our way to meet *les autres,* unless it's in our best interest to do so—in which case, such an encounter will happen. Until a way to alter this tendency of people to seek the company of others like themselves is found, the mixed-use tunnels will probably continue to attract working city folk, who seem destined never to be as idealistic as the urban visionaries among us would like.

I am concerned, however, about a certain metaphoric loss to our language these submerged malls will likely bring in their train. If developers keep providing vast subterranean pathways as utterly benign and non-sinister as those under Toronto, future generations may not understand what writers of the last two centuries have meant when they spoke metaphorically about "underground men," the "anti-fascist underground," and the like. Trodding the washed marble tiles under Toronto's financial district, moving through those immaculate and almost shadowless corridors, one finds none of those characters typically associated with the undergrounds in legend and story—sexual desperados, outlaws, mad hermits, wild boys who rule whole terrifying tracts of the dark world, and dangerous monsters, like the Minotaur, whom we descend into the underworld to fight.

Instead of all that, we discover respectable, well-dressed professional people, come down from the towers to shop in the thousand stores of that underworld. Terror has been banished from the experience.

But the person who goes through the tunnels may come back with one peculiar memory—of just how the system erases one's traditional sense of the city core as a rhythmic ensemble of level streets, right-angle intersections and high edifices. Twisting and turning among the roots of tall buildings, the particularity of each structure above ground cannot be sensed. Little other than a change in the pattern and composition of the floor tiles signals the passage from the basement of one building to that of another. Everything tends to meld into a continuous spectacle of shopping and regular movement, of sparkling glass and light travertine wall-facing, of broad-leaved tropical trees and upmarket fast food, all backed by the faint, incessant hum of the electrical and mechanical devices which share the corridors with us.

With light and music and pleasant finishings, the planners and makers of the urban culture have created a new, very popular structure. But they have also begun banishing from the city its ancient cloacal darkness, its space of the sinister, perverse, untamed—the scintillating depths which have inspired so much fine modern fiction, poetry and cinema, from Dostoyevsky to Derek Jarman. But this vanquishing may be inevitable. As long ago as 1965—at the start of the great pedestrian underworlding—the magazine *Progressive Architecture* printed an article by American architect Malcolm Wells called "Nowhere To Go But Down." His title has proved prophetic of what was to come; to walk Toronto's underground system is to feel oneself in the future of cities, and the slow turning of urban experience from the natural rhythms of day and night into something like unending day.

# Suburban Idylls

*Mall Path, Scarborough*

# REVISITING MISSISSAUGA

Though I'd never before seen it in print, I must have heard
a story like Andrew McAlpine's, published in *The Globe
and Mail* just after Christmas, 1992, a dozen times.

His tale was about a recent, wintry drive by his childhood
home, where his parents lived twenty-five years before moving
to the Ontario village of Fergus. Memories rushed back from
1963, when Andrew, aged seven, decamped with his family to
a new tract house at the end of a remote, idyllic cul-de-sac, out
among apple orchards and strawberry patches and deliciously
inviting country vistas of suburban Mississauga.

The idyll was short-lived. Andrew's mother soon found
herself bored silly. And the boy himself lived there long
enough to witness the burial of the orchards under concrete
and asphalt and lawn, and the building of "more houses and
shopping malls and high-rise apartment blocks and glass office
towers." Returning to suburbia after a decade abroad,
McAlpine found it all "as awful as I had feared. The mindless
patchwork of banal and ugly speculative development that
passes for a planned city has continued its cancerous growth."
The question that came to mind as he motored down the cul-
de-sac, noting the present-day residents, was whether the
dream his family bought thirty years before was theirs as well.

I would expect not. The suburban family-folk I know

personally give quite practical reasons for living out there: more house for the same money, big yards for the kids, a non-specific sense of security, and the good, long distance living there puts between the secure fortress of domesticity and the downtown towers they earn the mortgage money in.

Except for a brief time many years ago, I have never lived in suburbia, so I cannot say how much of what suburbanites, past and present, say is true, and how much delusion. But that the original inhabitants of Toronto's postwar sprawl were dreamers is beyond reasonable doubt. If the tract-house advertisements and "modern living" supplements in magazines for the years between 1945 and 1955 tell us anything, the dream—or commercial come-on—was about freedom and fresh air, a healthy young, white-collar Dad coming home from the office, Mom hard at work among her delightful children and miraculous appliances. It was about stability, and a few square feet of ground to call one's own. It was about predictability, security, solidity.

I am inclined not to hate postwar suburbia, if only because it delivered on its promise, at least for a while. Too, I can just remember the conditions under which McAlpine's parents may well have grown up in—the scarcity of the war years, the abandonment of children to whomever was handy while Mom went to work at the bomb plant, the absence of men and the constant worry that those absent men might never return from the conflict in Europe or Asia. And I know more than I wish to know about families demoralized and embittered, even ripped to pieces by the Great Depression. Given the miseries of the years between the Crash and VJ Day, it is no wonder that developers found the marketing of the tract-house dream easy in the postwar period. It was not a meretricious or absurd dream. So what went wrong?

The current wisdom puts the finger on greedy, speedy developers, money-grubbing townships wanting to up the tax base, and utopian planners slap-happy about the power of bulldozers to make real their concrete New Jerusalem, express-wayed, malled and bungalowed. All these ingredients were present at the beginning, at least in the ill-planned suburbs. (There were others which were *not* ill-planned.) But a recent book about sexuality and city planning called *Gendered Spaces*, by urbanist Daphne Spain, raises the possibility of yet another factor in the reported unhappiness that descended on the subdivisions: the obsolescence of the social ideals suburbia's endless rows of neat, secure ranch-styles were trying to re-create.

Spain's book throws interesting light on, among much else, the boredom of McAlpine's mother in her paradise of Tupperware and gadgets. For almost a hundred years, she tells us, North American house-builders and their middle-class clients had been inundated with books insisting on the "home" as the physical expression and enforcer of social stability. All these books "glorified the wife's role in creating a calm and peaceful retreat for her family." It was the "faire ladye's" lot in life—the ridiculous spelling is from one of these tomes—to preside over a parlour furnished in "simple, elegant and harmonious style," and to provide her husband with a "sanctum" worthy of the "master of the house." Meanwhile, the tide of reality was running another way. Since the mid-nineteenth century, women had been steadily winning more and more rights—to vote and work, to keep their earnings, to own property. Most women, it appears, liked what they got. A labour research team has discovered through recent interviews, for example, that women who spent the war years making machine-guns in a Toronto plant again and again recalled those years of financial independence as the best in their lives.

Then, in 1945, Rosie the Rivetter, Molly the Machine-Gun Maker and myriad other Canadian and American women were abruptly demobilized, and displaced by returning male veterans, then subjected to a stunning mass-media campaign aimed at turning them into the women depicted in those Victorian architectural handbooks: serene housewives, busy consumers of new commodities, and contented, fertile queen-bees making cookies while hubby was out earning the cash. Many young wives went along with this vision, and tried to make it work. And it all seems to have worked, for a time, at least for some people. But a century of gradual emancipation from rigid expectations of what women should and must do had done its irreversible work. Even if it was, is and always will be desired by many men and women, stability in gendered roles will probably never again be sustainable for very long. It was the fate of Mrs. McAlpine, and that of millions of other women, to come of age at precisely the moment when the old, old human hope of snug security was briefly rekindled in mass culture, and their destiny to live long enough to see it snuffed out, this time perhaps forever.

## THE STRANGEST HOUSE ON PARKHURST BOULEVARD

Shady under its old hardwood trees, East York's Parkhurst Boulevard is a comfortably modest street of family homes, none grand but none particularly mean, arranged side by side on narrow lots with mid-sized aprons of lawn fore and aft.

The small brick houses, with their neat flower beds out front, seem to have been grown from the seed of country cottages; they imply coziness without crowding, the rural hearth without any of the heartbreak of urban living. There are no signs of institutional life (churches, offices and so forth) on the street. Rather, the word *family* is brought immediately to mind—just the word itself, free of sociological or critical qualifiers such as nuclear, extended or whatever, and comfy with connotations of poignance and warmth.

I cannot say whether all the people who dwell on Parkhurst enjoy warm, comfy family lives. But if they don't embody such values, the nostalgic visual rhetoric of their street surely does, with plain conviction if also with rather too much emphasis on social uniformity, or, to use the nicer word, *community*.

Along with everything else on the street, the house at 160 Parkhurst, built about 1948, conveys this message, with its warm brick front, the petunias nodding by the door, the stately maple on the lawn and the white picket fence. But not much human kindliness was ever generated under this house's gently pitched roof. Walk through the tall white front door—as I did with Jim Balmer, manager of operations for the East York Hydro-electric Commission—and you find yourself on a red-tile floor, standing among huge, loudly humming and whining metal boxes. Into these boxes, explained Balmer, come 13,800 line-volts of electricity, supplied by Ontario Hydro. The power is reduced inside the house—known in the business as the Parkhurst Sub-Station—then sent on for further reduction by small transformers affixed on hydro poles along the street, and thence to the local residents' toasters and TV sets.

The building at 160 Parkhurst, then, is a house, but hardly a home. It just looks like one. Or, more to the point, it is an instance of modern technology (without which suburbia would not be possible) resolutely disguised behind an explicitly anti-technological mask.

And it's not alone. Around 1987, Toronto artist Robin Collyer, who lives in Willowdale, became fascinated with these non-homes of suburbia and has since photographed some forty of them, which are only a fraction of those built. Collyer's subjects have ranged from the Toronto Hydro installation at 555 Spadina Road, elegantly disguised as a Forest Hill mansion in the Georgian style, built about 1951, to ones which amount to little more than a skimpy lawn and tacky bungalow façade dropped in front of a clump of buzzing transformers.

During the same three-year period, Collyer has also been taking pictures of "monster houses," a suburban blight of more recent vintage, which, in the photographer's view, embody urban values precisely opposed to those of the transformer houses, and much less desirable. Monster houses show "no consideration for the character of the neighbourhood," while the concealment of transformers within home-like structures was a "quite honourable decision" which showed "sensitivity to the neighbourhood."

Since this phenomenon of "sensitivity" happened right across Toronto during its postwar suburban building boom, it is clear that builders and home-owners were giving the hydro authorities the same message, which, in turn, became a remarkable architectural fact. But what exactly motivated it? What was it that Torontonians in the postwar era didn't like about transformers? To say people thought them "ugly" and therefore wanted them camouflaged explains nothing, since it doesn't make clear how these ruggedly handsome, tough items of technology came to be perceived as ugly, hence undesirable.

You'll get an idea of how that happened if you take another walk along Parkhurst Boulevard, this time thinking about its history.

Like that of countless other suburban streets in Toronto, the architecture of Parkhurst is an artifice created in response to trauma. As the first houses began to go up, the Great Depression was still a vivid, terrible memory. The last houses were completed in the years immediately following the Second World War. The architects of Parkhurst showed how well they knew their clients when they crafted a street of small, old-fashioned homes redolent with memories of happier times.

The result was a kind of hospital disguised as a street of homes, instituted for the healing of souls damaged by some fifteen years, first, of economic breakdown (which hit the borough of East York very hard) and, next, mechanized warfare. In the closely related styles and closely aligned sizes of the houses, the street speaks of a uniform commitment to an idea of family life from the earlier twentieth century—the benign, companionable patriarchy which succeeded the more rigorously hierarchical Victorian one. By offering a continuation of the suburban building styles of twenty years before, the builders proclaim the street's continuity with the pre-crash, pre-war world of the buyers' childhood. There was to be no place here for reminders of disaster. In a therapeutic setting such as Parkhurst Boulevard, a bald reminder of the modern network of industrialized electric power would indeed have been out of place—hence, its designation as undesirable, and its concealment behind an ideological façade.

Since the Second World War, Toronto has been a thoroughly modern city, yet its urban modernism, like Janus, always faced two ways. One view was towards the future—towards mastery over urban and human disorder by means of the strict, serious command of space and planning, and by technology and industrial power. The other has typically faced the other way, preferring a nostalgic play with masks, façades and the known styles of the past.

Any Toronto suburb presents evidence of this kind of nostalgic modernity, which, since the building of suburbia itself began, has a kind of visualized anguish for lost roots and interrupted traditions. Normally, and as often as possible, expressions of the two modernities—soaring American-style office tower and English story-book cottage—are kept from meeting publicly in the same place, on the same street.

Occasionally, however, the technological fact and architecture of roots are required to share a street. Hence, the transformers disguised as houses, in which Toronto has proposed an interesting solution to the enduring conflicts between ideas of what it means to be modern, urban, free.

## DON MILLS

In 1953, with the Convenience Centre ready to go up on the bull's-eye of the 2,058-acre mixed-use project at the intersection of Lawrence Avenue West and Don Mills Road, and with houses, schools and churches (coordinated in colour, materials and design) already arising on the lanes of its meticulously planned residential quadrants, Don Mills was ready to receive its founding families.

Those first Ozzie and Harriets, for whom this innovative town of up to thirty-five thousand souls seven miles north-east of downtown Toronto had been projected on the Ontario countryside, found themselves in Modernity's postwar Emerald City, radiant with the New—new cars, new babies coming along, the dads' new careers opening up, new houses to outfit with gleaming novel appliances, new neighbours to meet.

Their immediate vision is commemorated by two relief sculptures still affixed to Glen Gordon Court, a modest garden apartment emplacement near the Convenience Centre. On one panel is stalwart father, happy baby and serious little girl; on the other, dutiful mother, healthy boy—and, naturally, the family pooch. Given their preoccupation with making this vision real, few of the Don Mills pioneers of '53, I suspect, had much time to ponder what their town would be like forty years on—and, even had they taken a moment to do so, few could have believed that this experiment in Modernist social engineering would be more fascinating in 1993 than ever before.

True, Don Mills is today a place less refined and astute than the paradigm of Modernist probity decreed in the early 1950s by Macklin L. Hancock, the gifted Harvard undergraduate whom Toronto financier E. P. Taylor picked to mastermind his giant real-estate scheme.

Urban jumble long ago nudged its way into Don Mills' green belt, intended by Hancock to quarantine the self-contained community of commercial, residential and industrial facilities from precisely this sort of encroachment. The low horizontal lines of architect John B. Parkin's Convenience

Centre (completed in 1955)—an historic work of mall construction—has been broken by the recent erection of an office tower, and its serene autonomy smudged by isolated fast-food and mini-mart agglomerations with no architectural reference to the commanding central structure.

Worst of all, some condominiums in hideous French Provincial and neo-Georgian flavours have muscled their way into the small, well-spaced parks between the older flat-topped concrete and brick buildings around the intersection of Lawrence Avenue and Don Mills Road.

What's remarkable, given the project's compromised bounds and disarrayed centre, is the dedication with which the quadrant residents are keeping together the crisp Modernist coherence of their instant neighbourhoods, and the distinctive poetics of their streetscapes.

If the odd maverick has been demolished or turned into a garage, the single, open carport—the domestic showcase of postwar consumerism and mobility—is still the standard place to find the family auto in Don Mills. One can find the occasional monster house, loathsome pink and frantically ornate, its cavernous multi-car garage crowding the street line. But for the most part, Don Mills folk have rebuilt and remodelled modestly, and with consideration for the relatively small scale, style differences, simple lines and material harmonies—beige flagstone, tan and grey brick, dark brown wood trim—dictated by the original plan.

*Dictated*, by the way, is hardly too strong a word for what Macklin Hancock, his assistant Douglas Lee, and his backer— E. P. Taylor's Don Mills Development Corporation—effected on that countryside once just beyond Toronto. Don Mills was not to be just another monoform subdivision, or merely another add-on to Toronto's suburban supernova. The project was to be a new creation, its every detail and distinction strictly supervised, its amenities and houses constructed by the best architects available, and carefully directed towards the technological and architectural satisfaction of human desire, as understood by Hancock, his Modernist teachers at Harvard, and the now much-despised social and urban theorists of mid-century.

The free spatial movement afforded by cars—the analogue to the free social mobility so highly treasured by these theorists—was understood as a basic need and pleasure in the Don Mills model of human nature and urban culture. Hence the scarcity of sidewalks—a presumed "fault" balanced by the extensive system of discreet off-street paths—and the complete absence of corner stores and local hangouts within Don Mills' residential precincts. It was expected that one would cruise over to the Convenience Centre, when in need of such services. In this model, similarly, the need for articulated visible order, wide and regular spacing of houses, and the sharp curtailing of visually jarring variances and innovations, is taken for granted.

Anyone inclined to dismiss as boring and sterile the result of such thinking should spend a day roaming the pleasant residential quadrants of Don Mills. The street, dedicated to cars, is each sector's central architectural fact. But, because no street is straight, the eye is always being led onward, round yet another turn in the road, both by the gentle bending of pavement over the rolling landform and by the broad strips of neat lawn bordering each thoroughfare. Residents, by and large, have honoured the designers' intent when it comes to these continuous green street margins. Only rarely does one find a front yard transformed from oblong of lawn into a garden, thus "individualized."

And though the original houses are closely attuned in shape, size and colour—a changelessness of programme perhaps meant to recall the changeless virtues of grace, good taste, good form—the progress of the house line along the street is restrained from tiresomeness by its graceful curving with the street, and by the uncrowding that allows each house to *rotate* with respect to the passer-by, revealing various curt angles as the observer moves along. (Le Corbusier, whom the anti-Modernists blame for every urban ill short of flat tires, issued a refreshing challenge to modern planners in the 1920s, to see if it were possible to "impose an architectural character on the winding street." Macklin Hancock obviously picked up the gauntlet, and won the battle.)

If Don Mills didn't work out quite as its planners hoped it would—the expected mix of persons of differing means and ages did not materialize, and Don Mills people have remained stolidly middle class, and ever older and greyer—this most famous of postwar Canada's new towns is still a monumental rebuke to Modernist idealism's numerous enemies, and an instance of the moral seriousness that characterized the best Modernist urban thought and architectural practice in its heyday, some forty years ago.

## THE TROUBLE WITH SCARBOROUGH

Retired accountant Tom Abel and his neighbours, founders of a pep squad called Friends of Scarborough, are "fed up" with their Metro city's reputation as a crime-ridden, decaying and centreless bore. The tiny group's goal is to "build pride" among the 500,000-odd dwellers in the vast east-Metro suburb. "We have a lot to offer," proclaimed *West Hill News,* a Scarborough community paper in late 1993. "Scarborough is the most ethnically diverse city in Canada. A lot of good things are happening...but more needs to be done to foster a positive attitude."

The crusade of the Friends and of *West Hill News* is doomed, of course, simply because the Metro member-city is a crime-ridden, decaying centreless bore. Between 1988 and 1992, Scarborough's muggers, rapists and murderers increased their business by almost 40 per cent. This visually inert expanse of bungalows, shabby strip malls, mass-designed schools and factories is regarded by many Torontonians—with justice, given the prevalence of ethnic gangs—to be our town's likeliest launch-site for any future race war. Prostitution and drug trafficking are on the rise, right along with poverty. Apart from the Scarborough Bluffs, jutting in rugged grandeur into Lake Ontario, I can think of few reasons for any non-resident to go there—unless, like me, you happen to be fascinated by the phenomenon of postwar suburbia, its successes and failures.

I do not wish Scarborough ill. Nor do I share the cool hatred for the suburbs oozing from much contemporary writing by academic urbanists and architectural theorists. Indeed, I am convinced that it is time to show mercy on those whose highest earthly hopes were embodied in bungalow and lawn, comfortable conformism, freedom from ideology and the liberty to consume in a leisurely fashion.

That having been said, Tom Abel and his comrades should take a long look at the historic errors made in the creation of the place and state of mind known as Scarborough.

Nowhere in this suburb do these errors find more eloquent expression than in the so-called centre of this political unit, which in fact has no architecturally designated focus or edge. Even that official "centre"—the ensemble of buildings situated south of expressway 401, between McCowan and Brimley roads—is multipolar, disparate, centrifugal. The generic names of the streets in its surroundings suggest, not specific site, but slow drift through a dictionary of names of nothing: Estate Drive, Production Drive, Corporate Drive, Grangeway. The visual force giving a sense of location, presence, to all else was supposed to have been Toronto architect Raymond Moriyama's Civic Centre (1969–1973), an extravaganza roughly circular in plan and theatrically angular in elevation. Sprawling northward from the Civic Centre is Scarborough Town Centre, a regional shopping mall linked to the municipal building by a row of huge steel arches.

What makes this otherwise boring place interesting is the innocent exuberance with which its planners embraced Modernist development doctrine as a cure for what ailed Scarborough after the patient was already moribund, and got the medication wrong to boot. If by the late 1960s the city was feeling all the psychological and social ouches of aimless sprawl—so the thinking went—the thing to do was create *ex nihilo* a centre to give focus where there had been none. (The success of Don Mills is largely a result of the anticipation of sprawl problems, particularly ones caused by vast over-sizing of uncentred "neighbourhoods," and coordinated attention to them before they arose.) And if the rising incidence of gang conflict and plain fear was due to factional alienation in the huge, cheap-built residential sectors, then civil harmony could be attained by providing a forum in which persons from all classes, races and tax-brackets might gather to celebrate the one transcendent sacrament remaining in secular culture: the consumption of commodities and public services.

The complex that resulted from this meditation is anchored by its two principal structures. The enclosed mall features imposing department stores (Sears, The Bay, Eaton's), between which are strung numerous little outlets for Canadian and international retail chains, such as Taco Bell, Japan Camera, Cineplex Odeon theatres, Baskin-Robbins, Pro Hardware. Like virtually every shopping mall, it is nowhere and anywhere—the topographical equivalent of the raceless, genderless, non-sectarian and hence ideal citizen which secular humanism would have us be.

For such a soul was Moriyama's Civic Centre erected. While the smiling attendant did not appear to understand the quite simple question I asked on a recent visit—where and when the lecture by the project architect would begin— she was quick to point out the wares on sale at her information desk: Scarborough ballpoint pens, Scarborough scarves, Scarborough baseball hats, tickets to Canada's Wonderland. In

*Fire escape, Scarborough*

fact, the Civic Centre advertises almost as many products as the Town Centre: an Italian cultural festival; innumerable "educational opportunities"; social services for persons with any need, deficiency or ailment, or none; a programme of regular brisk walks and health lectures among the Town Centre shops, co-sponsored by city and mall management.

In this strange non-place of amusements and consuming and servicing, we have an excellent instance of the unlimited hedonism deployed as a cure for the disorder of non-planning, non-thinking. Government is presented no longer as the restrainer of desire, but its coordinator and satisfier, and the provider of "culture." In this view, however, it also becomes the parody Theodor Adorno called "a manifestation of pure humanity without regard for its functional relationship within society." Which is only an abstract way to name the hectic round of Scarborough's (and every suburban government's) ethnic singalongs, minglings, festivals and other unreal events. Burdened with such deeply flawed idea of governing, and a hopelessly wrong-headed idea of culture, is it any wonder that Scarborough can't understand what is going wrong with it? At the Civic Centre, every politician and speaker at the Moriyama event—a homage to the architect on the twentieth anniversary of his building—drivelled on about what a "people place" Scarborough is. If there's something wrong, well, the citizenry and politicians just have to work harder to make it a "people place." That is, a place devoid of *real* people, and populated only by quiescent phantoms of Adorno's "pure humanity."

Into the vacuum created by the failure of any government to make constraint, restriction and the enforcement of sensible ethical standards its first duty, brutality and injustice are always quick to rush. So far, three hundred bannings of young people, most of them Filipino in origin, have taken place in the mall during the last year. A young Filipino was hauled by guards out of a hamburger line, charged with trespassing, and told to sign a form saying he would never come into the mall again. Another Filipino, a Taco Bell employee, has alleged harassment by guards as he tries to get to work.

Apparently, the problem is that some Filipino youths hang out—gasp!—use naughty words—shock!—and dress flamboyantly. They are *not* vessels of the "pure humanity" Scarborough would create. Or so I gather from the warnings throughout the mall. "Loitering makes shoppers uneasy... Running, littering or swearing in the mall upsets other shoppers... Disguises unnerve shoppers." That is, in the course of just being teenagers these people threaten the compulsion to consume, while it is precisely this compulsion, suburbia's real law and hope, that lies at the heart of its tragedy.

## TROUBLE IN NORTH YORK

Some years ago, during an informal chat with Mel Lastman, North York's eternally electable mayor, I inadvertently called His Worship's vast suburban turf a "borough," which it indeed once was. Whereupon the usual cheery demeanor vanished from Lastman's face. He fixed upon me a stern gaze, and firmly, very deliberately, said: "It's the *City* of North York. Not borough. *City.*" The mayor was appalled.

On a Sunday afternoon in early December, 1992, Lastman was appalled again. This time, the occasion was a customary holiday ceremony on North York's civic-centre plaza, which the mayor has graciously allowed to be named after himself.

It seems that about a thousand Greek-Canadians had turned up in front of North York City Hall to stop the hoisting of a flag by about the same number of people from the transnational Balkan region of Macedonia. In the shoving and shouting match that ensued, the mayor suffered a bloodied shin. He also suffered an even more severe blow to his optimism about life in Canada.

"I'm a nervous wreck," Lastman told a reporter the day after. "I saw hate for the first time in my life yesterday, real hate. Here were people with their eyes bulging out and their mouths frothing....When people come to Canada, they've got to leave their hate at home." Alas for North York, which proclaims itself "The City With A Heart."

I cannot explain, and do not pretend to understand fully, the historic feud that led to that Sunday's shoving in North York. And if Lastman's complaints in the newspaper stories about the tussle called to my mind that trivial *faux pas* I'd almost forgotten about, I mention the two incidents together here not to suggest their equivalence, which would be absurd and tasteless. Rather, I do so to call attention to the widely held, flawed notions of urbanity suggested by Lastman's comments, both then and now—notions that, it seems, still pervade political culture in the gigantic suburban terrain north of the City of Toronto.

When Lastman gave me a comeuppance over the "borough" remark, it came as a sharp reminder of how attractive and sophisticated-sounding the word "city" had become to politicians in Toronto's suburbs, and how readily these chieftains bristle at the suggestion that their jurisdictions are—as many a hard-core urbanite deeply believes—occasionally interesting but largely misbegotten superblocks of tacky boxes somewhere north of beyond.

Of the five boroughs that joined Toronto City to bring Metro into existence in 1953, all but East York have proclaimed themselves "cities" in name. Since their incorporation into the titanic Metro conglomerate, a number of these entities have rushed (or are rushing) to become cities in fact, with impressive city halls and other public amenities, large libraries, galleries and theatres, clusters of soaring, gleaming office and apartment towers, and other emblems of high urban aspiration.

But Lastman's dismay and astonishment after the showdown between Greeks and Macedonians suggest a curious lack of realism, at a couple of levels, about the sparkling city life he and other suburban mayors seem to want so dearly.

Real city life is, after all, a matter of continual conflict as well as glistening tall buildings, a matter of ethnic passion as truly as it is a commitment to wheelchair-accessible theatres. More doggedly and longer than newcomers to the United States, recent immigrants to Toronto treasure the national chauvinisms and ancient grudges they brought with them in their trunks and bags. This reluctance of the recently arrived to join hands with others, even tangentially or nominally, and thus create a homogeneous "Toronto citizenry," is not their fault. As an immigrant myself, I can testify to Toronto's myriad ways of letting the newly landed know—even if they come from another Canadian city—they are allowed and tolerated, but not really welcome. More than any large city I know, Toronto is clannish to the core, characterized by tightly circumscribed ethnic and professional networks and old circles of friends, and by little open psychological space in which any new centres of real political or social power can be established. The message is: stay with your own kind. The only alternative is to ingratiate yourself with an existing power network—a nearly impossible task for many an immigrant—or be so brattish you cannot be ignored. If you have no kind to stay with, and are not able or inclined to be ingratiating or conspicuously obnoxious, then stay alone and out of the way. Don't look for a glad hand here.

Everyone who lives in Toronto knows and, most of the time, abides by the codes of this frigid civility. Except for the odd visit to an "ethnic" restaurant, we *do* stay with our own kind. Perhaps this is a reason Americans, on holiday from their disintegrating cities, find Toronto such a peaceable and agreeable place. What they do not appear to realize is the extent to which this "peace" is a result of extraordinary self-policing and self-segregation.

Pandemic in the satellite-cities of the Metropolitan Toronto complex, and perhaps especially in North York, is the fantasy of being the Great Welcome Wagon which Toronto City certainly is *not*. In this suburbia, the vision of true democratic urbanity would prevail, mediating conflicts instead of ignoring them, and bringing people together into a commonwealth of difference, celebrating rather than fearing variety.

Or so we are to believe, if we subscribe to the politicians' twaddle, and their architecture. The great public square, with its entertainments and opportunities for meetings of the citizenry, is an inevitable part of this notion's substantial rhetoric; and Mel Lastman Square is an excellent example of how it's all supposed to work. Located on Yonge Street just north of Sheppard Avenue, a belated architectural cluster installed at the centre of absolutely nothing, the North York City Centre is as eloquent a witness to this dizzy urbanism as we are likely to find anywhere—one in which historical memory and the strife such memory engenders are supposed to be eliminated by unrestrained consumption, opportunities for self-improvement and unlimited distraction.

If the sumptuous Romanesque bulk of Toronto's Old City Hall speaks to us of solemn encounters between wayward citizens and socially superior, strict magistrates, the North York Civic Centre is supremely about citizenship as a kind of permanent state of bliss. The welcoming, open City Hall, with its smiling receptionists, occupies one side of Mel Lastman Square. On the south side is the Board of Education, and facing it is the city's central library. A theatre lies next to City Hall, and just north of the library is a hotel, and a marble-lined shopping galleria, its glass roof opening towards a slit of sky defined by the sheer glass walls of office towers.

Elsewhere in the complex one finds a swimming pool, offices of dentists and doctors, and a city-operated parlour for weddings. Outside, in Mel Lastman Square, we have a bandshell and an ice rink, an amphitheatre and a box office—satisfactions for almost every need and desire, short of religious or sexual ecstasy (or a fine bookstore or superb restaurant), one could imagine.

It could be argued, and Lastman is obviously prepared to argue, that members of a free and privileged society should behave themselves better than the Greeks and Macedonians did that Sunday in Mel Lastman Square. He was shocked. But how seriously should we really take this shock? Human nature being the potentially horrific thing it is, I should think the mayor would prefer a little hooting, pushing and uproar to the kind of thing that goes on in places where no public social space is provided for dissent—in the rural districts of the world, for instance, where death squads, barn burners, lynch mobs and other furtive, elusive actors have always been the main performers in the rituals of difference. Other than the mayor's scraped shin and jangled nerves, little real damage appears to have been inflicted during the Greek-Macedonian melee.

What the politicians in the new "cities" want, apparently, is neither country-style marauding nor Toronto-style coldness, but apolitical Eden. In the long history of the city, nothing has ever been quite so unreal, so remote from the true fact and face of urbanity, as the "centres" of these suburbs longing to be cities. Big-city reality has a way of invading even the enchanted gardens of the suburban politicians, of which fact I submit the faint scar on Mel Lastman's leg as Exhibit A.

# Concrete Dreams

*Column, Gardiner Expressway*

# CAR ARCHITECTURE

Officially, it was just a proposed highway that died that summer's day in 1971, when the Ontario government decided to swing its bulk behind a grassroots coalition of environmentalists and neighbourhood-minded folk, and stop the southward thrust of the Spadina Expressway towards the heart of Toronto.

But as many on both sides of the issue realized at the time, the more important casualty of the decision was a certain idea about Toronto's future. Its devotees called this idea Progress. To its detractors, what was stopped was an ideologically driven programme of therapy that would kill the patient, by destroying virtually all the things that make cities worth living in. Since 1971 until now, Progress has been an idea suppressed in Toronto. And so it is that this remains perhaps North America's only metropolis with expressways that abruptly stop, and empty their load onto ordinary streets—the Allen Road, as the Spadina Expressway is known today—and soaring ramps, like those at the eastern end of the Gardiner Expressway, that suddenly lose their surge, go limp and sag to the ground in the middle of nowhere.

And as intended, comfortably antique neighbourhoods approximating the anti-Modernist visual ideal have survived downtown—at least in the minds of the aging urban professionals who took up the populist slogans of Stop Spadina, and occupied and gentrified the Victorian houses of Cabbagetown and the Annex. The massive internal migrations of well-heeled citizens during the astonishing real-estate boom of the 1980s, incidentally, did more to destroy the social fabric of "traditional neighbourhoods" than the Spadina Expressway ever would have. But the visually homey streetscape is as important to the architecturally savvy as to the upwardly mobile. It's also the principal criterion of what's a neighbourhood and what's not. A number of mobile Torontonians I know staunchly claim they live in "vibrant neighbourhoods," even though they don't know the names of the people next door. Nor do these educated, middle-income invaders, of which I am one, spend much time wondering publicly where the indigents, addicts, students and artists who once found cheap housing in these zones have gone.

Before the 1971 death of Spadina, the vogue for high-speed modernity had enjoyed a career in Toronto quite as remarkable as it had anywhere else on this continent, reigning virtually unopposed in the planning departments and the minds of theorists after the Second World War. The soaring expressway was democracy visualized, social mobility given infinite physical tether, the decisively right use of heavy technologies after a half-century of brutal misuse. In the sacred name of Progress (or using it as an alibi), civic planners and private real-estate developers wiped out city blocks and nearly the whole of the large warehousing district just west of downtown, raised office towers in the avant-garde Euro-Modern style from the scraped-down ground, blitzkrieged the urban fringe with subdivisions, constructed regional shopping plazas ringed by parking lots. The halt of the Spadina in 1971 did not, of course, instantly stop this upheaval, so conspicuous in the buckaroo days of Modernist bulldozing. But it did reveal—even to us beneficiaries and admirers of the Modernist ethos and *élan*—that the quasi-religious belief in the power of wrecking balls to set us free was, like most other optimistic gospels, fatefully vulnerable to error, and open to loss of credibility.

Few Torontonians under forty nowadays, and not a great many over that age, require much convincing on this point. The tight, comprehensive weave of expressways, conceived by Modernist planners and brought to full realization in many an American city, is a bad thing; such is general conviction today, almost never publicly contested any more—more a matter of sincere sentiment, that is, than a talking point in the politics of the urban future. It suffuses the contemporary literature on urbanism, like a dogmatic truth that should be self-apparent to all but psychopaths and the benighted.

In common with most other fellow-citizens, I believe Ontario's decision to halt Spadina, and the dramatic expresswaying of Toronto, was the right one—not because it would have ruined Toronto, but because it would not have solved anything. Or so I believe today, some twenty-five years after the fact. It was a sentiment that did not spring spontaneously from my heart, in which the love of expressways had taken root long before. Growing up in the rural American South, I was trapped in a small community by narrow, pocked roads that seemed to have been designed with my imprisonment in mind. Then, just as adolescence struck me, the Interstate Highway came through—a huge gash in the red clay of the Louisiana hills, later filled with concrete stretching away to the far horizon. The first spring the expressway was open, the din of trucks and cars that fell on my ears sounded like a song of freedom. I wanted to go where those cars went, and I did. To be sure, the first sizeable city down the line was pretty pokey when it came to civilized pleasures. But to me, it was Babylon and Paradise, all rolled into one; and the expressway got me there.

Even today, when I know better, I still feel primitive excitement when whipping along an expressway, or banking hard

*Parking Lot, Queen Street East*

along a ribbon of concrete at a basketweave interchange. Nor is such mystical regard for expressways, I suspect, uncommon among those who hit adolescence thirty years or more ago. I recall a newspaper article written by Toronto sociologist Arnold Rockman in the mid-1960s—I read it some years later—in which the newly completed Don Valley Parkway is praised as "sculpture in motion." In a 1991 interview, Rockman recalled his excitement upon driving on the Don Valley Parkway for the first time, the admiration he felt for "the way it conformed to the landscape." The article was, in his words, "a futurist rhapsody" of a sort, he believed, could not be written in the 1990s.

If not the expressway, at least what flies along it *was* being rhapsodized in 1991, though neither Rockman nor I knew it. Dutch architect Moshé Zwarts was writing these words, destined to appear in a little anthology called *Architecture Now:* "I propose that starting from tomorrow we all privately and publicly declare our love of cars. For our profession, this would mean having to treat cars affectionately in our designs. I say this because I dare to recognize that the car is an almost ideal form of transport…unrivalled by any other vehicle in the amount of freedom it offers…apparently affordable for most of us…environmentally friendlier per passenger kilometre than the train." The problem, in this view, is not the car, but the failure of architectural imagination in accommodating our stubborn allegiance to it—a failure that is nearly universal, except in one spectacular instance: the invention and development of the expressway. While not the only tool in the kit of transportation planning, the high-speed, limited-access highway has proven itself to be an extraordinarily versatile one. Now we need others—many others, so far unimagined—that, like expressways, will enhance the pleasures of metropolitan choice and movement.

# THE GARDINER

Admirers of urban form and transformation can never afford to doze, since there is simply no way of telling just when and where a city will start telling stories you never heard before. Such was the unexpected lesson that came my way on a wintry day, when I was trying to get a good look at Fort York.

It's easy to get a view from inside what's left of Toronto's Georgian imperial defence, such as it was. A magnet for tourists and school tours, the fort is open to the general public most every day. The hard part comes when the would-be spectator tries to find an instructive standpoint *outside* the structure, in the gritty downtown clutter of factories, expressway ramps and truck yards, smokestacks and tall electric signs that has long hemmed it in, shutting it away from almost any long view.

It was during a search for such a viewpoint that I found myself slipping and sliding on icy, mucky rubble beneath the traffic deck of the Frederick G. Gardiner Expressway, where it billows upward and soars between Fort York and the lakeshore, just west of Bathurst Street. No scenic prospect presented itself—until, that is, I gave up trying to get a useful topographical glimpse of Fort York and abruptly noticed the sublimity of just where I was.

Few sites more forsaken lie this close to Toronto's busy, dense downtown mountain-range of glass. Overhead, the wide steel belly of the Gardiner's traffic level lies like a flat green snake on a series of tall, water-stained concrete brackets. Underneath spreads the expanse of loose gravel, some of it used as a gathering place for trucks, some of it the dusty yard of a factory in which big cement blocks are fabricated.

One hesitates to use the word *beautiful* of such a forbidding place, though the word fits the bill. There is strong visual surge and power here: in the dignified rhythms of the expressway's tapered reinforced-concrete supports, marching away into the distance like an immense Baroque colonnade, in the tough muscularity, in the ensemble of cement factory and rumbling trucks. There is a gruff beauty here that the swank towers nearby can't touch.

In penning this hymn to the Gardiner and its industrial aesthetic, I mean no insult to those who fought hard and successfully to stop the total expresswaying of Metropolitan Toronto, or to people for whom expressways are the very incarnation of urban menace. But the battle *is* over—really and forever. The opponents of freeways can sleep soundly at night, and need not fear the presence of one aficionado of the grand idea and the massive architecture they stopped. Indeed, had the concept of salvation by expressway so much as a flicker of life left in it, the Metropolitan Toronto government would probably not have dared inaugurate, in 1991, its new archives building on Spadina Road with the handsomely fair visual and documentary exhibition called *Concrete Dreams*.

Drawing on the extensive holdings of pictures, maps and other resources conserved by Metro council, archives exhibits manager Michael McMahon, historian Rosemary Donegan and photographer Jim Miller assembled a lively, engaging evocation of Toronto's period of heroic urban Modernism (roughly 1950 to 1970), and a memorial especially to Frederick "Big Daddy" Gardiner, first Metro chairman and our Robert Moses (urban planning czar of New York City), a massive schemer and bully who was the power behind the plan to drop a comprehensive net of interlocking expressways on Metro. (Gardiner is regarded with affection by Torontonians. His motto: "You won't leave your footprints on the sands of time by sitting on your ass on the beach.")

If Big Daddy and his gang on Metro Council were hardly Modernist visionaries and original theorists, they did believe sincerely that any city, to be great, must have expressways; and they very much wanted Toronto to be great. The crumbling, crowded neighbourhoods sullying Toronto in 1945 were disgraces reminiscent of the Depression, and were best done away with. The future expansion and glory of Metropolitan Toronto, Big Daddy's baby, lay in blitzing the blight and stinking small-industrial zones, and raising from the rubble a new town of high-rises and parks, populated by well-to-do cosmopolites working in shiny, tall buildings that would say *cosmopolis* to the world. His agents were to be, and were, the newest generation of planners and developers, who believed, also with undeniable sincerity, that the path to urban peace and private wealth would have to be cleared by bulldozers.

In this scenario, the cure for the city's image problem was a radical dose of demolition, followed by big spoonfuls of high speed. As McMahon put it, Space (the neighbourhood) was to be conquered by Time (the car). Significantly, official documents from the early 1950s, in which plans for the new elevated lakeshore expressway were enunciated—it was later dubbed the Gardiner—made much of speed and volume of traffic flow, but said virtually nothing about the homes and streets and buildings of historical interest that would be swept aside to make way for this river of heightened mobility. The latter did not exist in Big Daddy's dream. Fort York, for instance, turned out to be in the way of the lakeshore expressway. The solution proposed by Gardiner was simply to move the fort. His plan was given solemn blessing by city engineers, who proclaimed that pulling the proposed highway around Fort York would involve a "sacrifice (of) design standards, resulting in unsafe driving conditions." Such was the tenor of thought in those days, at least among bureaucrats, politicians and real-estate capitalists devoted (for various reasons) to the "urban renewal" taking place in American cities. At its worst, the project was driven by greed, naked political ambition, foolish chauvinism. At its best, such Modernist super-planning was driven by compassion and idealism, honourable civic boosterism combined with holy hatred for Depression-era slums and for what they were doing to the miserable souls condemned to live in them. But Modernist urbanism was never what Jane Jacobs, as recently as 1993, was still denouncing as "fraud" and intellectual treason. Nor do I believe anything more noble than the usual hesitancy about American influence was at work in the late 1950s, when the Toronto citizenry and press forced the imperious Gardiner to leave Fort York *in situ.*

## BURYING THE GARDINER

No document more eloquently conveys the romantic mood of current planning orthodoxy than *Regeneration,* the 530-page final report of former Toronto mayor David Crombie's Royal Commission on the Future of the Toronto Waterfront, released in May, 1992. It is suffused by the piety that cars, and the architecture they make necessary, are both horrid.

To the surprise of many observers, however, the report stopped short of calling for the wholesale knockdown of the Gardiner Expressway. "Shying away from the enormous cost," lamented urban activist Colin Vaughan in *The Globe and Mail,* "engineers and planners were timid about the removal of this elevated eyesore that blocks access to the city's lakefront." But, we learn in another newspaper story, if there's no simple solution to eradicating this "wedge between Toronto-area communities and Lake Ontario," the commission "suggests that burying part of it would make the Gardiner less of a barrier without increasing traffic woes in the process."

While it did not strike me as odd that Toronto activists, such as Colin Vaughan, would use this occasion to bash the now-heretical view that limited-access elevated highways are balm for gridlock, other early responses to the report were stranger. It struck me as odd, for example, that anyone could refer to the Gardiner as an "elevated eyesore," without qualification. Those who rode it in the early days remember it much differently. Back then, the expressway was illuminated by parallel lines of fluorescent tubes recessed into the guardrails on either side. Coming from the direction of Scarborough, one came onto the ramp at rapidly accelerating speed, climbed into the sky, the equivalent of some three storeys in only fifteen seconds, and then was guided off into the distance by ribbons of light. Ahead lay the flashing Consumers' Gas flame, and the shining city. Nobody complained then about the expressway's ugliness, nor should anyone do so today. It is Toronto's largest and most spectacular monument to the tragic utopianism typical of Modernist culture as a whole—and, at an instantly more mundane level, still a good, fast way to get downtown, thus worthy of preservation on both counts.

Nor do I sympathize with the claim, very often heard from its critics, that the Gardiner is somehow impeding our access to the lakefront, like the former Berlin Wall, an insuperable obstacle between landlocked Torontonians and a realm of forbidden delights we can now only dare dream about, or see on television. Is it *really* paradise over there, among the Florida-style condominium towers that East York's wretched bungalow-dwellers, imprisoned behind the Gardiner Expressway, can only lust after from afar?

Such a bizarre vision of the glories of living beside Lake Ontario—the vision informing much of the wildly inappropriate tropical architecture at Harbourfront—caused even David Crombie to marvel. The designers appear to have simply overlooked the fact of our bone-chillingly damp winters, Crombie told *The Globe*'s Craig McInnes. "Most of the buildings along the waterfront in the public realm are built as if they are in the Mediterranean. If you think about it, that's crazy. We have winter here every year."

What exactly, then, is the Gardiner blocking our access to?

Nothing. You can drive or walk or take the light-rapid-transit car under it or over it at many points.

And what does one find in this wondrous Land of Oz south of the expressway ramps?

Well, for the discerning few, there's The Power Plant, a public art gallery which often displays contemporary Canadian and international art of outstanding quality. There's also a couple of other interesting cultural facilities—a dance theatre, a workshop for making and displaying crafts, a forum for literary readings and so on. For the tourists, there's deluxe shopping at Queen Quay Terminal—though less deluxe, and a lot pricier, than similar shopping north of the Wall. You were supposed to be able to stroll for miles along the alternately blisteringly cold and blazingly hot waterfront, if that's your idea of a good time, but the condo developers have put considerable swatches of the harbour off limits to ordinary folk.

Once upon a time—indeed, for a couple of years after I first arrived in Toronto—the harbour still possessed a certain wonder. It was a run-down Great Lakes port, past its best days, which had never been very good; but still a port, with ships and sailors hailing from all the world. The cracked concrete docks and corroded cranes and little tin service buildings were mute reminders of the era when the Lakes provided a great marine highway from the Atlantic into the very heart of the continent, linking Toronto to Cleveland and Chicago, to Montreal and London, Capetown and Leningrad with the strong cords of trade. Then the cords snapped one by one, the marine traffic declined, and the docklands became Harbourfront: soaring, boring condo towers and hotels and well-kempt parkettes and promenades, all nakedly exposed to the winds that sweep inland from the lake most months of the year.

The winds do die down in May, and Toronto experiences a seasonal miracle: the fleeting moment when the waters of our cold, dangerous lake briefly sparkle brilliantly, and all seems balmy. This moment is usually cut short by the regular summer die-off of small lake fish, whose silvery, stinking corpses mass in the boat slips. If I dislike Harbourfront, and never go there except on business, it's perhaps because I was not born in Toronto, and therefore never knew the rough romance of its zenith as a port town. Nowadays, when I peep over the Gardiner, all I can think of is the good job this mammoth expressway is doing, just by keeping phoney Miami out of sight.

## THE MOTEL STRIP

If you've always meant to do a dirty weekend in a cheap room down in the Etobicoke armpit known as the Motel Strip, and just haven't gotten around to it, take heart. There's still plenty of time.

That's despite the 1993 decision of Ontario's highest zoning power that put an end to twenty-five years of wrangling among builders, politicians and citizens over what should be done with the notorious fifty-acre lakefront site at the west end of Metropolitan Toronto, and gave the green light for the bulldozers to move in. When they do, the motels will go, and in their place will rise gleaming condominium towers, a hotel, upmarket retail stores. The idea is to attract, as a *Globe and Mail* reporter put it, without a trace of irony, an "influx of stable, community-minded residents." The scheme also includes the construction of another of those waterfront parks Toronto planners keep wanting us to have. (When will the planners realize that anyone of sound mind will not want to frolic beside the cold waters of Lake Ontario? And, for that matter, haven't they figured out that Torontonians don't like to frolic *anywhere*?)

The reason why the window of opportunity for sleaziness remains open is the flat Toronto condo market, which is not expected to pick up until the mid- to-late 1990s, if ever. But if I were you, I wouldn't put it off too long. Nobody will shed a tear when the Strip's famous culture of sex and drugs, and the refuge it's historically provided for Bonnie and Clydes on the lamb, falls victim to the full-scale gentrification now on tactical hold. When the wreckers start to move, nobody is going to stop them.

Speaking of tears, a motel operator burst into them one cold day late in 1991, when I told her that I found her establishment's streamlined, luxury-liner styling and *haut-moderne* glass-brick touches all quite interesting, and surely worth a hail-and-farewell in *The Globe and Mail* before it all gets knocked into oblivion. The distraught lady's fear, I learned, was that I would write something which would get her motel designated a protected historic site—when all she wanted was *out.*

No such designation has taken or will take place, with or without my help. But some note should be taken of the fifteen-odd boarded-up or feebly operating motels on the Strip before they slip away beyond the edge of city memory. Apart from a similar row of one-night-stand motels on Scarborough's Kingston Road, this one-kilometre stretch of Lake Shore Boulevard West is Toronto's last substantial preserve of an architecture specific to the Great Automobile Age. It was during this period—launched by the high-speed expressways of the 1940s (including the Queen Elizabeth Way, Canada's first controlled-access road) and brought to an abrupt halt by the oil crises of 1973 and 1979—that the popular worship of the car-as-sex-symbol reached its zenith. The motel styling on the Strip is the sacred architecture of this cult of the fast, sleek, daring, hedonistic.

Before this moment, the North American automobile traveller could expect to find accommodation in an old-fashioned hotel. For those who preferred, however, on the outskirts of every city there was always a row of huts called "tourist cabins," cheap digs which nostalgically connoted pioneer dwellings, and recalled slow, purposeful journeys across great expanses. (There used to be such a place in Scarborough called Wagon Wheel Court.)

Since the 1950s, however, the temporary shelter of choice has been the "motor hotel" chains—low stacks of prefab hotel rooms, without room service, virtually identical in design coast to coast, typified by Holiday Inn and Howard Johnson's. These motor hotels have always been camouflaged as apartment buildings. On occasion, their architecture merges seamlessly with that of recent hotels, so that one cannot tell the difference any more. It's all the same beige broadloom, easy-care plastic wall coverings, uniform windows that will not open, Formica table tops. The inner environment suggests "home away from home," by creating mediocritized, generic versions based on the domestic bedroom of the moment.

These mass-replicated environments—along with fast-food outlets, among the world's first such items of commercial architecture—were an instant hit with the mobile public; their success was also an excellent instance of capitalist industry's ability to meet a genuine need with speed and considerable technical sophistication. This need on the part of travellers was begotten by the notorious unevenness and unpredictability of overnight accommodation during the Motel Strip era. Beyond not knowing whether the bed would collapse, or you'd find roaches in the bathtub, there was always the possibility of a chance collision between motel cultures: the older one, involving hookers and the clandestine rendezvous and next-door noises very hard to explain to a curious six-year-old; and the newer ethos of the happy, typical nuclear family on holiday.

The Brady Bunch, in other words, would *not* stop off at the Motel Strip, hence its decline—but also its value for recollecting a distinctive architecture and unique style whose day is past. These buildings draw their aesthetic and connotations from neither the pioneer sod-house nor the Home, but from the Car. Like '59 Caddys, most are long, low, brightly coloured, easy to slip in and out of quickly. The sleek red stripes of the Strip's Cruise Motel echo the chrome stripes on the automobile. The smooth wrap-around design of the boarded-up Lake Edge is reminiscent of the wrap-around windshield of its postwar epoch.

Both car design at the time—roughly the mid-1940s through the 1950s—and the classic motel architecture on the Strip express the new, permissive erotic style which came into the open in North America during the early *Playboy* period. The tourist cabin was still, after all, a cabin, a kind of home, often set among trees. The Strip motel of the 1940s and 1950s, on the other hand, takes its cue from the back seat. It's a row of bedrooms parallel to a row of parking spots. The motel acknowledges the new mechanical sexiness by dropping the discreet lobby, the seemly vestibule—the separation of sex and street characteristic of stately hotel design—and offers unencumbered instant passage from the erotic zone of the car to that of the bed.

If the car overcame the distances between cities, it also eliminated an interesting new kind of interval, between the motel and the rest of town. It was commonly known in the small Southern American town I lived in that a local pillar of the community, when his wife went to visit her sister in Dallas, always met his girlfriend in the motel in the next town along the highway, just over the Texas line, five miles away. He imagined his meetings were secret, of course, and my buddies and I thought we were the only ones who knew. As I later learned, everybody in town knew, though no one talked. Like the car, the motel was a zone invisibly cordoned off from proper small-town morality, in which one could easily imagine getting away with fantasies and acts prohibited in town. (Hence the understandable surprise of televangelist Jim Bakker and Jessica Hahn, and Jimmy Swaggert and his hooker, when their strip-motel trysts were discovered and frowned upon by contributors.)

The classic modern motel, such as those we find in Etobicoke, does not pretend to be a home away from home, or a cozy guest-house or anything other than what it is: a partner with the car in the uniquely mid-twentieth-century culture of high-speed travel, fast and novel powers and sex.

## CONCRETE REALITIES

Until the early days of 1993, city critics could credibly claim to know the exact death-date of architectural Modernism, and its lofty dream of mass cleanliness, urban rationality and salvation by skyscraper and park.

All that idealism bit the dust, so the old story goes, in April, 1976, in St. Louis, when city authorities dynamited the giant Pruitt-Igoe housing project. Hailed as a model of progressive urban renewal when put up in the early 1950s, by the early 1970s Pruitt-Igoe had become a cluster of horror-houses, raddled with violent crime and abandoned by all but gangsters, rats and a few victims too poor or frightened to move out.

While acknowledging the historic importance of the spectacular demolition in St. Louis, Modernism's steel-and-concrete vogue has certainly continued, enjoying new significant anniversaries. I here propose to add one to the calendar: a new one, just as spectacular, and accurate not merely to the month or even day, but to the very minute: Friday, February 26, 1993, at 12:18 p.m.

This was the moment a powerful bomb exploded in the parking garage under one of the two immense towers comprising New York's World Trade Center, killing seven people and injuring about one thousand in the skycraper above and the rapid-transit station below.

In addition to the human harm inflicted, the blast knocked out the 110-storey building's communications systems, air-conditioning apparatus, fire and smoke alarms, and 2,721 toilets—virtually all the unseen or discreetly tucked-away equipment which made this titanic structure convenient and safe for the 50,000 people who came to work in it every day.

The St. Louis and New York stories are linked, interestingly, by two facts. Both Pruitt-Igoe and the World Trade Center became important architectural events only with the help of high explosives—safely, professionally set off in St. Louis, detonated with deadly intent in New York. And, by a curious irony, both architectural settings—the St. Louis development (1952–1955), the Manhattan office tower (1962–1975)—sprang from the quintessentially sub-modernist mind of U.S. architect Minoru Yamasaki.

For those of us who've lived much of our lives in high-rise apartment buildings, Yamasaki's St. Louis fiasco has never seemed as significant as anti-Modern critics have made it seem. Some of the thousands of housing blocks cobbled together from concrete slabs, steel beams and prefab windows and doors during the last forty years were bound to fail, for reasons of structural faultiness, or because of the sorts of people who live there. Pruitt-Igoe was among the flops. The clean, handsome, completely prefab thirty-storey Toronto block near High Park, in which I rented a well-proportioned, inexpensive apartment for sixteen years was a success by any standard. I could have lived there all my life, had renting not become uneconomic, and had we not simply run out of room.

All we learn from the recent history of apartment construction is that some modernist megastructures work, some don't. But the 1976 lesson wasn't grim enough to slow down developers from carrying right on with the erection of tall modernist residential and commercial buildings—though without the dolling-up with perky hats, glitzy brooches and marble high-heels popular nowadays.

Once its full significance sinks into the minds of architects, developers and urban planners, the New York bombing may be recalled many times as an instructive event, even an upturn in the hopes for the tall building.

If decorative beauty in an edifice meant to be used by more than a couple of hundred people is optional, an underground parking garage is currently unthinkable. True, since their introduction parking garages have been dangerous places, especially for unaccompanied women. But the person who touched off the bomb under the World Trade Center brought us face to face with the fact of how dangerous they can become, instantly, for up to fifty thousand people at once—and how relatively harmless. The explosion did not blow out the perimeter columns of Tower One, bringing down the whole edifice; the blast damage was largely confined by various structural barricades to the garage itself and to underlying structures. While it did reveal the vulnerability of a great building's electro-mechanical, electronic and safety systems to so powerful a detonation, it also demonstrated the sturdiness and containment powers of a reinforced concrete parking garage, properly buried and technically isolated.

My optimism is qualified by only one fact: that the underground garage built as sturdily as the one below the World Trade Center is rare. We may never again be able to trust entirely this benign, useful building-type, created by and for the car, as we once did. What security systems are now in place to prevent a fanatic or lunatic from driving into any subterranean parking garage, under any residential or office tower anywhere, with enough explosives to make his point?

Be that as it may, these structures will endure, we will continue to use them, and New York will not affect our practical decisions to park underground. Nor will parking garages rapidly lose their practical interest, or their air of novelty. From time immemorial until the invention of the subway, the vehicles of transportation were always kept above ground, in a stable or (in any case) stablelike, free-standing building. At least that's where my great-grandmother kept her buggy and horses, until my great-grandfather turned the stable into a garage for his new car, the first ever seen in Palestine, Texas, and a gadget which attracted great public curiosity.

The descent of car barns underground, City of Toronto architect Robert Glover speculated in an interview, may have begun with "basement parking" in domestic or small office structures. While it's hard to say just when the true underground "parking garage" came into existence, the earliest instance I've found of an office tower with parking facilities built into it is Chicago's Pure Oil Building (1924), with the Title Insurance Building (1928) in Los Angeles a close runner-up. But never mind. "Going underground," says Glover, "was the only way of maximizing parking without losing open amenity space."

And, of course, it still *is* the only way. We shall probably never see the end of underground parking. But while I don't know about you, I'll never again feel quite the same about driving off the street, down the long, winding ramp, past the robot that burps out my ticket, and into the concrete-lined semi-dark under the belly of the city.

# *Streets*

*Curbside, St. Clarens Avenue*

# FORSAKING KENSINGTON MARKET

If the millions of people who live in North America's cities don't appear to care that the casual bump, shove and commotion of traditional big-city street culture is dying, Spiro Kostof cared very much. This outstanding American architectural historian, who died young in 1991, wrote about cities past and present with rigour and verve, and with a handsomely broad command of his subject. But he also did his scholarly work with evangelical militance, as though commanded by an angel to stand at the gates of the city, defending what was left of untidy, organic, unpredictable urbanity from the rational Modernist barbarians and planners camped without the walls.

We learn from a headnote in *The City Assembled*, his final testament, that Kostof died on the barricades, revising and sharpening his arguments almost to the last. It is in this lavishly illustrated book that Kostof paid his final, most passionate tribute to the old-fashioned street, and thundered forth his most dire prophecies about its future, and our own fate without it.

"In the past," Kostof writes—exactly when and where this *past* was is not specified—"the street was the place where social classes and social uses mixed. It was the stage of solemn ceremony and improvised spectacle, of people-watching, of commerce and recreation…both school and stage of urbanity…" He suggests that all this goodness has been diminished or destroyed by our recent inclination to "keep our own counsel, avoid social tension by escaping, *schedule* encounters with our friends"—his emphasis—"and happily travel alone in climate-controlled and music-injected glossy metal boxes." Change your ways and revive your streets, warns the author, lest they become "the burial place of our chances to learn from one another, child from bagwoman and street vendor from jock; the burial place of unrehearsed excitement, of the cumulative knowledge of human ways, and the residual benefits of a public life."

Kostof's is a moving appeal to the urban soul; it is undergirded, as well, by perhaps the most venerable of all perennial visions of urban utopia. Writing in 1913 from a point of view similar to that of Kostof, C. J. Cameron declared that "from almost every country in the world the immigrants come to Canada like the magic assembling of a hundred constituents to form a chemical compound. …Canada is the vast laboratory of grace in which God is fashioning the final man. The final race will not be any one nationality, but will be composed of elements from all races."

In every view informed by such apocalyptic pictures, the street is the "laboratory of grace" *non pareil.* With all the respect due Kostof, however, we are not likely to change our ways—simply because most of us have willingly chosen the new anti-street alienation, and have no intention of reviewing our choice.

If the word "street" has a certain charm to it, our scepticism and apprehension about this urban setting is revealed in the adjectival uses we make of the word. "Street people" are those unfortunate souls with no place to sleep. "Street kids" are teenagers who have descended into the hell of drugs, violence and prostitution that "street culture" has become in every large city. To be "street wise" is not to be wise at all, but merely clever at defending oneself against the predators who currently dominate "street culture." The gaudy, most sordid sections of Yonge Street, the sites of "street culture" with a vengeance, are not what Kostof had in mind. In search of some remnant of his dream-streets in Toronto, he would certainly have ignored Yonge and gone to Kensington Market.

Out-of-town visitors enjoy being walked through its narrow lanes and streets to savour the spirited open-air commerce now vanished almost everywhere except here, in the densely peopled, hectic retail and residential district of downtown Toronto south of College Street and east of the high Victorian brick façades, from the 1880s, lining Spadina Avenue. The Market is no neat theme park of Shopping Past. It is living, bruising, sweaty history. Elbowing your way through the mob on a sunny Saturday morning is probably as tough today as it was in the early 1920s, after Jewish merchants had established a thriving open-air market with "a shtetl atmosphere," an historian has affectionately recalled, on the narrow sidewalks of Augusta and Baldwin, Nassau and Kensington.

Every wave of immigration since then has left its mark, its particular commercial trace—jobbers and kosher butcher shops, West Indian roti joints, Portuguese cut-rate clothing stalls, Vietnamese restaurants, the bakeries and spice stores and greengrocers perfuming the air, brightening the street on the greyest winter day. And especially the earlier immigrants— Jewish and pre-war Italian—brought their political passions, leaving the area (as playwright and journalist Rick Salutin has written) "a centre for every kind of opposition and alternative to the sober Upper Canadian mainstream." The last struggle of anarchist Emma Goldman was waged there, on behalf of Italian anarchists, you tell your guests; and there she died, in 1940. As recently as the late 1960s, Grossman's Tavern was a hangout for black American draft dodgers and a drop-in centre for elderly Communists, while guys down from the

University of Toronto double-dog-dared each other to lead the way into the Victory Burlesque (formerly a Yiddish theatre), where you could see some of the dirtiest hip-grinding west of Times Square. (It's now a Chinese movie house.) The stench of fresh fish and a hundred kinds of cheese mingles with loud socializing in a dozen languages under the awnings of the open-air marts, and we and our visitors are charmed, especially because that's not the way we have to provision or entertain ourselves each week.

But that's just the point. Very few immigrants not forced by poverty to do so continue living in Kensington Market voluntarily. Some people still call Kensington "the Jewish market," and Jewish it was, from the turn of the century to the 1940s. At that point, prosperity, education and assimilation opened the way out, and the Jews sensibly took it. Ukrainian, Hungarian and Italian immigrants flooded into the Market after the Second World War, and by the 1960s Portuguese from the Azores had become the local mercantile ascendency. While the campuses of North America were ablaze with protest in those years, the Market's fame as a hotbed for political and social dissent had evaporated. The postwar immigrants are now following the Jews into suburban enclaves, and being replaced by East and West Indians, Koreans, Filipinos, Latin Americans, who will soon do the same. No amount of hand-wringing and nostalgia about what Toronto is losing with each flight will make one person stay, or anyone come back.

To my knowledge, the residents of the Market today are almost all recent immigrants too poor to do otherwise, university students playing poor, and a handful of sophisticated urbanists who, for some reason, *want* to live among the Market's rats, racket and odours. There is something touching about Spiro Kostof's decision to include in his superb final book a cheer for the busy old street, and a heartfelt appeal to those who've deserted all that for backyard barbecues and family rooms, private decks, *scheduled* encounters and life in "climate-controlled and music-injected glossy metal boxes." May Kostof rest in peace, undisturbed by urban humankind's firm rejection of street culture, and may he remain in everlasting ignorance of our complete absence of guilt or remorse about having made the decision we did.

## NOT FINDING MAIN STREET

The front-page news stories about Toronto's rampage of May 4, 1992, was dominated by the facts of what actually happened, musings about what caused it, and speculation about the ultimate social and dollar costs of it all. There was much public curiosity about the event, simply because it was exotic. Unlike U.S. cities similar in size and ethnic diversity, Toronto has rarely witnessed a widespread social blow-out of any sort, let alone a major uprising of citizens. The last memorable outbreak of equivalent civil violence here was, I believe, in 1837.

Be that as it may, the otherwise exhaustive coverage of this affair overlooked at least one aspect: the aimlessness of the route of both the peaceful demonstration and the violent display that followed. Toronto, it revealed with unusual force, lacks a Tienanmen or Wenceslas Square, an open place of celebration and conflict which Torontonians identify as uniquely our own, and a traditional crucible of our history. Nor could one escape being struck by Toronto's peculiar lack of a proper main street, along which a parade or violent demonstration could move with spectacular effect.

The affair began at about 4 p.m. on that spring Monday, as a peaceful gathering by about five hundred people in front of the United States consulate, an unimportant New Deal edifice huddled behind ugly anti-terrorist cement barricades on lower University Avenue. The demonstration had been called to protest the weekend shooting of Raymond Constantine

Lawrence, a young Jamaican-born man, by Toronto police, and also the recent acquittal of four white Los Angeles police officers in the videotaped beating of Rodney King.

While there may have been some symbolic reason to protest in front of the U.S. consulate, no real public effect could have been expected. That's because University Avenue is a grand and sociable boulevard only at first glance. On closer inspection, it reveals itself to be a failed main street, grandiose in concept but dead in fact, where people neither live nor enjoy themselves. If, long ago, University was a spacious thoroughfare lined by stately houses, today it is just an especially broad boulevard fronted by government buildings, insurance companies, financial institutions and hospitals. The employees who work by day in these buildings were all packing up their briefcases to go home by the time the demonstration began, and were tucked into the family room by the time it became ugly. Virtually the only people left who could possible appreciate the spectacle in front of the U.S. consulate would have been those sick or dying in the hospitals. A less promising street for a demonstration of outrage could hardly be imagined.

The crowd, still more or less peaceful, next made its way north to the mid-town intersection of Bloor and Yonge. The demonstrators then sat down, blocking what traffic there was for about an hour. Again, fact and perception collide: for if Bloor and Yonge is famous for marking the principal interchange of the Toronto subway system, its importance as Toronto's main vehicular crossroads is a thing of the past. The intersection only *sounds* important, and even then only to Torontonians. Like declaiming on near-deserted University Avenue, blocking Bloor and Yonge should have been recognized for the hopeless exercise it is. The net of wireless communications, particularly the traffic and news reports available on car radios, makes it easy for any motorist simply to take another route. And in any case, most sensible drivers heading out to suburbia or into the heart of downtown avoid Yonge Street at all times.

The trashing and looting began in earnest after the mob started milling around the toney shops near the intersection, and drawing in teenagers who had not taken part in the demonstration at the consulate. The untidy gaggle of demonstrators and mere vandals next started rambling down shabby Yonge Street, yet another of Toronto's main streets *manqué*.

Now Yonge Street *is* famous, because *The Guiness Book of World Records* has declared it the longest street in the world. Built early in the city's history to serve as a northbound escape-route from maurauding Americans, Yonge now measures 1,178.3 miles from its intersection with Front Street in Toronto to the bridge at Rainy River over to Minnesota. It also sports a handful of refined and important architectural monuments, especially along its lower blocks. But Yonge south of Bloor is, for the most part, gaudy and raucous, day or night—a showcase for male and female meat for sale, a stew of rock record stores, sex shops, electronic outlets, sleazy fast-food outlets, a hangout for drug dealers and destitute teen runaways. Could anyone realistically imagine that storming Yonge Street could have the effect of storming the Winter Palace, or the Bastille?

After milling and mobbing all the way back down from Bloor to Queen, the crowd then found itself at New City Hall. The great plaza in front of Viljo Revell's curving, embracing towers structure is perhaps the nearest thing Toronto has to a Winter Palace courtyard, though the effect of spaciousness has been largely negated by the clutter of bandshells and skating rink and peace monument and a Henry Moore sculpture—hardly a suitable or desirable place for a full-tilt demonstration.

Whatever was left of the peaceful element of the demonstration was then completely swept aside, and a more violent mob began moving back up Yonge. Now there is venerable Toronto tradition of crowds taking over Yonge Street for a night of merry wildness on special occasions, usually victories in sport. What happened here, however, was a perverse twist on this tradition: an angry rampage of trashing cars and looting shops, with the hooligans fighting the police, bystanders and, it seems, each other, all the way back up to Bloor, where the complex series of events finally fizzled.

The habit of remembering such civil upheavals by the names of city sites—Chicago's Haymarket riots, the storming of the Winter Palace, Watts, and so forth—is old and stubborn. It is still with us, despite the fact that organized demonstrations are now everywhere staged mostly for the benefit of the mass media, not to summon the local citizenry to arms or to frighten an offensive despot, holed up in his castle, into quick abdication.

Because the 1992 riot had no urban focus, any more than Toronto does—because it had no real main route or geographical aim—this almost unprecedented occurrence is doomed to be quickly forgotten, and will certainly not colour the meaning of Yonge, University or Bloor in popular imagination and urban mythology. Within days, police had downgraded its importance from "race riot" to "giant swarming," and mostly the work of teenagers greedy for the jackets on display in the Giorgio Armani shop. The drunken post-game looniness on Yonge Street will doubtless continue unto the ages of ages—while Toronto will have again absorbed and buried a memory by the sheer fact of its curious lacks of focus, ghettos, "festering zones of poverty," even *neighbourhoods* in any sense except that used by real-estate agents.

## THE END OF UNIVERSITY AVENUE

Just as the century began, Edwardian Toronto's prosperous and powerful took a long look south, at the urban transfigurations under way in Buffalo, New York, Boston and Chicago, and they very much liked what they saw. In those transportation and commercial hubs, akin to what Toronto had become, public power and private wealth were combining forces to make their cities as magnificent in visual form as they had become in financial and commercial fact. Displacing the low downtown jumble were long spacious boulevards and plazas, from which gracious residential streets branched. Grand theatres, heaven-defying steeples, parks and monuments were being deliberately sited and built to impress and delight, and to advertise urban prestige and glory. Here were cities ablaze, as Toronto was not, with the angelic fires of Progress and Refinement, sweeping away the old and stuffy to make way for "The City Beautiful."

When Toronto's plutocrats and politicians looked back at the old home town, they did not like the miserable buildings and crowded blocks they saw. In 1905, The Guild of Civic Art, inspired by the 1893 Chicago world's fair, had called for a major revamping of Toronto in accordance with City Beautiful notions—but nothing had come of it. "For me it is not a question of the city beautiful," said financier Sir Edmund Walker the next year. "It is just a question of practical common sense. Do we really believe in the city of Toronto?"

Had he been in the audience that day, architectural historian William Dendy would surely have responded with a resounding *yes*.

Dendy, who died at age forty-five in 1993, exulted in the cultivation, public intelligence and self-confidence of so much built in Toronto during its first two hundred years. That was the easy part. More remarkable is the sturdiness of his interest in Toronto throughout the writing of his prize-winning 1978 book *Lost Toronto: Images of the City's Past,* and the arduous updating of this indispensible work in the last months of his life.

Dendy was a connoisseur of lost chances. It bothered him to think, especially, about the doomed proposals for University Avenue which sprang from pre-war City Beautiful enthusiasm.

In a lovely drawing by Earle C. Sheppard, done for City Council in 1929 and reproduced in Dendy's book, we are shown a breathtaking proposal for the southern termination of University Avenue. The great street would broaden just south of Queen Street into an immense plaza, to be called Vimy Circle, focused by a tall, slender war memorial. As though paying deep homage to the fallen heroes of the First World War, refined and dignified civic and commercial buildings—none too high, all appropriately conservative and martial—would line the curving edge of this urbane *place*.

Traffic continuing towards the lakeshore from Vimy Circle would be angled slightly eastward, along a wide radial street intended to terminate, at Front Street, in another focused opening, to be called Britannia Square.

As things turned out, however, neither the Circle nor the Square ever got built, though the street did—producing one of the most unattractive conclusions of a great city street imaginable. Today, the broad part of University Avenue simply fizzles south of Queen, narrowing into an ignominious "extension." From the north start of this tightening, University Avenue continues southeastward stingily to Front Street West, where it twists and dives into a loathsome tunnel under the railway tracks, disgorging its traffic at last onto the waterfront.

This is not to say the last passage of University has been deprived of all architectural punctuation. What's wanted, of course, is a splendid exclamation point, such as the proposed Britannia Square. What the southbound motorist gets instead, just before the plunge into the sewerlike tunnel, is just a smudged comma, in the form of Citibank Place. Though only nine years old, its silvery twenty-storey façade at Front and University is already stained and shabby—unfortunate even (or especially) in a building that was as charmless as a public toilet fixture on the first day of its occupancy.

Anyone brave enough to get out of the car and walk around this confused, hectic tangle of crossing streets will see that Citibank Place is hardly the only offence against eye and good taste. But before the architecturally well-advised Torontonian hurls this book into the dustbin, I hasten to acknowledge that, yes, the intersection *does* feature two of Toronto's great twentieth-century buildings, the Royal York Hotel and Union Station. As William Dendy pointed out, both were briefly considered for deployment as framing and focusing elements for the magnificent Cambrai Avenue proposal. This thoroughfare would have begun its straight northward passage at the portico of Union Station, concluding above Richmond Street in a vast open circle to be known as St. Julien Place, in memory of the Battle of Ypres. Had Cambrai Avenue been built, Dendy wrote verily, "Toronto's downtown would have had a focus and grandeur it sadly lacks." It could also have provided a highly imposing initiation into urban sophistication: a grand and thoroughly urbane street, lined with elegant towers and galleries, fine shops and exquisite restaurants, all dedicated to the highest civilized pleasures and pursuits for the some seventeen million travellers and commuters who arrive in Toronto via Union Station each year.

As matters stand, the arriving passenger steps from the train, descends through an indifferent passageway, and is deposited into a low-ceilinged, meanly appointed arrivals room located directly below the station's justly famous Great Hall. The traveller can then come up directly from the swarming hall onto Front Street, as from a basement flat, to be greeted by a welcoming committee out of nightmare, comprised of an escarpment of giant buildings, all staring down coldly upon the hapless newcomer.

The alternative is to make a beeline for the network of man-made caves fanning out northward underground from the Station, leading to hotels, shops, subways. But whatever you do, however—scram in a cab, flee into the underground maze, jump on a subway—the only appropriate response is panicky retreat.

I realize that to utter negative thoughts about Union Station is to invite arrest on a blasphemy charge by Toronto's architectural preservationists, who, more than two decades ago, fought long and successfully to save the Station from the wrecker's ball.

The nub of the problem I'm pointing out is that all the architectural ceremony of Union Station is, and was originally designed to be, reserved for people who are *leaving* town. Arriving by car at the Front Street portals, the traveller passes though a magnificent colonnade into the Hall, with its fine tiled barrel vault overhead and everywhere the luxurious rhythms of warmer and cooler stone. One passes to the trains from this triumphant (though hardly pompous) space down a brief, luxuriously appointed ramp guarded by tall pillars topped by flourishing Corinthian capitals, the city's last bouquets for its *departing* guests. Does Toronto *always* have to save the best until last, the climax for the conclusion?

## THE BURYING OF THE WIRES

We seem prepared to go to almost any length to flaunt certain accomplishments of modernity—soaring towers celebrating technical and financial mastery, cars conspicuously loaded with chrome, or compact to the verge of ostentatious minuteness—while relentlessly hiding others. In this latter category, I'm thinking of almost everything that has to do with electricity. The visible net of communications technology (telephone, television cable strung overhead), for example, and the physical apparatus of energy supply. (The CN Tower is, technically, an exception, being the tallest communications mast in the world; but its function as a TV and radio mast is incidental to its presumed usefulness as a city status-symbol, an emblem to be stamped on endless souvenirs, a stalk for a revolving restaurant from which nothing can be seen except water and Buffalo, and so forth.)

Most hateful, apparently, are the street wires, the burying of which was briefly a hotly debated public topic in Toronto early in the 1990s. Until then, I had never thought of hydro and phone wires as either homely *or* lovely. In fact, I'd never thought much about them at all. City councillor Howard Levine had been thinking about them a great deal, and come to the conclusion that they are things we should all give grave thought to indeed.

"If we live in an ugly environment," reasoned Levine, in a utopian-Modern (or Ruskinian) mood, "it stimulates ugly social patterns. A beautiful city is important." I suspect that most people are sympathetic with the sentiment, even if the behaviouristic social theory that produces the equation "ugly wires equals ugly acts" is, of course, quaintly false. But even if they disagree with Levine's philosophy, no Torontonians will take to barricades to stop Ontario Hydro's enormous programme of burying its wires beneath the sidewalks.

Now underway, the great interment will cost taxpayers an estimated $1.5 billion and take twenty-five years to complete. The occasion of this project is a massive changeover, for which Toronto Hydro has argued persuasively, from the 4.16-kV (kilovolt) grid, in service since early in this century and now approaching its limits of service, to a more capacious and otherwise up-to-date 13.8-kV system. According to the official Hydro proposal, the new high-voltage network need not be buried, though aesthetic considerations about poles "out of proportion to the street" and about "industrial-type hardware... not fitting for residential communities" have combined with practical considerations to make burial the chosen option. (The vulnerability of exposed wires to Toronto's occasional savage windstorms, which, to my mind, is the best reason to put the things underground, appears to have been only a minor consideration.)

Not every wire in the new 13.8-kV distribution grid, incidentally, will be put underground. In industrial areas—around

Toronto Harbour, in the Eastern Avenue wasteland of junk yards, and around west-downtown's crumbling, vanishing factory district, among others—the new cables will still be strung between and from tall poles, as before. But on many arterial and commercial streets, around public parks and along what are being called "historical streets"—mostly in the vicinity of Queen's Park and in "olde York"—the concealment of transformers and conducting wire is intended to be total. Street lighting will be provided, in all districts where burial is complete, by lamps mounted on stalks or walls.

As for residential streets, Hydro is going halfway. The transformers, and the primary 13.8-kV lines serving them, will be put under the sidewalks, inside tiny burrows excavated, for the most part, by remote-controlled mechanical moles. Each house on a given street will be served by a slender bundle of secondary, reduced-voltage cables strung from an eight-metre pole. The effect, then, will be to reduce the overhead clutter in residential neighbourhoods, but not to return them to the appearance of premodernity altogether.

Unless, of course, one is prepared to pay for it.

Under Toronto Hydro's so-called "local option," residents of each urban area will get the choice of eight-metre poles at no extra cost (beyond the increased hydro rates made necessary by the city-wide conversion), or total undergrounding at a cost of between $4,000 and $5,500 extra per property, payable by the owner. Complete burial will require approval by two-thirds of all property owners in a given area, and will then be mandatory for all. Thus, having hydro wires on your street, or not having them, will become, for the first time in the history of urban electrification, expressions of neighbourhood status.

Once they're gone underground, the swags and festoons of wires now overhead on every street, and criss-crossing in loose weaves at most important intersections, will probably not be missed, if only because we have not been much aware of them for most of a century. Only at the odd time when they get in the way—when we're trying to take a snapshot of the factory we live in, to send back to Texas cousins who can't believe we really would live in such a place—do we actively dislike them. Long past is the day when the incising of those lines against the changeable Toronto skies was a moment of excitement on a given street or in a given neighbourhood—the very herald and sign of modernity, coming to pierce the dark of pre-electric night with steady brilliance.

Removing the wires will not make us beautiful people, as councillor Levine thinks; indeed, it will give new visual expression to the turn of attitude towards the city long underway—from a certain delight about our machines and electric devices to a downright dislike of the things, and a will to rid ourselves of the very sight of them.

## CHRISTMAS LIGHTS

Now while we're on the subject of electricity and streets, and ridding the latter of the former, I wish to register a complaint about the one electrical custom I don't like, which is the ritual of Christmas lights. Our single strand of outdoor bulbs, manufactured to cheer the hearts of passers-by, lay heaped in a chair in the bedroom all through the last Christmas season, a sad example of the unstrung and the unlit.

Blame it on the dragging economy or rumours of an impending jack-up of the provincial sales tax or whatever: most people I know have had problems revving up the old Yuletide cheer the last few Christmases, and a number have failed, as we have, to put up our outdoor lights. No one should conclude that I and my crowd are grinches; we aren't. I will advance an alternative theory of our behaviour presently. To be fair, it does seem that most other Torontonians except us have been merrily stringing their estimated ten million lights, inside and out, around Metro. (The estimate came from Noma, Inc., a Canadian company and the world's largest manufacturer of Christmas lighting.)

This last Christmas, few households in my downtown neighbourhood were content merely to put an old-fashioned glowing orange candelabra in the window. The more usual style has been increasingly Las Vegas post-Modern. Galaxies of big bulbs in nail-polish colours, set on rapid-blink, in the trees. Strings of twinkly green or poisonously red lights outlining fence, porch railing, roof. Whorls of brilliant white pinpoint bulbs around evergreens, programmed to light up one after the other at blinding speed, like casino marquees.

The festoons of Christmas lights which bedeck, year-round, a local front garden shrine of the Immaculate Conception was enhanced for the holiday season with a mini-Niagara of gently luminous blue bulbs. Less pious decorations included innumerable glowing plastic Santas, Rudolphs and such.

But, in any Christmas season, to motor along the wide streets of Toronto's outer suburbs is to find mere front-yard showoffishness replaced by a war of spectacles, with everybody on a street aggressively trying to outdo his neighbours. Vastly long snakes of twinkling bulbs in the trees surround the ranch-styles in delirious fantasias of colour and light, flood-lit mechanized reindeer rock stiffly back and forth, while Santa's arm wags back and forth on rooftop or lawn. What is more wondrous? The army of glowing gnomes in Yard A, or the full-sized, flood-lit tableau of the Holy Family in Yard B?

Hoping to feel noble about my abstention from doing an outdoor display, I rang up Ontario Hydro to find out how much money everybody wastes, province-wide, on the Great Christmas Light-Up. To my disappointment, I found it's very little, comparatively speaking: only about $21,000 an hour on top of the hourly $1.3 million that Ontarians would ordinarily be spending on electricity at that time of year. If Hydro statistics cannot be used to make us feel thrifty, and virtuous in our concern for the environment, those who dread the onset of Christmas—the decorating and partying and shopping, as well putting up outdoor lights—could take comfort in the notion that we may well be avant-garde, yea! the very Spirits of Christmases Yet To Come.

It should be obvious that what is dreaded is not Christmas itself—which means nothing to those who aren't Christians, and something wonderfully important to those of us who are—but certain "traditional" elements that have come to be associated with it. The enforced conviviality of obligatory parties, for example. And the shopping in bad weather or in crowded malls. And the virtually unavoidable overeating, over-drinking, overloading on chocolate. And lights. While pigging out on Christmas Day is perhaps a custom of high antiquity, the pre-Christmas party at office or school appears to be an invention no older than the 1920s. And, says a spokesman for Noma, outdoor Christmas lighting only goes back to the latter 1940s. Thus, the exhaustion some of us feel at the very idea of Christmas may not be a sign of impending Scroogehood or grinchness at all, but just a sign that the latter-day novelty of Christmas lights may be going the way of other fads, such as the rib-crushing corset and the boogie-woogie.

## LANEWAYS

A history of the residential laneway, which nobody has gotten around to writing, would make colourful reading; and the Toronto chapter would go farther back than you might imagine. Leader Lane, in the heart of downtown, is thought to be from circa 1850, while Grand Opera Lane dates from around 1874. The oldest alley of which the City has official knowledge—this information from public works planner Julius Keddy—is a century old, and, unlike most of its counterparts

*Emerson Alley, Morning*

throughout the metropolis, has a name, Mincing Lane. I only recently learned that it was called that after the ancient London street. Until then, I had wondered whether the *mincing* had to do with what you do to meat, or from the way tall men walk when attired in spike heels; I considered no third option.

The practice of putting paved lanes between rows of back gardens endured into the early 1930s, principally in Toronto's working-class residential neighbourhoods. By the thirties, of course, its principal original uses—the removal of kitchen garbage and night soil from privies—had been rendered antique by the installation of underground sewage pipes. But architectural habits die hard, and zoning habits even harder. If you do have a lane out back, it's fairly certain you've bought into what was and may still be a workers' neighbourhood. (The notion of the residential laneway as mews, for the discreet movement of horses, groceries and servants, is Old World; though a grungy version of this older idea can still be seen in the commercial alleys, full of dead lettuce and soggy cardboard boxes, running parallel to market thoroughfares.) By the same token, the more upper-class the neighbourhood, the rarer the lanes. Some can be found among the late Victorian brick houses of gentrified Cabbagetown, but only a few in comfortably middle-class north Toronto or in generally posh Forest Hill (on the really posh *east* side of Spadina, anyway).

As it turns out, Keddy said, the overhauled circa-1915 factory I live in lies in the heartland of Toronto's 233.6-kilometre system of laneways. It's that stretch of town south of St. Clair Avenue, between Christie Pits and the Junction, transformed quickly from vacant cropland into a tract of industrial plants and workers' houses shortly after 1900. Apart from a complete overhaul in ethnic makeup—from British, to a current mix of Portuguese, Italian, Asian and Yuppie—it remains the densely populated, unspiffy and unstylish territory it was *ab origine*.

Like every other planned city site, the typical lanescape in this district is in constant, often contradictory architectural process. The outhouses that once stood at the alley-end of the properties have long ago disappeared, but the rickety old wooden garages that replaced them are falling down, and sturdier brick ones are everywhere under construction. Many of these newer buildings are not used for parking cars. In garage-looking structures behind my factory one can find a little auto-body shop, a meticulously well-organized welding operation, a tiny furniture factory, a junk dealership, a storage facility for Volvo parts—the infrastructure of that display of individual initiative known as the "underground economy." After some older garages have collapsed, however, homeowners tired of mowing and weeding have mercilessly paved their back lots, while others have plowed them up for the spring planting of tomatoes and grape vines.

This physical environment is the stage for volatile live action of the alley, the urban theatre which is too little known, and too little appreciated. For the kids, it's a winter battleground for snowball fights, and a summer street-hockey arena. For our Sikh neighbours, it's a place to gather in tight bunches and chat quietly, even on very cold days. For the tubby, ugly Siamese tomcat who lords it over all the other cats in the area, it's turf to be guarded with fang and claw, and, when he's lovesick, where he howls for his passion of the evening.

We dwellers in the factory know that spring has come when musclebound guys pull a sputtering car into the lane, put some heavy metal rock on the boom-box, plunk down a styrofoam cooler full of iced beer, and spend a Saturday afternoon ripping out the engine's guts. Or when the car-washing begins, spattering the pavement with frothy suds. We know it's nightfall in summer, when all the little kids abruptly stop bashing each other and vanish indoors, and the lanky pimp in a Kermit-green tracksuit slouches to his post up by the fender-mender shop, and settles in to do business.

And we'll know it's September, and nearly the end of another summer of gardening, when a broad streak of transparent ecclesiastical purple appears in the middle of the lane's grey concrete pavement one morning—the evidence of grape-dregs, clandestinely dumped by our wine-making neighbours into the storm sewers in the dead of the night before.

# Gardens

*Fence and Rose Bush*

# GROUNDS AND FRONT GARDENS

O nly the wealthy few in any metropolis have what can properly be called *grounds*. Almost everyone else has unwalled yards, fore and aft, with a walkway or drive of varying width running perpendicular to the street between one house and the next.

While I have neither grounds nor yard, most of the people in my district of west-end Toronto have front and back gardens. Almost every one has been endowed with a specific character, giving the neighbourhood a character entirely different from the uniformity attempted in suburbia, with its regular, uninterrupted lawn-strips and "foundation plantings," or in the upmarket zones, where gardens have been reduced to ostentatious monotony by imperious designers. Low, inconspicuous fencing is common, and an important aspect of a streetscape rhythm of enclosure and disclosure, what's mine and what belongs to everybody, or what can belong to both me and everybody, to varying degrees and at different times. Most front gardens around here are clearly laid out to be beheld by passersby, and not strolled in by anyone, including the owner—a crucial departure from the aristocratic European garden, designed for the owner's eyes only—while the front porch overlooking it is arranged as a quasi-public area, a proletarian belvedere, for neighbourhood gatherings on summer evenings.

A few of the small front yards in my territory have been allowed to go weedy and scruffy. Such a fate is rare, because universally disliked. The more usual attitude taken by my neighbours is one of idiosyncratic attention towards the front patch as an infinitesimal state under absolute monarchy. The experience of the streetscape, then, is one of pleasing, wild variety, as one might have found in nineteenth-century *Mitteleuropa*—an archipelago of minute principalities, each with its own currency, cuisine and customs.

One front yard will be a strictly uninflected rectangle of grass, sown and grown with exquisite care, and chemically encouraged to resemble Astroturf, each blade clipped to precisely the same length. Another will be laid out in beds of red and white petunias, alternating with a pattern as regular as houndstooth, and set in rigidly straight rows from which, one imagines, it would be certain death for a petunia to wander; while yet another will be dotted with annuals selected, it appears, to illustrate the heraldic colours of the owner's home country.

A front garden around the corner lies almost invisible under an overwhelming scramble and tumble of pink roses, while the one next to it is a square slab of smoothed, uniformly grey concrete, perforated in its exact centre by a small hole stuffed with lurid impatiens. Nearby is an exceedingly neat, faintly tragic garden of devotion to Our Lady of the Immaculate Conception, whose sacred image, bedecked year-round with Christmas lights, stands in a finely constructed brick shrine—tragic, because its creator clearly wishes his front garden to be a great place of piety and quietude, a refuge not unlike Lourdes, while his property is small, and abuts one of the busiest streets in the area.

If there is one frequently recurring plant in the various front-yard arrangements, it is a kind of astonishingly abundant, climbing rose with screaming red blooms, giving many a porch the appearance, in high summer, of having been hit with rocket-launched bombs filled with nail polish. Whatever one makes of the contribution to beautiful urbanism by this strange rose—a bit of genetic fallout, surely, from the same progressive postwar moment that gave us Tang and Teflon—virtually everyone seems deeply concerned about the effect of their little front yards. I should add that many people on my street eschew all spectacle, making quietly eccentric, flowerful or fruitful yards, lovely and visually melodic despite (or perhaps because of) their makers' angelic ignorance of "good design."

Now I have nothing against good garden design—the real and inventive thing, as preached and practised by the likes of Gertrude Jekyll or Vita Sackville-West. It's just that good garden design can rarely be found here, and most rarely of all in the pretentious, predictable, unfelt deployment of flowers and shrubs one sees on the front yards of one carriage-trade street after another. Such plantings express no joy, declare a lack of abiding care, and reveal a ballooning surplus of image-anxiety on the part of the owners.

My thoughts on front gardens were not prompted, however, by unhappy drive-bys of the front yards of the downtown rich, or by affection or disaffection for the way my unrich neighbours utilize their little lawns, but by the surprising discovery of what little information is available about the history of this commonest site in Toronto and every other North American city. It happened when I reached for the architectural dictionary I keep ever at my elbow—a fat, recent book abundantly endowed with entries on everything from aedicules to zoophoria. In it was not a word about yards, most ubiquitous of North American urban forms, their development or the stage they provide for the enactment of the rites of metropolitan culture. It was like finding no article about God in a large, authoritative dictionary of Christian theology. The yard appears to be to contemporary architectural historians what toilet activities were to our great-grandmothers: universally known to exist, though something absolutely not to be mentioned.

So far, I have been able to find only one reason most of Toronto's working-class tract houses, quick-built on farmland, between the 1880s and the First World War, have front and back yards and narrow corridors between; and it is a legal one. The British Parliament's Public Health Act of 1875, urged on legislators by the squalidly crowded, disease-ridden slums which blighted Britain's cities during the Industrial Revolution, set strict standards for intervals separating domestic dwellings, in the name of health and well-being. The result of this law was the development of a model for urban housing throughout the Empire, which, in turn, gave us pre-suburban Toronto, i.e., most of downtown constructed before air-conditioning and central heating. The standard working-class house of this period is a detached structure, or, perhaps more commonly a semi-detached one—an architectural peculiarity in North American building history, very common in Toronto—with large windows to allow free ventilation, small front "gardens" to provide distance from the dusty street and unenclosed by walls, to assure proper air and light—a novelty, coming from a European culture much given to walling up gardens, yards and farmlands. Some space was required between houses, again to allow ventilation, with long backyards behind each structure—not for growing beans and tomatoes, at that time anyway, but to provide a decent separation between back door and privy.

The death of the privy allowed the transformation of the backyard into a garden for flowers or vegetables or both. Paving and guttering of streets, and the running of storm and sanitary sewers underground, left the unwalled front yard without function as a sanitary interval. But California urbanist Dean MacCannell is probably right when he suggests that peculiar obsessiveness lavished on the front garden in a district like mine may well be grounded in the need of the immigrant labourer—alienated from homeland, expected to obey strange laws and customs, shut out by the native élite—to control at

*Lappin Avenue*

least *this* much of the land he's come to. Assimilation will undercut the desperation feeding this need; upward economic mobility, and the move on to suburbia, will largely eliminate it. But for now the front gardens on my street are objects of this curiously intense caring—whether what's being attempted is floral fantasy or salad-growing, the obsessively cute piling of rocks to create a miniscule Hobbit shire, or, in the case of a yard directly across the street from my factory home, a primly maintained grassy shrine of the Lord Buddha.

## Essential Urban Gardening

In 1891, a young man working in a Manchester factory put an ad in a local newspaper, asking for help in planting a window-box three feet long and ten inches wide. He knew nothing about growing things. Would someone kindly give him advice?

Fortunate was that man, for the ad turned up on the breakfast table of a portly, myopic, middle-aged Englishwoman, known to her friends as Aunt Bumps, who decided at once to take the boy and his box firmly in hand. "The post brought him plants of mossy and silvery saxifrages, and a few small bulbs," Aunt Bumps recalled later. "Even some stones were sent, for it was to be a rock-garden, and there were to be two hills of different height with rocky tops, and a longish valley with a sunny and a shady side."

Now she who so promptly answered the working-boy's appeal—the lady known outside her inner circle as Gertrude Jekyll—was accustomed to gardening on a somewhat larger scale than a window-box on a working-class street. Her home turf in Surrey covered fifteen acres, and kept a half-dozen workmen busy year round. In the remaining forty years of her very long life, Jekyll would design, directly or in consultation with fifty architects, some 350 gardens, large and small, for a galaxy of wealthy clients, including the Duke of Westminster, Prince Alexis Dolgorouki and Vita Sackville-West.

But, as she knew perfectly well, and as snobs never learn, creating a wonderful garden has very little to do with money or grand space. It has everything to do with rigorous attention to both detail and ensemble, a thorough grasp of plant structure and behaviour, reverence for the *genius loci* expressed in the suite of lights and shadows that informs the shape of site, even the tiniest window-box, making it unique.

A passage on gardening, and gardening tips, may seem like an odd addition to a book on city sites. My reason for putting it in is simply that no city site is so common, or numerous, or various than the garden, created under the particular constraints of city living; and no city site is less complex or various. On it converges every sort of desire, longing, hope and love of pleasure, and into its creation goes peculiar and intimate knowledge, disciplined by restrictions the country-dweller does not have to face. This, then, is very much a personal story; but it is also an experience, I believe, that is not unlike that of a million other people who, for some reason, have taken it into their minds to make a garden in the midst of metropolis.

Fortunately, I discovered the example of Aunt Bumps before building the boxes on my third-floor deck garden and putting my hands into the dirt, thus saving myself from doing what I usually do in practical matters, which is put cart before horse. Instead of rushing out and buying a lot of nice-looking plants, I first amassed a small library of botanies, practical growing guides, works on the history and philosophy of gardens, and handbooks on successful container gardening, then went to work, studying and drawing and planning. The principal difference between gardening on a deck and on the ground had to be dealt with immediately—the absence on rooftops of any possibility of dialogue between the given and the constructed, that is. Up there, *everything* is constructed, even the dirt—or "dirt," as this fluffy ersatz compound should properly be called. My first idea was to create a belvedere from which to contemplate the housetops, chimneys and laneways to the south, with birches framing the roofscape and focused on an old-fashioned black metal watertower in the distance. After the first summer, however, I decided to turn the deck into a *hortus conclusus,* or monastic garden—an enclosed dead-end for meditation and retreat, since the view definitely did not turn out to be as interesting as I thought it would be.

Never mind that all my schemes have gone awry, and few of the plants behaved exactly as the books said they should. Aunt Bumps's advice is still sound: the plan comes first. Much of the value of doing things this way is psychological, for I might not have been able to summon up the courage to make my first garden in the only place I had—a bare oblong of outdoor deck opening south over the rooftops and backyards of my neighbours—without a detailed strategy in hand.

Jekyll brought me the benefits of the great change that took root in the British garden in the 1860s and 1870s, the years she was coming of age. The older, exclusive ideals—the outdoor botanical museum, the stiffly geometrical planting, the carefully disposed rhythm of copse and field, the garden as intellectual exercise or stylishly novel showpiece—were already under attack by garden designers flying the flags of wildness, the romance of colour, the irrational, the natural and intimate.

She would eventually give such ideas some of their most glorious and influential expressions. As a young woman, Jekyll was aware of this horticultural revolution afoot, and would shortly begin contributing the first of hundreds of articles to the journals promoting it. She perhaps could have struck out as an independent leader of it, because her comprehension was brilliant. Instead, this deeply mid-Victorian soul for many years devoted herself to the traditional womanly crafts of her age and place, from textile design to embroidery and watercolour.

It was while taking these steps into art that she drifted effortlessly into a circle of romantic writers and artists including John Ruskin, with whom she shared the worship of Turner, and William Morris. And there were the Jacques Blumenthals, who hosted musical evenings, and the Duke of Westminster, Princess Louise—Victoria's daughter and a talented artist—the dashing amateur watercolourist Hercules Brabazon, the painters Edward Burne-Jones and Lord Leighton, the odd Anglican prelate and many another genteel and cultivated persons.

From our late-modern overlook, Jekyll's social scene seems (as the title of a book about her puts it) like an endless glide through "gardens of a golden afternoon," *English* in the tea-and-crumpets sense that would die in the trenches of the First World War. Yet this gentle cultural loam nourished in young Jekyll a blossoming interest in fine hand-crafted design which would finally find its fulfillment in one of the great creative friendships of modern times. This relation began in 1891—the year of the Manchester window-box—when she met an ambitious young architect named Edwin Lutyens. Aided in his rise by the socially well-connected Jekyll, this last of the great English country-house architects returned the favour by commissioning her to do more than one hundred gardens for his projects.

One wonders what Gertrude Jekyll would find to do nowadays. As the gardens of Toronto's poshest neighbourhoods testify, the rich want show, not subtlety—a big visual impression, not art, invention, fugitive delights. And most of us non-rich are too busy making a living to spend the years of patient experiment and rigorous self-education that it takes to create a garden on the large scale. So we borrow the concrete ideas about plantings and such from Jekyll and her heirs, just to kick-start ourselves—working out designs with a colour wheel, studying up on heights and textures and colours so as to avoid making a mess, and so on. Only later do we begin to find that gardening the Jekyll way is as much a spiritual discipline as a hands-on craft. The joy of it is in learning how the sunlight of each summer hour falls on every leaf, petal and twig; of noting how an autumn shower changes the colour of one's late-blooming clematis and hydrangeas, of learning to listen to the fragile soul of the world, speaking in every garden's ever-evolving, evanescent beauties.

Not that many serious plantspeople outside cities would consider my deck-top boxes of dirt a real garden. Perhaps in self-defence, my use of the word is promiscuous. I am prepared to allow the word to be used of an island of hot-pink impatiens on a flattened, poison-green suburban lawn, and also my neighbour's tiny plot of exuberantly abounding salad greens. A clutch of potted petunias on a twentieth-storey balcony is a garden, and so is a capacious estate planned for a cowed client by a tyrannical landscape architect and maintained by a battalion of weeders and trimmers. So is a row of shrubs, or a line of proletarian annuals plunked down each May to mask an unsightly concrete foundation.

Some private gardens are actually quite public, like the little patches in parks allotted by the city to apartment-dwellers. Others are (or are meant to be) secret, like the secluded patch of tomato and marijuana plants I discovered a summer or so ago, while scouting an abandoned railroad right-of-way for wildflowers.

Now that I've defined *garden* so broadly that it includes whatever you do—from gently putting in *Cypridedium insigne* to growing pot on the sly—you'll probably be wanting some practical tips. I don't have any, except the obvious ones. Just because you like a plant is not good enough. It must fit the plan. Learn how to refuse, firmly and finally, cuttings spontaneously proffered by friends trying to be helpful. Their helpfulness will turn out to be your downfall. At the same time, develop polite strategies for getting your friends to give you cuttings that will fit your plan. Be brave in your retromania, since it is a grace given to every plantsperson who works and prays. Above all, *think*. And be imperious. Every really good gardener is.

What counts is the development of a correct attitude. And this is my reason for recommending to all city plantsfolk V. *Sackville-West's Garden Book*. If notorious for the oddity of her marriage to Harold Nicolson—she, lesbian; he, gay; the marriage, idyllic (most of the time); the children, smart and charming—the late Vita Sackville-West was also probably the best horticultural journalist ever to write for a newspaper. The *Garden Book* is a selection of weekly columns contributed to *The Observer* between 1947 and 1961. After its publication in 1968, this volume went through ten subsequent impressions in hardcover; and, since coming out in paperback in 1987, it's been reprinted twice. Read twenty pages, and you'll understand the reasons for its durable enchantment.

Just remember that Kent isn't Canada; and few of us have the barrow-loads of money, the land, time or willpower to create anything like the world-famous gardens at Sissinghurst, the country seat of Sackville-West and her diplomat-husband. What counts in this book, apart from the marvellous writing itself, is the columnist's exemplary stance, which any city gardener will do well to mimic, even if his or her garden is, like mine, just some insulated boxes on a rooftop.

Central to the Sackville-West position is an unflinching ruthlessness, coupled with an unbounded delight in experimentation. "The true gardener must be brutal," she advises, "and imaginative for the future." Every plant must please. If something doesn't please, for any reason, it must be ripped out and thrown away. Move things around, add, subtract, try anything, but never rest until everything is exactly right. Since nothing about a garden comes out exactly right, you'll be at the job for the rest of your life.

Of course—here I go again—you won't get anything right if you don't have a plan. Sackville-West was an architect at heart, who chose to realize her plans in the ephemeral, unpredictable stuff of plants, with their infinite variety of colour, texture, volume, shape, seasonal variation. Like any relentless designer, she is exasperated when something goes wrong. But every exasperation is just a jumping-off point for a revision of the plan, and the next try. In a fabulous understatement, she reminds us that "one has a lot, an endless lot, to learn when one sets out to be a gardener."

In addition to everything else you have to do, you should learn the sheer botany of it all. You must know exactly what such-and-such really is, when and how it blooms and droops and dies, where it comes from. (Vita has a lovely column about the origin of Bourbon roses on an island off the east coast of Africa.) You must know the minutest detail of every bloom's powers to lure butterflies or repel them, what sorts of bugs will chew it to death, and what house-pets its leaves, lunched upon, will kill.

It follows that flowers must do more than just look nice on a sunny day. They should be interesting in temperament and history, as well as in appearance. Her opinion of campion (*Lychnis haageana*) is that it's "rather untidy," with "ugly leaves" and "shaggy flowers"—but she finds its tendency to come up from seed in unexpected colours amusing, so its life is spared. The attraction of *Narcissus triandrus albus* is its liking for "broken shade, where it looks like a little ghost, weeping."

But she would rip all the ivy off those venerable English walls, because "one gets so bored by its persistent stuffy evergreen." If a terrible snob in private life, Sackville-West is militant about reversing the bad rap given the humble Virginia creeper, after she discovers one in its autumnal scarlet phase, not "glued to red-brick houses," but hung in "great swags and festoons" on a silver birch, and glowing like "wine held up to the light."

So here's a rooftop toast to Vita; and a toast, too, to all my fellow city-dwellers who are planning or learning the beauties we want to spring, someday, from our most intimate city site, be it yard, pot, box, planter, tub, or whatever other bit of dirt to which we have decided to lay total, imperial claim.

## ALLAN GARDENS

Newcomers to Toronto are still warned by friends and old-timers to shun Allan Gardens. While I don't remember getting this advice when I settled here a quarter-century ago—not in so many words anyway—the idea of this once-fashionable downtown park as a sordid open-air drug-and-sex bazaar, and a noisy preaching-field for the famously fundamentalist Jarvis Street Baptist Church nearby, somehow got stuck in my mind. Not needing heroin and being certain of Heaven, I stayed away—until one very cold Sunday afternoon in 1991, when I discovered what many another wary immigrant has probably missed for as many years as I had.

It is the charming domed and winged pavilion of glass that stands on Allan Gardens' west side, designed by city architect Robert McCallum, and known as the Palm House. This little structure was put up between 1910 and 1913 to replace a whimsical pagoda of 1878, famed for its concerts, balls and high teas, and which burned to the ground in 1902. At the time of the completion of the Palm House, the posh Edwardian district around Allan Gardens and the Palm House was poised on the edge of decline, which urban decay would inflict in earnest after the First World War and largely destroy by the end of the Second.

In 1910, of course, Robert McCallum did not know what was coming, and so envisioned his building as a gleaming brooch on the ample, upper-class bosom of the neighbour-hood. I have not been able to track down the likely inspira-tion for McCallum's project, and am inclined to think he had no specific structure in mind. Rather, the Palm House appears to be a little chamber rhapsody on several large, lovely themes current among *fin-de-siècle* French and English builders of canopied and winged conservatories, market halls, exhibition palaces and the like. The lanterned central dome recalls the one Victor Baltard had provided for his Halles Centrales in Paris, though McCallum has given it an exotic taper, perhaps to remind his Toronto viewers of India and Raj. The closest thing to the Palm House McCallum might have known directly was the great glazed tent of the Palm Stove, created by Decimus Burton and Richard Turner in the mid-1840s for the Royal Botanic Gardens at Kew.

The Palm Stove is really an ordinary rectangular greenhouse writ large, with all its angles smoothed into an elongated bubble of glass. It looks like a domed railway car, and seems about to turn from architecture into engineering before our very eyes. Toronto's Palm House does not go so far, nor become so modern. If it glances at the Palm Stove and contemporary pavilions, it also has an air of the old-fashioned garden temple about it. In McCallum's work, the central temple is turned from stone to glass, and outfitted, not quite convincingly, with wings that are really just traditional hothouses.

In the Palm House, there are a number of palms from Africa and equatorial America, some of them surprisingly tall, surging like green fountains towards the dome's clear glass lantern. But strolling through the wings of this sunny palace of plants, the visitor will also find a gallery of cactus, variously sinister, impudent and piquant; a tiny swamp; and splendid orchids suspended aloft in many small baskets, as though enjoying a sociable afternoon of hot-air ballooning. In a sweet, cold gallery, there are banks of white narcissus, those good-natured proletarians of the garden, and beds of pale, neurotic camelia, flowerdom's Blanche Dubois.

One finds no long or panoramic vistas here. Everything is very close, inviting scrutiny rather than admiration. Walking along the Palm House's narrow, meandering flagstone trails, one is usually nose-to-leaf with swags of vine or palm-tree fans, or about to crush splatters of moss underfoot, or bruise fingers of creeper clinging to the path's edge-stones.

While devoted to plants, and rich in everything that destroys artworks—bright sunshine, air that's hot and moist—the Palm House is surely less garden than museum, of a peculiarly old-fashioned sort. The modern museum of art or science is, after all, a place in which the exuberant jumble of reality is tamed, arrayed by type, given an air of order it never has in the real world. The whole idea is to make sense out of South Yemeni tattooing practices, Renaissance easel painting, toed feet in their large but finite variety, and all else serious people become interested in and spend lifetimes studying. The emphasis is on revealing—or, more likely, creating—a system in the apparent chaos of existence.

The Palm House, on the other hand, embodies a notion of the museum as a cabinet of curiosities and wonders, a heap of booty hauled from the world's farthest corners to amaze and delight, and to accustom Toronto's rising colonial middle class to proper respect for the immense expanse of the Empire. It was an idea of both museum and gardening obsolete in Britain and North America when the Palm House was built—though this ideology, enshrined in the midst of late-twentieth-century Toronto, is too delicious to pass over without a notice.

I know no better summary of it than Canon Henry Ellacombe's *In a Gloucestershire Garden,* first published in 1895. The book's twenty-five chapters are columns written between 1890 and 1893 for *The Guardian* by the vicar of Bitton, a village lying under the clement skies of southwesterly England. They deal with matters ranging from the chief floral beauties of February—rather a cruel column for a Torontonian to read—to "the easy cultivation of hardy palms," and how most pleasingly to plant an ancient, ruinous garden wall.

As Canon Ellacombe was penning his articles, he perhaps did not notice his early Victorian concept of the garden as a museum of botanical curiosities was swiftly passing away, dethroned by the new spirit of sheerly aesthetic garden design being spread by Gertrude Jekyll. If the gardening idea coming into ascendence had to do with textures and colours, iridescences and shimmering ambiguities, effect and show, Canon Ellacombe's credo led him to plant less for colour than for botanical or historical interest. Thus, his trees and flowers mentioned in the Bible—palm, fig, olive, "the willow of Babylon," hyssop—for the edification of "garden parties of mechanics, young men's associations, school teachers, etc." He found it "very pleasant" to see growing, side by side, the Antarctic bramble and the Iceland poppy, simply because one is the most southerly, the other the most northerly, of flowering plants. He would grow anything mentioned by the ancient Greek and Roman writers, just because they mentioned it; and he put down a yucca after reading a poem "by the late poet-laureate" which begins: "My Yucca, which no winter quells…"

Toronto's Palm House plantings belong to the spiritual world of Ellacombe, not Jekyll or Sackville-West. Even when mimicking one, a planting in the Palm House replicates no real environment elsewhere, and every one is a fiction. The little swamp in the north wing is a pleasing fiction composed of Egyptian papyrus, sweet flag from Japan, Ontario pond weed. Similarly, the thick jungle vignette under the central dome is a jungle from nowhere—a silver thatch palm from Trinidad, Madagascar's screw pine, poinsettias from Mexico.

As we wander through these fragrant galleries, it's always best to do so in a leisurely late-Victorian frame of mind: charmed by the opulence, sharply attentive to details of pistil and stamen, delighted to practise strolling in this improbable spot, surprisingly reminiscent of the architectural vogue of our own *fin de siècle* for cleverness, the cute, the *quel surprise!*

## AND THEN THERE ARE *LAWNS*

Each year in May, everyone in my household wakes up with blinding headaches, scratchy throats and stuffy noses. Soon, we gather round the breakfast table, smiling at each other through the tears of joy drizzling from our reddened eyes.

"'Tis spring at last!" I muse aloud to my gasping wife and coughing daughter.

"From the great aprons of green spread before the ranch-styles of Etobicoke to the long yards behind Scarborough bungalows"—I continue between sneezes—"the plucky buzz of the Toro and the 4.5-hp Noma Brute, and the mighty roar of the 12.5-hp John Deere STX38, arise from the land.

"The folk, both great and small, have again begun their timeless ritual of shaving their grass down to the suburban standard variation of between 2 and 2.5 inches, filling the air of our city with the music and fragrance of their noble industry.

"Soon, out of the metal shed will come the clippers and edgers, fertilizer spreaders, weed whips, poison sprayers, Speedy Weedy Weed Removers, black rubberized lawn edging, the 72-position oscillating sprinkler, lawn food, insect killers powerful enough to kill whole species at a whiff, and herbicides able, like smart bombs, to pinpoint the enemy weed and annihilate him, while leaving the good and kindly grasses to grow—the weaponry, that is, in the unrelenting struggle of Man against the Forces of Nature."

Then, taking the hands of my gagging mate and wheezing child in mine, I say: "If in the beginning there was chaos, we can be sure that in the end there will be The Lawn."

Weeping and uncontrollably choking—obviously so moved is she by my show of faith in Man's Progress Ever Upward—my little daughter asks between lung spasms: "But, Daddy dear and wise, how came this wonder, the Suburban Lawn, to be?"

Passing the family oxygen tank and mask to my wife, now lying half-conscious on the breakfast-nook floor after her most recent asthma attack, and after chasing some antihistamine tablets down my raw throat with a gulp of fresh-mixed powdered orange juice, I sit pensively for a moment, admiring the way the allergic rashes were turning my girl's winter-pale cheeks apple red—then begin my story.

"Once upon a time, in the wicked and dirty place called Europe, from whence we came to this new, free land, there were things known as Walls. Now I know you have never seen one in Toronto, but, believe, they did indeed exist.

"And awful things they were, these Walls, both high and forbidding. They were built of stones by the rich, the aristocrats and other degenerate persons to keep us common folk out on the dingy, grey streets, and to protect all the Lawns for their own use and pleasure. And what miserable things they were, these Walls of stone! Plague-bearing wild creatures, known as 'rabbits' and 'mice' and 'birds'—all extinct now, thank heaven—made their disgusting nests under and among the stones in the Walls, and the rich people allowed even hateful weeds, and flowers not certified disease-free by government authorities, to take root and flourish in the crannies."

My daughter shudders at the very thought, and hacks meaningfully into her paper table napkin.

"But then our stalwart ancestors quit that miserable continent of Walls, and came to this broad, fruitful and free land. After clearing it of trees, Natives and other impediments to Progress, they created Suburbia. There, each man could be a king in his castle, and rule his turf like an emperor. And did those yeoman pioneers, who made Etobicoke, North York and Scarborough what they are today, build Walls around their greenswards? No, not they, these men of democratic vision! For them naught but the Lawn in all its purity would do—the open Lawn, flawless, uniform, free of disease-bearing animals and perfectly green, and free to be seen by all!"

Choking back the sobs for a moment, my little daughter asks eagerly: "And all this wonder began right here in Canada?"

"No, no, my child," is my reply. "Like everything good in this country, the Lawn was invented in the United States. 'Twas in the year 1868, as I recall, that a great American named Frederick Law Olmstead was asked to create, near Chicago, one of the first real Suburbs. And it was he who ordained that all the houses in his Suburb be set back far from the street. All trees were to be uprooted and removed, so that each house would sit in a perfectly green and level rectangle, thereby making it easy to kill all disease-bearing animals, and slash vulgar weeds off at the foot.

"Then an Englishman named Frank J. Scott—one of the few decent men of his decadent nation—was granted a vision of Olmstead's cunning handiwork, found it good, and published a book in 1870 called *The Art of Beautifying Suburban Home Grounds,* in which he offered the Lawn to the world. Like Olmstead and every other person who is careful to include something from all food groups in every meal, and keep the head clear and the bowels open, Scott hated the Wall. 'It is unChristian,' he wrote in his wise book, 'to hedge from the sight of others the beauties of nature which it has been our good fortune to create and secure.' "

With darkened countenance, I go on thus: "And so, my child, you see why we must be ever vigilant. Whether with poison or shotgun, leg-hold trap and caustic fertilizers, the Lawn must be kept green and pure at any cost—else Christian Civilization itself be lost!"

Visiting my wife in hospital later that day, I comfort her with these words: "Sorry I was so wrapped up in our daughter's instruction that I didn't notice that you'd passed out after a windpipe seizure on the kitchen floor. But now our darling understands everything. Family values. Lawns. The importance of chlorinated hydrocarbon pesticides in keeping it all together. Think about it. Isn't the maintenance of our hard-won Civilization worth a couple of months a year in an iron lung, recovering from pollen-induced respiratory failure?"

She can't speak, of course, because of the feeding tube pushed down her throat. But I know the tear running down her cheek says *yes*.

# *Moral Management*

*Suburban Crescent, Number Two*

# 999 QUEEN

In 1989, a young man in a stolen car hurtled down Ossington Avenue, jumped Queen Street, crashed through the glass-fronted main entrance of the Queen Street Mental Health Centre, continued through the lobby and drove ninety-one metres down a glassed-in corridor before the car was stopped by a broken wheel.

Whatever the driver's intentions may have been—one story has it that he was trying to free an incarcerated friend—they probably didn't include a demonstration of how permeable the recent architecture of mental hospitals has become.

But that was one lesson that came out of the caper. Built by the Ontario government in 1956—most of the other structures on the site date from the early 1970s—the building in question fronts Queen Street bluntly, with much glass and concrete pushing out. The lobby is on the edge of the sidewalk, like a store-front. This lobby, and the long corridor which was turned briefly into a speedway, are both at street level, suggesting a smooth continuity between life inside the institution and life outside it. Before the crash-in and the erection of anti-terrorist concrete planters, it was easy to drive in—almost as easy, in fact, as it is to walk in.

Absent are all the standard things about older mental hospitals that would once have made such a spectacular drive-through impossible: the high perimeter walls, the wooded park in which such institutions were frequently set, the flight of steps up to the portico and vaultlike door leading into the vast, mysterious asylum beyond. Instead of being open, *porous,* the structure would have been opaque, solid, resistant to the glances of snoopy passers-by.

Until nearly twenty years ago, as many a Torontonian will recall, the centrepiece of a rural asylum-complex of this sort did stand on the site, just south of the modern building on Queen. That remnant was the Provincial Lunatic Asylum—popularly known as 999 Queen—North America's facility most finely attuned to the psychiatric ideologies current at the moment of its construction. The cornerstone was laid in 1846, in what was then countryside west of Toronto, and the first patients arrived three years later. Designed by the ubiquitous John Howard of Colborne Lodge, it was first acclaimed for its design—said to have been inspired by the National Gallery in London—then later much criticized for practical faults, downright despised by staff and patients after the Second World War, and finally demolished in 1976 to make way for the present scatter of successor-buildings. In its declining decades, the immense edifice was noted for its peculiar and unforgettable stench.

But whatever blame was to be heaped on it in later years, at the time of its opening the Lunatic Asylum was at the forefront of the revolution in asylum architecture and the treatment of mental illness then sweeping North America. Optimism about the curability of mental disorder was in the air. The ill were being unchained from the walls of ordinary prisons, in Ontario as elsewhere. The radical treatments of former times—whipping and starving and purging—were everywhere being rejected in favour of what was called "moral management."

This was first of all a theory of treatment: "activity without excitement, progress and the combination of self-government with appeals to the intellect and sentiments," in the words of a Victorian psychiatrist.

But new systems of treatment required new places in which treatment could appropriately take place. Anything reminiscent of the stinking cellars where the mad had been kept earlier in the nineteenth century would clearly not do; hence the rapid development, at mid-century, of the new theory of asylum design embodied in John Howard's building on Queen. The new mental hospital, wrote U.S. madhouse theorist Thomas Kirkbride, "should have a cheerful and comfortable appearance, everything repulsive and prison-like should be carefully avoided, and even the means of effecting the proper degree of security should be masked." In its classical visual balance, the building should express stability, order, permanence. Its architecture should itself be a kind of therapy, complementing the moral management going on inside.

The Toronto incarnation of these lofty notions was Howard's building at 999 Queen Street West: a forceful expression of what was then fashionable, but soon reputed to be too big, too forbidding. Before it was finally ripped down, historian Tom Brown has written, it had come to symbolize, "for many generations of Torontonians, all the terrors and horrors of the dark and hidden world of the mad." During the debate in the 1970s among architectural preservationists, provincial officials and historians over the proposed demolition, one frequently heard the argument that the worst thing about the building was the fact that it was simply sending the wrong message.

Today, there is almost nothing left of Howard's edifice or its message, except for a gloomy wall running intermittently around three sides of the site, and an old service building tucked away at the back. The general impression given by this large provincial medical facility is less one of asylum than of community college. Most of it has been built in the last twenty years, in the campus style. Low dormitory towers are connected by glassed-in walkways, and bordered by parking lots and tennis courts and grassy lawns. There's even a pleasant student union building—it's called the "community centre"—with a large central lounge, a swimming pool, a coffee shop, a bank.

This is no place of incarceration, or even of treatment, but of education. What's being dealt with are not terrifying illnesses, but ignorance. Those resident or occasional users of this place are not dangerous psychotics, or the compulsory objects of police scrutiny, or people whose personalities are being held together merely by powerful and destructive drugs, but *students,* coming and going as they please through those glass doors and long, open corridors. They will not be there forever. They will graduate.

Or so the architecture of the present Queen Street facility insistently tells us. The reality is different. Reality and architecture usually are different, with architecture playing the role of making rhetorically forceful the myths and theories reality stoutly denies. Like John Howard's old asylum, the new centre is a visible expression more of expectation than of anything real—this time, the fond, recurring hope that the asylum-as-prison is nearing the end of its long career, and that soon all the insane will "graduate," walking out into the world to resume life as productive and happy and creative citizens. The vogue enjoyed by this fantasy among psychiatric professionals in the 1950s helps explain both the extraordinary hatred of John Howard's building, as well as the style of the "campus" subsequently built on the site. The recent discovery of a new family of antidepressants, Eli Lilly's Prozac chief among them, has inspired yet another flutter of optimism among the doctors, who long so badly (and curiously) for their own obsolescence. I should be surprised to find a sensible psychiatrist who really believes the end of forced confinement and life-long heroic treatment is really going to come in our time. But architecture serves as the guardian of foolish fantasies about many things, the junior-college campus on Queen Street being one superb example.

## THE BOARDWALK

Toronto has a number of sandy shoreline expanses lapped by the waters of Lake Ontario, but only one known simply as The Beach.

Or, if you prefer, The Beaches.

Once you've decided what you'll call it, by the way, be prepared to stand your ground. The citizens of this east-end neighbourhood are notoriously touchy about what things are called. In 1985, some shopkeepers along its Queen Street getting-and-spending strip decided to have signs put up proclaiming the area The Beaches. As the entrepreneurs should have known, the denizens of The Beach are not folk to be dealt with high-handedly. They organized, they protested—while historians timidly tried to convince everyone that *both* The Beach and The Beaches have long histories in local usages. Residents who'd lived there thirty years had been calling it The Beaches, and thought The Beach a novelty. But, in the end, the loudest citizens' group won. Their turf was, and ever shall be, The Beach.

While perhaps the most pedantic uproar of them all, it was not the first time Beach(es) people had gotten on their high horses, and ridden off to war; nor would it be the last. In 1907, they stopped the greatest rail companies in the land from putting tracks along the lakefront. And in 1988, they again rose up in outrage, on this occasion against the building of a temporary 14.6-metre beaconlike fancy by the distinguished Italian architect Aldo Rossi. Rossi's $100,000 work, his contribution to an international art exhibit, was eventually built on the lower lawn of the R. C. Harris Filtration Plant, but only after anonymous threats of violence against the exhibition organizers and a near-riotous demonstration by Beach(es) activists at the construction site.

There has never been a dust-up about the name of The Boardwalk, though the stubborn Beach(es) residents have been fighting to save it from the lake wind and water since it was officially opened on Victoria Day, 1932. Severe storms sweep off Lake Ontario almost every winter, ravaging and dragging away whole sections of the structure. But walk along it some summer evening, and you'd never know a plank had ever been displaced. The unbroken continuity of wooden walkway along the district's three kilometres of lake frontage—from the Balmy Beach Canoe Club at the east end, to the more recently fashioned Ashbridge's Bay Park—is today the most conspicuous monument to the dogged determination of Beach(es) souls to preserve Toronto's last extensive neighbourhood to front directly onto an unexpresswayed and unrailroaded strip of public lake footage.

While I find the famous grouchiness of Beach(es) people diverting, I find the Boardwalk less so, and seldom go there. I would perhaps have enjoyed the earlier, fragmentary boardwalks more, judging from the surviving photographs and memoirs. Torontonians of late Victorian and Edwardian times seem to have understood boardwalks, not as places of idle relaxation, but as occasions for the costume and ceremony characteristic of Toronto's first great age of middle-class consumerism and the shortened work-week.

One did not merely walk on the extant portions of boardwalk in former times, for instance. One promenaded: if male, in best suit and tie, and if female, in elegant hat and high collar, long sleeves and long skirts, all as part of a continuous unrushed display of pride in the white-collar class and its perks. When picnicking, one did so carefully and uncomfortably—in full afternoon dress, dining off china, never forgetting the show of propriety which was one's duty as an actor in Toronto's rather new pageant of respectability. Or one played; but only as a member of a disciplined, uniformed team, which in turn reflected the disciplined, promenading and uniformed middle-class Beach(es) culture as a whole. Such regulated play was epitomized by the community's boating clubs, still popular at the present time.

The modern store, with its large windows stocked with mass-produced consumer goods, emerged on Queen Street East at the same time. If Queen was the place where Beach(es) people learned the new rites of acquisitive consumer browsing, the Boardwalk was where they learned the rituals of conspicuous leisure, and of free time attained. Recreation, in the contemporary sense of winding down or staying in shape, was not an issue.

By 1932, when the continuous Boardwalk we have now was completed, the cultural ideals and ethics that had brought the promenade into being were already passing into memory. The last time I walked the length of the Boardwalk, they had altogether vanished. It was this discord that struck me most forcefully: the contrast between the lost historic purpose of the Boardwalk as architecture for conspicuous enjoyment, and the use to which it is now put by virtually all its comers.

Today's joggers do not parade; they run along with ears plugged into taped music, seemingly oblivious to everyone else around them, except as obstacles to their onrush. Little groups, twos and threes, walk along more slowly, equally oblivious, talking loudly about such private topics as their lovers and their sex lives, the impending death of parents and so on, as though no one were listening and watching—when the whole point of the boardwalk-as-idea is in fact to listen and watch, and be watched. Granted, this is the age of Oprah, when confession has taken the place of conversation. But *must* people be constantly divulging?

If discourse proper to boardwalk spectacle is gone, the costumed formality of yesteryear has also been replaced. Its heir is what's euphemistically called "informality," but which usually means slovenly dress and swinish manners, pop cans and cigarette butts tossed on the sand.

I recall reading somewhere that the contemporary expressway is an accelerated boardwalk. The analogy certainly held true in the 1950s, when the shells of Detroit cars were designed to declare the power, wealth, suave sexuality, businesslike demeanour or other wished-for traits of their drivers. Be that as it may, boardwalks—like expressways—have lost that richness of spectacle, and become as devoid of stylish showoff as the styling of the cars clogging Toronto's streets in the 1990s.

## HIGH PARK

After a long lapse, interest in the public park, that wonder of nineteenth-century municipal design, is on the upswing. The reason, I suspect, is that North American parks themselves are so conspicuously and universally on the skids.

Talk to worried urban planners, peruse recent photographic surveys of parks, page through the books and reports coming off the presses, and you'll find generally the same story. It's about a brilliant social invention—an opening of green and sky in the midst of the industrial city—betrayed by stingy politicians, deserted by the hard-working city folk for whom its bandstands, flowerbeds and playing fields were created, and now colonized by addicts, rapists, prostitutes and other undesirables.

The tone of the reports is usually one of elegy, tinged with hope for restoration of the old ideal of the "people's park." But occasionally there's a dissenting voice. In a recent study, British urbanist Hazel Conway has denounced the public park as a tool of mass social control, designed by the Victorian patriarchy to instil good public manners, patriotism, team spirit, Christian respect for Sunday and other presumably imperialist values in a working class dangerously prone to waywardness, even revolution.

Had Conway been looking for Canadian proof of her thesis, she could have found it writ larger in few places than the 406.8 acres of High Park, Toronto's grandest contiguous green space and its most quintessentially Victorian British rest-spot for the common man. The core is a wildly beautiful lakeshore property donated in 1873 by John Howard, the city's first and gifted official engineer, who left another 45 acres, including Colborne Lodge, to the city in his will. In Howard's day, the park around the lodge was used by its owner for riding and blood sports, the obligatory rites of colonials (then and now) keen to display visible ties to aristocratic Englishry. But when deeding it over to the city, Howard made sure future users would be doing none of that. Perhaps with the precedent of Frederick Law Olmsted and Calvert Vaux's recently opened Central Park (1858) fresh in mind—a development promoted by New York's élite as a hoist for the dilapidated morals of the poor—Howard envisioned High Park as a school of uplift for the slum-dulled working family, and spent the rest of his life, which ended in 1890, planning drainage and changes in the landform, clearing the scrubby brush and proposing "improvements to the site." High Park was off limits to booze and questionable frivolity from day one.

At night, of course, like every other public park in the world, High Park was (and remains) a popular spot for erotic quickies between gay men, and for back-seat and blanket sex between consenting adults and consenting kids. But moral militancy reigned by day, at least until rather recently. In 1913, a playground was established by a women's group determined to provide an "antidote to slothful living." Grown-ups were allowed to stroll politely through the grove of oaks and among the roses on the Lord's Day, and expected to do nothing more vigorous or flamboyant than listen to band concerts. In 1937, more relaxed recreations were allowed on Sundays, though hockey and other team sports, along with tobogganing, were banned on the Christian Sabbath until 1961. We do well not to let our liberalism (or the present-day dogmatic commitment to the casual) be offended by such now-lifted prohibitions, simply because they interestingly reflected the Victorian park's forerunners, in the military parade ground and the field for public ceremonials, and similar institutions, such as Central Park.

Now no longer a training-ground for Victorian social decorum, or informed by any other strong, central idea, High Park is drifting in the same dismal direction as other big-city parks in North America—though drifting not so quickly, this being Toronto, hence slower to inflict destruction upon itself than American cities the same size. As early as 1904, on a return to his native New York, expatriate Henry James was shocked to find Central Park "overdone by the 'run' on its resources...It has had to have something for everybody, since everybody arrives famished." It took the 1985 murder of a homosexual schoolteacher in High Park by young gay-bashers, however—memorialized in Robin Fulford's remarkable play *Steel Kiss*—to make the once-peaceful park *seem* more dangerous, and at least alert Toronto officialdom to the decline of their best Victorian park.

The concern is well grounded. The fear of rape in broad daylight has made women afraid to jog there alone. And apart from the heavier threats we associate with American public parks, petty annoyances plague anyone using High Park. There's the unending rumble of car traffic on the north-south street bisecting the park between the Queensway and Bloor Street—it should have been blocked off year-round long ago, not shut, as today, only on summer weekends—and the difficulty of observing bitterns and herons at the marshy edge of Grenadier Pond without noisy runners galumphing by, terrorizing the wildlife. And there's the inevitable, annoying conflict between the rights of guys who've come down after work for a good knock-down, drag-out game of soccer, and those of drugged or drunk wanderers, of families letting their kids have a visit with the yak in the little zoo or run off some steam before bedtime, and of quieter folk who just want to contemplate the autumnal daylight's slow failing in High Park's beautiful ravines and shadowed copses.

While not yet in ruins, High Park is visibly buckling under the weight of use and the burden of conflicting demands. The salvation of the park from its perilous popularity was clearly on the minds of the City of Toronto's parks-and-recreation people when, in 1992, they handed their political masters a list of proposals for restoring and better managing this matchless resource.

The planners want less car traffic and a freshening-up of the gardens overlooking Grenadier Pond, increased protection for both the park's human users and its rare, vulnerable blackoak savannahs and moist forests of red oak and hemlock. They want people to enjoy Colborne Lodge, and the swimming pool, and the hockey rink. They want dwellers in the apartment complexes north of the park to continue growing zucchini and sunflowers in the tiny community allotment gardens, and they want nature-lovers to be able to stalk peaceably the shy birds that nest along Wendigo Creek.

In fact, the planners want *everything*, only "improved." They can't be faulted for that. High Park attracts millions of visitors each year, and it's the job of the City to see that these people enjoy themselves without undue stress, annoyance or danger.

But even if City Hall were to be enchanted by what was proposed in this report, and came up with the money to fulfil the bureaucrats' every wish, High Park would still be, in my view, doomed to continuing decline. This gloomy forecast has nothing to do with the goodwill of the city or its well-meaning planners, but is based on the peculiar nature of English Victorian parks in general. Though nobody nowadays wants to admit it, these parks worked best so long as they were institutions of official moral management, whose working-class users knew and kept to the rules, dutifully appreciating the exquisite views from well-defined strolling paths by day, refraining from undue noise on Sunday, and confining their sexual ramblings to discreet voluntary encounters at night.

But even then there were vexatious problems that only grew more obvious with time. The English Victorian inventors of the public park wanted their creature to be two things at peace with each other: a field for staid entertainments, and a green chapel for quiet meditation upon nature and nature's God. Almost no downtown urban space anywhere, and certainly not Toronto's largest park (after the harbour islands), is vast enough to serve both purposes. We are gradually learning, as Montreal has learned from Frederick Law Olmsted's splendid Mount Royal park—intended as a sort of church for the adoration of nature—that the North American public park has been beset from its beginning by its inner contradictions.

So far, however, High Park has not sunk to the level of wretchedness notable in some of its American counterparts, and may yet be saved, at least in part. It is bearing the traffic of use better, in fact, than most parks—which is not saying it's bearing it well, or without the inflicting of slow, incremental damage. Crime and the destruction of delicate environments—the old oak groves, the unique blend of forest types—are the most serious symptoms of decline. But what really can be done, short of police-state control, the outlawing of cars, and putting most of its sensitive natural areas off limits to human use? The result, of course, would be the true end of the Victorian mixed-use park in our midst, the death of another idea from the past, and the hastening of High Park's slow decay into a collapsed moment of redemptive urbanism in the city's heart.

## BANKING

When banking, my city-born Victorian grandmother always wore hat, gloves and girdle. She could not have foreseen a day when half-dressed and unkempt people would jump out of cars, stick plastic cards into an automated teller on a windy street or in a convenience store, snaffle up the bills burped out of these machines—and dare call this *banking*.

Now the notion that getting dressed up to cash a cheque for twenty-five dollars might be snobbish would have struck my grandmother as absurd. One dressed importantly to bank, simply because banking—along with shopping, lunching, attending Horticultural Society lectures and worshipping the Divinity—was an important rite of urbanity, requiring one to dress the part.

While such colourful seriousness has largely vanished from our increasingly lax social culture, many a dignified Victorian or Edwardian building still stands, often in the humblest of neighbourhoods, as a reminder of a certain urban grace and gravity we lost sometime around the middle of this century.

Vast, costly churches, for instance. Looming, turreted public schools, tributes to the Elevating Powers of Education. And, everywhere, banks in many architectural styles, but possessed of unvarying solemnity, appropriate to the respect they enjoyed in Canadian culture when built, and to the importance people once ascribed to the rites conducted in them.

Look around any turn-of-the-century residential zone in a Canadian city, and you soon find a bank that illustrates exactly what I'm talking about. It will be discovered in one of two forms. The less august of the commonest old bank-types is to be found on the ground-level corner of a larger commercial building.

Toronto has many good corner banks; were I pressed to pick a personal favourite, it might be the Canadian Imperial Bank of Commerce office at the intersection of Spadina Avenue and Queen Street West. A work finished in 1903 by establishment architect George W. Gouinlock, the bank graces the intersection with an angled entrance guarded by two stout Tuscan columns and watched over by a Renaissance Italianate balcony. The deep-cut rectangular windows are similarly framed by Tuscan columns, but "rusticated"—rude, primitive.

The result is a column that looks as though it were passing up through a series of fat Scrabble blocks. Such stylistic gestures, expressive of stolidity and "ancientness," are repeated across the whole office building's façade, impressing the prospective client with the antiquity and durability of the firm.

The more imposing of the two bank-types is the free-standing pavilion, impressively ornamented, and elevated above street level as a way to insist on the seriousness of the rituals of banking to be done within. In this category, I have many favourites that I never drive past without a nod of thanks: the Bank of Montreal's self-important little Roman mausoleum at the ignominious corner of Christie and Dupont Streets, for instance, and, in rundown Parkdale, the same institution's Greek temple, charmingly mongrelized by two vaguely oriental leaded domes stuck atop it.

For the record, however, Toronto's—perhaps even the world's—most exalted example of a bank branch in the traditional, conservative, free-standing "temple" tradition is neither old nor ponderous. Yet Mies van der Rohe's floating glass and steel banking pavilion at the Toronto-Dominion Centre outdoes all its predecessors, as an expression of banking's seriousness and urbanity. Despite the structure's Modernist formality—or, rather, because of it—my grandmother would have felt completely at ease doing business there.

By 1968, when the T-D pavilion was completed, the automated banking machine (ABM) was already making its way down the technological pipeline, headed for your street and Quik-Mart, and about to doom both the high rites of middle-class banking, and the imaginative architecture designed as a setting for them. Some twenty years after the introduction of ABMs in Canada, the number of bank branches across the country—about 7,600 at last count—is declining, while the 13,000 ABMs in use at present are multiplying like rabbits. Michael Bradley, an analyst with the Canadian Bankers Association and the source of these statistics, sees no end to the services that these machines may provide. We are likely soon to be using them for the processing of mortgage and loan applications, the dispensing of "postage stamps, travel services, transit passes, movie tickets," he says, in addition to coughing up bills and gulping down deposits.

The last time Bradley checked, there were some 14.5 million ABM cards in circulation in Canada. No Luddite, I have one and use it all the time—though with an increasing sense of unease about what this use portends for the future of urban rites. According to the Bankers Association, Canadians used ABMs for some 900 million financial transactions in 1992—about a 20 per cent jump over 1991. That was some 900 million transactions conducted without one person having to deal with another in a civilized manner. Or, to put it another way, that was close to a billion opportunities missed to perform the ordinary courtesies that have traditionally affirmed urban community and helped keep it intact.

But not to worry, says Michael Bradley. Even if we do most of our personal money dealings with machines, the branch and the face-to-face encounter will still have a place in the ecology of advanced capitalist finance: in the purchase of securities, for example, and the retailing of insurance.

Somehow I do not find this very reassuring. First, because any machine that can sell a transit ticket will eventually be able to sell an insurance policy. Second, because even if personal interchanges are still required by law for stock purchases and such, the branch in a less well-heeled neighbourhood, where people have little loose change to put into the equity market, is doomed. My much-liked Roman mausoleum at Christie and Dupont is slated for abandonment and probable demolition— if not this year, then someday not long off.

But the eventual end of all stately settings for city rites, including banking, is something we may as well get used to. Urban experience is everywhere changing from a complex web of publicly enacted social interactions—like going to church or synagogue services, or going to the bank, dressed up—to a diffuse, individualistic, informal and unritualized condition. It all may strike you, as it does me, as a denial of all the richness most of us moved off RR1 to Megalopolis to find. Every time I pass it, the garish back-lit plastic sign announcing 24-hour banking, stuck in the doorway of the splendid old CIBC branch at Queen and Spadina, strikes me, in words my grandmother might have used, as "simply not fitting."

## THE ROBARTS

Not that anybody is going to put on a belated funny hat and pop open a magnum of Dom Perignon in joyous celebration upon hearing the news, but I feel compelled to note that 1993 was the twentieth anniversary of the University of Toronto's John P. Robarts Research Library. I do so because the building is the city's most universally despised item of architecture, and also because it is our most celebrated monument to despair over the decline in student respect for law, orderly education and responsible use of resources. Its users have always called it Fort Book. It is certainly more bunker than shrine of learning.

To create the Robarts Library, the university's principal repository of books, maps, microfilm, rare printed objects and other resource materials, the New York firm of Warner Burns Toan & Lunde first bulldozed a downtown Victorian residential block, then formed their structure by pouring an estimated 100,000 cubic yards of concrete on the site. This cement thug today looms fourteen storeys over the houses in what's left of its neighbourhood—an interesting architectural mix of comfortably middle-class domiciles and a few august mansions still left standing on St. George Street, staid Victorian-Gothic St. Thomas' Anglican Church, and an ambitious, largely failed scatter of Modernist academic buildings introduced after the Second World War.

Monstrously bigger than anything nearby, it is also monstrously uglier, and incoherent. Soaring towards the sky are vast snorkels and sharp-nosed ship's prows and defensive parapets, while, at street level, the library is clad with blockish concrete slabs that appear to have been designed to withstand heavy artillery bombardment. Until quite recently, there was no ground entrance.

Crooked exterior ramps lead the visitor up to exposed, bitterly windswept expanses of yet more concrete, the level top of the "platform" on which the library appears to stand. Once through the revolving glass doors, the patron is immediately confronted with more expanses, more streaked, shabby concrete walls, identical to those outside, and the unceasing mechanical rattle and grind of the escalators that hang in the structure's central well. The books lie beyond yet more barricades and cyclopean walls of concrete.

The honesty of the name for this type of ruthless construction—New Brutalism—may be due to the fact that the moniker was meant as a joke. In 1950, so the story goes, Swedish architect Hans Asplund offhandedly invented the term to describe the style of a house being designed by colleagues. The term later spread, via the international network of professional chit-chat, to England, where it was enthusiastically and seriously embraced by young architects.

It appears that there are now two subtypes of Brutalism, one grand, the other mean. The first is Brutalism plain and simple, a term used by enemies to nail the more horrifying ideas and projects of Swiss architect Le Corbusier. Not all Le Corbusier's notions of urban planning and building design are bad, and some of his projects will be thought-provoking for as long as people think about architecture at all. (I am thinking particularly of the splendid church at Ronchamp, France.) Having said that, Le Corbusier's so-called "Voisin Plan," unveiled in 1925—a project calling for the demolition of six hundred acres of central Paris, to make way for a camp of tall

*Creeper Vine, Robarts Library*

towers X-shaped in plan, and a net of high-speed motor-ways—not only deserves the name Brutalism, but is horrific enough to merit an all-points police alert for the arrest of its mad creator.

He would probably get off with a parking-ticket, how-ever—since in the age of the Voisin Plan megalomanic archi-tectural proposals were thick on the ground, and all the rage. The New Brutalism, principally an English and British colo-nial tendency of the 1950s and 1960s, was "new" only inas-much as it was forced by circumstances to apply the old ruthlessness to sites much smaller than, say, all downtown Paris. During the Second World War, after all, the military had shown its superiority to architects when it came to devastat-ing vast areas. After Hiroshima and Dresden, architects real-ized they would have to be content with depredations on a small scale—the odd neighbourhood, downtown districts, and sometimes, as in the case of the Robarts Library, with just single city blocks.

The common denominators of every act of Brutalism, however, are the cement-mixer, the contempt for context, and the determination to devastate everything on a given site, then build monstrously and afresh from the mud up. British Columbia architectural historian Alan Gowans has given the wickedly funny name *Führerbunkerstil* to this manner of building. Curiously, it is perhaps the only defunct architectural style which brings to mind only melancholy thoughts, tinged with chronic depression. We are reminded, for instance, of the concrete Nazi pillboxes now lying half-buried under Normandy's coastal sands, structures movingly photographed and described by the French intellectual Paul Virillio. And then there are the seemingly indestructible Nazi-era concrete structures still uglifying some streets in Berlin, and, under-ground, disrupting the construction of new utility and metro systems—as though Third Reich nihilism was still at work, silently defying the practical re-creation of its principal city as the capital of a more humane state.

In *Styles and Types of North American Architecture,* Gowans chooses to illustrate, as his best example of New Brutalism, Australian architect John Andrew's Scarborough College, completed in 1965 in a far region of Toronto's eastward suburban sprawl. While I find justice in Gowans's choice, I am inclined to hold out for the Robarts as the best of Toronto's worst.

Yet the real question remains, not which is worse, but why such construction ever took place at all. Fighting my way towards the Robarts against the howling, bitterly cold winds of a nasty Toronto spring, I find myself thinking: How did so repellent an idea take root in architectural practice, spread, and find its way into the heart of the venerable, eclectically Victorian University of Toronto?

But if I understand the rationalizations given by its British theorists correctly, the question answers itself. It's the empirical "truth" it tells about the empirical world that is supposed to give Brutalism its cogency—its unmasking of the ideological obscurantism represented by, say, the University of Toronto's prevailing Academic Gothic. As Gowans explains, Brutalism "corresponded to a fashionable stance among sixties youths of 'brutal honesty,' 'no faking,' 'nothing plastic'..." It was the mirror image of the Victorian Picturesque, a discrediting of humanism in every tough, nasty angle and texture.

Though Gowans doesn't say so, Brutalism was also a quick and dirty way for an architect to gratify, safely, everyone. It pleased welfare-state bureaucrats, who wanted the shelters of postwar mass education built quickly and finished cheaply. It pleased university boards of trustees, by making buildings look like rough military defences of civilization against barbarian hordes of philistine students. And, surprisingly, it pleased the trustees' enemies, rabble-rousing anti-Establishment undergraduates of the 1960s, who thought they were seeing universities finally coming clean about their role as mere industries of knowledge, and assembly lines for information workers.

I intend never to stop mining the lode of some two million books in the Robarts Library, an activity which seems to me very much a part of being a civic, urban human being. And I hope never to lose my sense of revulsion at the wrapper thrown round these treasures twenty years ago—the kind of gut-wrench that reminds me that I still can recognize the architecture of mind control and crowd management when I see it, even when disguised as "truth to materials."

## THE SKYDOME

While no important city has a domed stadium—in fact, having one is a sure sign of urban second-classhood—Toronto sports fans love our immense reinforced-concrete bunker, and virtually all the amenities. Well, maybe not the food, widely reputed to be vile—but almost everything else: the sightlines and seating, the weather shield provided by the $90-million retractable roof, the $17-million Jumbotron—a glorified scoreboard operated by a crew of up to eighteen technicians—the handy washrooms and so on.

Torontonians not inclined to be game-goers think of it, if at all, as a gleaming pimple down on the city's backside. Indeed, the SkyDome is a homely and bulky structure, with a bug-like humpiness made only more egregious by the herd of smaller buildings hemming it in, and the soaring needle of the CN Tower next door.

But though not much of a fan (except at World Series time), I hereby distance myself a good nine yards from the building's most dismissive critics, and point out two reasons it deserves fair recognition, if not exactly a twenty-one-gun salute.

The first reason is the sheer effectiveness with which the SkyDome's bulk hides its faintly sinister elegance, both from fans inside and from passers-by. I am not suggesting that architect Roderick Robbie or engineer Michael Allen intended the public to believe the SkyDome to be really as simple as it looks. But the basic message the public gets from the concrete exterior is that the Dome is just another dumb jock of a stadium, only a lot bigger than most.

I got my first glimpse of the truth about the SkyDome in the summer of 1993, on a tour with SkyDome vice-president David E. Garrick. Our winding route, most of it between the outer walls and inner surfaces of the stadium—vast tracts ordinarily off-limits to the game-going public—took us through the semi-darkness under huge moveable bleachers, along corridors washed in cold fluorescent light, through private boxes (rental fees: up to $225,000 a year) and dining rooms and clubs.

But the rooms I found most fascinating were those resembling little skulls, crammed with the building's many unsleeping cybernetic brains, and peopled by almost unmoving men and women, made to seem irrelevant by the flickering banks of computer screens, flashing images relayed from myriad video cameras installed throughout the SkyDome, dials and read-out gadgetry, churning data-processing mechanisms.

Among our stops was the room that contains the electronic unlocking and tracking mechanisms, and the single button, controlling the retraction and extension of the roof's steel parabolic arches along its track-ways. Another was the top-security cell housing the optical and sensing devices which monitor every movement, the operation of every human and mechanical system, throughout the vast building, even every elevator. A glance at computer screens lets you know instantly whether any given lift-door in the entire building is opened or closed.

We naturally visited the elaborate Jumbotron control studio, and the nerve centre of Dome Productions, a deluxe $13-million facility hard-wired to forty-seven permanent cameras positioned throughout the stadium, and capable of transmitting images of a game to satellites in space and thence to everyone on the planet with a dish or cable and a TV set.

SkyDome officials are naturally pleased to hear their building compared to the Roman Colosseum, dedicated by the Emperor Titus in AD 80, and like to press the analogy on visiting reporters. Yet no two buildings are less alike, except in the trivial sense that both are big, and both are made of cement (though the Colosseum was clad in marble). And both were constructed in the round, to create the feeling of community, the experience of seeing both the spectacle and one-self simultaneously, which has been historically required of all sports palaces. Anyway, it's the difference between them that points up why the SkyDome is special. The Colosseum, after all, was a royal propaganda building, elaborately and monumentally ornamented on the outside, while the rounded façade of the Dome is democratically plain and functional.

More important, the Colosseum was merely a set of structurally sound, stepped bleachers for patrons, surrounding a wood-plank stage for the brutal games an architectural historian has called "ritual re-enactments of Rome's humiliation of the nations of the world"—while the SkyDome is principally an intricate mechanism of surveillance sheathed in concrete. Inside are machines for monitoring and sensing and interpreting information gathered from the field, and from every other nook and cranny, and from every electric and mechanical system on the site.

Only a tiny fraction of the information gathered and stored in the Dome—the game happening on the field, and pretaped advertisements—is transmitted to fans on the Jumbotron, and to Canada and the world via satellite. Most of the data flowing silently behind the concrete skin into the monitoring stations is used to secure—or control, inconspicuously—the movement of people through the gates, in the public corridors, in the stands, and to regulate the electro-mechanical and electronic environment that surrounds everyone. Seen from the perspective of one of its immaculate, equipment-jammed control rooms, the SkyDome seems less like an updated version of the ponderous old Colosseum than a mock-up for an ultra-high-tech prison, more dedicated to surveillance than any recreational facility previously built.

I raise this matter, not to criticize the SkyDome for being so pervasively wired, but to suggest how *comfortable* we have become in the midst of so many watching eyes. It has never been a secret that virtually all so-called "public" space, not just the SkyDome, is now under optical surveillance; or that electro-magnetic information-gathering operates every time we use a credit card, borrow a book, or write a cheque. If we are more aware than ever nowadays that video cameras and sensing devices are aware of *us*—whether we're whipping along an expressway, waiting in a bank line-up, or out on the town—there are two ready explanations.

In the first place, the sensing gadgetry is everywhere. We tend, I believe, to view these machines as mere deterrents to *someone else's* criminal thoughts or intentions, and are disinclined to think that someone, somewhere, is actually sitting there, recording our movements on videotape. With those little cameras oscillating back and forth across the teller area, who, after all, would stick up a bank? Anyway, it seems almost impossible that there could be as many observers as there are cameras—at least until one visits the SkyDome, and witnesses firsthand the vast network of people working the optical surveillance mechanisms.

The second reason we are conscious of this as never before has to do with the trickle-down into popular culture of certain ideas in Michel Foucault's 1975 book *Discipline and Punish*, which treats the modern history of incarceration. Certainly the most notorious and suggestive chapter in this book has to do with British philosopher Jeremy Bentham's Panopticon, first proposed in 1791 as a novel form of prison architecture. The jail would be round, with cells radiating from a central observation centre. From that viewpoint, one guard could keep watch over all the jailbirds. But once the inmates came to believe someone was sitting in the darkness of the watching booth, no one at all would be necessary to keep the prison orderly; and the inmates would then become their own guards. (John Howard's 1838 Toronto city jail, an unfinished structure, was influenced by Benthamite prison theory.)

To the consternation of writers on contemporary urban culture, we citizens of the late twentieth century have become indifferent to the cameras and sensing gizmos almost continually around us, and thus become our own cops. Nor is this phenomenon anywhere more obvious than in Toronto.

But why here?

That glorious night in 1993, when Joe Carter slammed the tiny white dot over the wall, winning the Blue Jays their second consecutive World Series championship, Toronto went crazy. Or as crazy at it goes, which isn't very.

In stark contrast with the four thousand rampaging baseball fans clubbed and gassed into submission before they tore up Saskatoon that Saturday night, the million or so party animals who took to the Toronto streets were real Sunday-school picnickers, hooting and hollering and honking, but doing little damage to property or each other.

Who would have had the situation be otherwise? While competitive with Montreal in many things, sports included, no sensible Torontonian would ever want a Hogtown replay of the riot that swept rue Ste.-Catherine following the Canadiens' Stanley Cup win in June, 1993. We'd be shocked silly if something that ill-mannered happened here.

A reason can be found, I think, by watching the slo-mo replays of Joe Carter's terrific hit. Here is sports television at its most beautiful: Carter, unsure at first about what he'd done, surging mightily off the plate towards first base, then suddenly becoming aware and almost incandescent in that awareness, then flying, free, ecstatic.

Now rewind, play the footage again. Ignore Carter and look at what's happening behind him. Emotionless uniformed

Metro police, previously invisible, swarming out of dugouts onto the field and quickly lining up, facing the stands. A fan has somehow made it past the cordon, and is running alongside Carter when the player rounds third base. There's a rush on the frisky fan by cops—but the camera moves on with Carter, so we do not witness the fate of the fan.

But this exception reminded watchers of the rule. Had even a small number of fans decided to leap the wall and mob the Jays, the police could have done nothing at all to prevent them from doing so. A predictable inner restraint kept, and always keeps, such a decision from being made by Torontonians; and all goes more or less smoothly.

Ditto later on, when the post-game bash got going on lower Yonge Street, consecrated by generations of Torontonians as our promenade of playful rampage. In theory, the doings on Yonge could easily have become dangerous. Were this Detroit or Chicago or Montreal, they quite likely would have. But Toronto isn't, and the doings didn't. "Police who lined Yonge Street in case of a Chicago- or Montreal-style ruckus," we read in Monday's *Globe and Mail,* "seemed to turn a blind eye to those who swigged beer. They mingled with the crowd, as they high-fived or gave the thumbs-up signal to passers-by." Mel Lastman, the everlastingly boosterish mayor of North York pronounced with pride: "When people see us on CNN, they talk about how well behaved we are, what a world-class area Metropolitan Toronto is. It's good for business, it's good for tourism."

Yet once again, the niceness reminded this city-watcher of Toronto's never-slackening sense of righteous force, ever poised for instant deployment against wrongdoers. This comforting thought is gratefully noted by visitors up from the Republic of Fear. The rarity of overt violence by the Toronto police—against white people, anyway—coupled with their omnipresence and unfailing smiles, their firm pleasantness in crowd situations, only makes the atmosphere of dread, and each citizen's duty to behave himself decorously and carefully in public, more keenly felt.

But woe betide the non-conformist in our benign Toronto police state!

The culprit I'm thinking of here is *Globe and Mail* reporter Kirk Makin, who supplied readers with a delightful World Series column called "The Fan," about being just that, throughout the playoffs. Perhaps so the burghers can sleep soundly again, Makin confessed all in his "Fan" the Monday after.

It appears that Makin took a home-video camera to the game that Saturday night and actually used it. He was immediately spotted by the good-behaviour boys, and apprehended. "My moving appeal to the home-town loyalties of an officious security twerp and a Metro Toronto cop fell on deaf ears," Makin writes. "Their steely grip on my arms, I was thrown out of the SkyDome in front of 20,000 revellers. Bad boy, go home."

My only regret about this episode—other than Makin's ouster—was that our reporter did not get caught videocamming *in flagrante delicto* by the roving eye of network TV. It would have happily besmirched the ghastly PR picture of Toronto as a "well-behaved," "world-class area" in American eyes, and proved that even a Torontonian can act really bad when he feels like it.

I am nevertheless happy to report that such a thing did happen during gametime one night in early 1990, just after the SkyDome opened for business.

While engaging to most fans, the baseball game had become boring to a man and woman lodged in one of the expensive, large-windowed hotel rooms overlooking the field—or so we concluded, when they casually doffed their togs and did It, in full view of forty thousand spectators.

This sexual coupling may well have been seen directly by more people than any other sex-act in world history. High historical significance aside, however, many patrons of the stadium reportedly got a real kick out of it—and probably nobody was really scandalized.

Nobody, that is, except SkyDome brass, who reacted with indignant, horror-stricken splutterings to the news media, and the issuance of stringent new rules governing guest conduct in the hotel rooms. "After all," reported *Globe and Mail* sports columnist Stephen Brunt with a smile, "a quickie today could turn into orgies by the all-star break and then what? The moral fabric of the town might be forever torn asunder."

That must not, of course, be allowed to happen. We are very *good* in Toronto. But on behalf of forty thousand delighted spectators, I'd like to thank the randy couple for doing something spontaneous in the one Toronto structure constructed precisely to prevent the unexpected from ever, ever happening.

# Moderne *Variations*

*R.C. Harris Filtration Plant*

# THE R.C. HARRIS FILTRATION PLANT

A few summers ago, friends handed me the assignment of showing the best of Toronto to their Parisian cousins. Father was a professor of Italian social history, mother an art historian, teenaged daughter an uncertain university student, pre-teen son continually on the lookout for McDonald's golden arches. I got just one afternoon to do the job, so deciding what to show them was easy. First, whatever it was, it had to be Depression Modern, simply because Toronto is peculiarly blessed with structures designed in this conservative interwar manner, which preceded the onslaught of full-scale glass and steel Modernism after World War Two. Surveying the available *moderne* variations, I had little trouble coming up with a choice: the R. C. Harris Filtration Plant, our Greta Garbo of public architecture, and among Toronto's grandiose expressions of building in the Depression Modern style.

The immaculately manicured site, just east of the Toronto city limit on the Scarborough bluffs, has long been cherished for its panoramic overlook of Lake Ontario. Between 1878 and 1906 a rambunctious amusement park called Victoria Park operated there. Though gone for almost a century, its name survives in Victoria Park Avenue, the long north-south street that ends there. And, to the endless exasperation of vociferous community groups in the adjoining Beach neighbourhood, its reputation as a terrific place to get drunk and party wild and long into the night has persisted in the folk memory of local teen culture down to the present day. The complex of buildings, begun in the years between 1933 and 1935, and completed in the 1950s, was first known as the Victoria Park Pumping Station; it was given the name it now bears in 1946, to honour Rowland Caldwell Harris, czar of Toronto public works from 1912 until 1945.

No lifeless relic of yesteryear's technology and architecture, it remains fully operational, pulling in, processing and pumping out an average 140 million gallons of fluoridated, chlorinated lake water each day, or roughly half the water required by the lawns and begonias, coffee-pots and showers, toilets and kitchen taps and public water fountains of Metropolitan Toronto.

In this array of buildings, closest to the lake stands the tall-windowed pavilion sheltering the huge intake turbines, sumptuously appointed inside with brass railings and brackets, and a wall-mounted panel of great brass-ringed numbers, back-lit to show which mighty pumps are operating. Outside, the limestone cladding bears carved bas-relief patterns of sleek, simplified turbines and waterfalls. Nearby a tall tank of alum, a chemical required in the purification process, rises camouflaged inside a slender tower reminscent—but only vaguely reminiscent, as typical of most Depression Modernism—of a Roman watchtower.

A tall, rounded entrance gives the finely balanced plant administration building the general look of a triumphal arch, fronted by a fountain and by a stately balustraded belvedere from which to view the lake—on a clear summer's evening, one imagines, in formal attire.

The two skylit wings of the filtration hall crown the green slope. The hall's immensely long galleria is among Toronto's most stunning interiors, sumptuously appointed with beige marble flooring and trimmed with brass inlays and fixtures, and lined with costly green marble. Exactly in the middle of this dramatic expanse is a sleek, sculpted tower and bank of dials and switches.

Sun-drenched on a cloudless summer day, the sweep of its buildings drawn hard against blue sky and immaculate green lawns, Lake Ontario at its foot, the site of the filtration plant is one of the grand overlooks in a city otherwise notably short of natural summits. We all love it—party animals, picnickers, sun-bathers, people who just want to sit alone, and gaze at the lake's blue waters and think. My Parisian guests were enchanted, by the way—especially by the interior contrasts between the swank decor and mighty engines, ducts and tanks.

For those interested in the history of building, the R. C. Harris plant holds still more charms, and even a pleasant bit of nostalgia for a modern architectural path that has been abandoned. For this coordinated ensemble of structures comes at the climax, and almost the end, of the great era of stream-lined, subtly decorated, stripped-down-classical waterworks, incinerators, pumping stations, power plants and other public utilities—architectural works which sum up for us the patriotic, heroic aspirations of R. C. Harris and public servants like him. Their projects were grandiose; but for cities crushed by the Great Depression, as Toronto was, the grandeur of the Victoria Park Pumping Station was exactly what was needed to return to a defeated citizenry the reasonable hope for a decent life. Harris's choice of a crisply modernized Roman shell for his water plant—a late application of academic styling to contemporary building—was part of this architectural scheme "to proclaim the grandeur of the city," as historian Alan Gowans says of all academic architecture, "to help citizens perceive themselves as part of it, to make individual lives somehow nobler by being set in relationship to a grand past."

The use of streamlined Classicism for reviving patriotism and public spirit was pervasive in Depression-era Canada and Franklin Roosevelt's America, but was hardly limited to the democracies. Its widespread deployment by populist totalitarianisms in the years between the wars—whether Nazi, Fascist, or New-Deal—was the key force behind the style's sudden obsolescence in North America after VE Day. By the mid-1950s, when the R. C. Harris plant was being completed, its chic styling and all it stood for—strong national revival, government-sponsored public order and uplift, renewed mass politics—was dead. The current moment, and the next twenty years of North American architecture belonged to the presumably anti-ideological International Style introduced to the United States by Mies van der Rohe, Walter Gropius and Marcel Breuer and adopted with enthusiasm by the post-war capitalist élite.

Yet the wheel of fortune never ceases to turn, and the International Style and all it stood for are now things of past affection—to be admired for their ambitions, and studied for the lessons they teach us, but no more to be emulated than the Depression-era styling and ideological scheme of the R. C. Harris Filtration Plant. Let us praise them both, for their expansive public ambitions, their vast intellectual programmes, and the contributions they have made to the built ensemble of urban forms we inhabit.

# 620 UNIVERSITY AVENUE

To my knowledge there is no corporate site anywhere quite like the one on which the successive office blocks of Ontario Hydro stand shoulder to shoulder on the west side of University Avenue immediately south of College Street. Here, between 1915 and 1975, Hydro built three head office buildings. Not clumsy add-ons or replacements, but three distinct, distinctive buildings, together comprising a remarkable anthology of our century's changing ideals for the architecture of public works. It is a collection also undergoing drastic internal revision, as the Toronto firm of Zeidler Roberts prepares to drop the new nineteen-storey Princess Margaret Hospital inside and behind the two older Hydro headquarters.

Few people will rejoice to learn that the third Hydro office building will remain untouched. I belong to the tiny minority that likes it. Opened in 1975, this thick concave arc of mirroring glass, curving around the intersection of University and College, never fails to remind me of the Horseshoe Falls at Niagara—arc, cascading sheen and all—though I imagine the Falls were not on the mind of the glass-bedazzled architect (Kenneth R. Cooper) who designed it.

You would not necessarily be aware of all the change going on, while motoring up or down University Avenue in rush-hour traffic. In fact, as important downtown dig-ups and knock-downs go, site preparation for the new medical treatment and research facility has been notably inconspicuous, because the work has been mostly veiled by the existing structures the hospital will eventually absorb. The main giveaway that something's afoot is the heavy web of steel girdles and garters holding up, until recently, an ornate Italian-Renaissance façade, the lingering architectural smile of the first headquarters at 610 University, now otherwise vanished.

Commissioned by Adam Beck, Hydro's visionary and despotical chairman, in 1915—five years after the utility started delivering power to Ontario communities—George Gouinlock's Hydro-Electric Building is (or was) a pretty, academic étude on Florentine themes, advertising the renaissance in electrification about to dawn all over Ontario by referring us back to an older, grander Renaissance. We should spend no time mourning the loss of the indifferent building itself, especially since the hospital master-builders have decided to attach the nicest thing about it, its exuberant Italianate mask, to the street-front of their facility.

Luckier than 610 University is the Depression-Modern edifice at 620, Hydro's second head office, destined to survive intact as a hospital office tower. Put up six storeys high in 1935 by Sproatt & Rolph, and topped off by the same firm in 1945 with a tower of ten more storeys, the Ontario Hydro Building is among Toronto's most comely stepped tower blocks. The ascent of smooth, warm stone moves up from the sidewalk along lovely steps, while the lower courses of the building are graced by expressive ornaments of open-handed refinement. Water imagery is everywhere: in abstracted cascades, carved on the streamlined classical pilasters on either side of the entrance; in the shimmering curtain of waving glass brick under which one enters the marble lobby; in wave-forms cast in the horizontal bronze elements which accent and lightly restrain the gracious visual upthrust of the exterior cladding.

It has become customary to emphasize the progressive, upward-yearning aspects of stepped structures, which were first seriously proposed by Louis Sullivan in 1891, an immediate hit with architects and their clients, and, at best, still among the finest results of twentieth-century building art. We are inclined to cherish the soaring sophistication and sculpted styling of such buildings, which have been made to seem only more attractive by the classic postwar office slab, bluntly confronting the sidewalk, or retiring from the street behind windy plaza. Such admiration of a beautiful object from the past is entirely appropriate, though one should not see a proclamation of heroic triumph in the sonorous vertical lilt of 620 University. From the standpoint of architectural history, it dates from the twilight of the expressive North American skyscraper construction in the stepped Sullivan manner, with its judicious ornamentation, street-aligned façade, allusions to past glories of civil engineering in the service of the people. Much of the beauty of 620 University is in its affirmative conservatism, and its skilful visual management of upthrust on a comparatively low scale.

But to understand 620 University fully, something of its immediate historical context should be known. By 1935, when the office building was opened, Adam Beck's dreams of universal, free electrification had been brought near death's door by the Great Depression. Plans for expanding the provincial power grid were stalled, some 134,000 Ontario farms were still without electricity, and the whole idea of "power at cost" had fizzled out. Seen against the storm clouds of dire days, the Ontario Hydro Building seems less like a victory monument than a promise to keep the progressive faith in the midst of evil times. The incorporation of noble touches, fluted columns and dignified, balanced ornaments recalls commitments to what endures, as the water motifs are pointed reminders of the mighty torrents that never cease, even when humans are temporarily unable to harness their immense power.

## THE HORSE PALACE

Although railway trains had replaced horses in inter-city haulage as early as mid-Victorian times, it wasn't so long ago that this most beautiful and intelligent of domesticated animals was still the principal engine for moving people and things around town, hence a common sight on Toronto streets. The combustion engines first startled big-city working horses, then abruptly displaced them, leaving only the mounts of Toronto's police on our streets, and those ponies now used for dragging tourist-laden buggies around Olde York on summer evenings. But if the civilian working horse has disappeared from the city, the fascination of urbanites with horses has not. Hence, the electricity that seems to flicker in the cold air down at Exhibition Place every November, as the annual Royal Agricultural Winter Fair gets ready to kick off its world-famous Royal Horse Show.

The first event is usually the $5,000 McDougald Open Jumper. But the official opening event—the $150,000 Crown Royal Cup Finale, often featuring such international equestrian superstars as Ian Millar and Margie Goldstein and Mark Leone—is what we all really wait for, and always find an unsurpassable thrill.

The steeds seen over the ten days of the Royal are, as you might expect, the peerage of the international equine world. Unlike most other revolutions, the one initiated by the automobile quickly eliminated the proletarians and left only the nobles, who now enjoy endless brushing and cossetting by their human servants in luxuriously appointed stalls.

The revolution that swept away the working horse was, of course, long over by 1931, when City of Toronto architect J. J. Woolnough finished building the first suitable temporary quarters at Exhibition Place for these splendid animals. If the excellent swine that turn up each year at the Royal get rather mean little pens, beneath their dignity, and the bovine breeding stock are assigned merely a bed of straw in the drafty, unadorned eastern shed of the Coliseum, the equine visitors and their human valets are quartered in Woolnough's Horse Palace, which may well be the most illustrious and interesting hotel for horses in the world.

With 1,200 stalls in several sizes and designs spread over eight acres, the Horse Palace proclaims the importance of both horse and Horse Show in every graceful detail and dashing line. Woolnough dressed its plain steel box-frame with a smooth skin of Queenston limestone trimmed in copper, bronze and brick, all of it ornamented with stylish equine motifs. A bas-relief frieze of horse heads parallels and accents a horizontal course of windows, full-bodied prancers adorn the dramatic stone curves of the Palace's main entrance. The doors are of glass, decorated with red and black woodwork. And, with a touch of humour we would not expect from a sober sided official architect, bas-relief horses' rears—to be sure, so streamlined one can just make out what they are—grace the exterior entrances to the toilets.

Inside the Palace, we find the same careful attention to

detail. The charcoal-dark elm wood and cream-painted *moderne* ironwork of the stalls provide a luxuriant visual harmony, while the sleek, ceremonial banisters on the ramps connecting the vast structure's two principal floors also declare this a palace in more than just name. The lighting, naturally, is neon.

In the late 1980s, the City officially put the Horse Palace under the protective wing of the Ontario Heritage Act. But, as we find in the official memos leading up to the structure's designation, nobody appears to have been quite sure what to call its distinctive architectural styling. Should it just be called Modern? After all, an article in the September, 1931, issue of *Construction* magazine did hail the Palace as "modernity itself." But other writers, responding perhaps more to the building's delightful Jazz-Age ornamentation than to its resolutely Depression-Era horizontal streamlining, have tended to use the term Art Deco, from the 1920s, for it.

In fact, the Horse Palace was built in the midst of the architecturally uncertain period between the Crash, which ended the feverishly exuberant Twenties and took the always costly, high-style Art Deco with it, and the 1933 Chicago world's fair, which was to set the tone for the super-streamlined, sleekly unornamented nationalist fashion in everything from toasters to skyscrapers in North America for the next decade. Commissioned to make a grand building on the very cusp of two historical epochs—a collapsing era of luxury and display, a rising era of shortage and constraint—the earnest but pedestrian mind of J.J. Woolnough came up with a design of such nice ambiguity that it shouldn't work. But it does work, beautifully—expressing in ornament and line both the passing extravagance of that new, horsey money which brought the Royal into existence in the early 1920s, and anticipating, with surprising accuracy, sweepingly stern, horizontal post-Chicago styling at the same time.

Not that the magnificent and expensive horses housed

there care much about architecture, or about anything else except the regal treatment they're used to. But horsey Torontonians curious about architecture may well want to give the Horse Palace a closer look than usual from their limousine windows, as they sweep onto the grounds for the next Royal horse gala.

## MAPLE LEAF GARDENS

There are reasons for ignoring Maple Leaf Gardens. Maybe, like me, you're not a hockey fan. In that case, the historical detail that Foster Hewitt broadcast the play-by-plays to all Canada from the Gardens' booth for fifty years is just a fact, not a holy truth of Canadian Identity. And unless you're heavily into nostalgic trivia, the facts that Elvis wiggled, Billy Graham preached, Buster Crabbe back-stroked and manic girls screamed for the Beatles' bodies under the Gardens' roof won't be tidbits to cherish forever.

You may, however, have noted that mammoth, routine modern buildings on the slide—even places as widely venerated as the Gardens (or, say, Exhibition Place)—never age with ruinous and melancholy grace. They just get shabby and faded, and appear all tuckered out, like the down-and-outs hustling spare change on nearby Yonge Street.

Or at least such were my thoughts about Maple Leaf Gardens before I stopped and took a long look at the inside and outside of what I'd been casually ignoring for years. For those who appreciate ambitious modern engineering, the interior of this 16,000-seat arena is the most interesting part of such a look-see. There is drama in the canopy of corrugated metal, held aloft, without internal columns, by four arched ribs bearing all the ceiling weight down on four concrete stumps, one at each of the building's corners. In an era that's brought us the telescoping roof of the SkyDome, the sight of the Gardens' roof won't be a transcendental experience, but that cover is still one of Toronto's most inspiring interior instances of steel's defiance of gravity, and its almost animal will to leap across space—a property of this wonderful modern material noted ever since the Brooklyn Bridge and the Eiffel Tower.

To those more interested in architectural styling than in engineering, and who've never given the Gardens' style much thought, a close look at the exterior of this huge box will come as yet another kind of pleasant surprise. But the finesse of the exterior is hardly news. During the recent controversy over whether the 1931 structure should be named an official "heritage property" by the city of Toronto—eventually it was designated just that—consultant A. M. de Fort-Menares effectively pointed out how the streamlined upsweeps of brick and window elements were joined with strong horizontals of grey concrete and "stylishly modern detailing" to make a distinctive building both staidly traditional and cautiously *moderne.*

But in her report, Fort-Menares also argued against giving the Gardens an exalted place in the story of Toronto's large-scale architecture done between the world wars. Compared with what used to be Eaton's flagship College Street store, a block away—a work of very high quality done by the same designers—the Gardens is characterized by "coarseness of materials," "utter functionalism" in its interior arrangements and "superficiality" of exterior ornament.

And if it wasn't great even on opening day, the building was only made tackier by thoughtless changes to the facade, and by numerous needless uglifications, removals and renovations. Inside, the rich curtains of the top rank of windows, and the huge ceremonial portrait of the sovereign, were swept away to make room for more seats. And outside, there are those hideous panels of mortared stone chunks adorning the entrance to the private Hot Stove Club.

Then we have the more general havoc wreaked on the Gardens in the 1970s, when the bosses decided to clean the building by sand-blasting, thereby blowing away the cladding's distinctive glaze and dulling the porous yellow brick, and making it defenceless before all the city acid and dirt. (The more recent cleaning, completed only a year or so ago, was done with gentler, water-soluble detergents.) The Gardens is more architecturally engaging than it's reputed to be, yet hardly as fine as Toronto's finest examples of interwar architecture. But who cares? When you're talking about the Lourdes of hockey, it's the miracle of winning in overtime that matters to those millions of Canadians glued to their TV sets, not whether the Art Deco styling in the brickwork over the marquee is quite up to snuff.

If originally a sceptic about the Gardens—or, more accurately, an indifferent bystander—I am no longer. After seeing the place, and reading its history, I now understand the broadcast gasp of CBC's Morningside host, Peter Gzowski, upon his learning that Maple Leaf Gardens had been given official "designation as an historic building" by the Toronto Historical Board. "Designation?" Gzowski spluttered in disbelief. "It didn't need designation! It's always been an historic building!" Much the same note was struck, in more measured language, by Toronto historian Michael Bliss in an impassioned 1989 memorandum to the Historical Board, at a moment when demolition was threatened. "Maple Leaf Gardens is one of this country's most historic buildings…the cathedral of Canadian hockey during the sport's Golden Age," wrote Bliss, "a time when hockey became part of the fabric of the culture for millions and millions of Canadians." Being a young country, Canada has few symbols of national identity. "If in 1989 we no longer believe that Maple Leaf Gardens has been a historically significant building—if we are happy to let it disappear under the wreckers' ball—then we might as well give up."

Well, the building did not disappear, as its owners wished and wish it would, and Canada did not give up. And at least one outlander, this writer, finally figured out why the Gardens must never go, so long as there are people alive who remember it in its most happy moments.

Now if you're wondering why a huge, steel-roofed square box in Toronto should get the name Gardens—spelled always with an "s" but always used in sentences as a singular noun—the story goes like this.

It started with the designation of a famous sports facility in New York as Madison Square Garden (spelled without an "s"). Madison Square wasn't a garden either, but it was built on the site of an amusement park called Gilmore's Gardens. In 1912, Toronto borrowed the name, or nearly, when the Montreal firm of Ross and Macdonald built a sports palace called Arena Gardens, on Mutual Street. In a little over five months in 1931, the same firm built Maple Leaf Gardens, for the same ends as Madison Square Garden, but adding the "s" from Arena Gardens (demolished 1989). All of which may explain how gardening and hockey got mixed up in the Canadian imagination.

You always wanted to know that. You really did.


PARK LANE

In a tribute to the brilliant pianist and theorist of technology Glenn Gould, *Globe and Mail* music critic Robert Everett-Green observed that the artist's "playing was a thoroughly modern phenomenon, more akin to the uncluttered lines of modernist architecture than to the Beaux-Arts exuberance of, say, a Rubinstein."

As it happened, Gould spent the last twenty years of his life in a spectacularly messy penthouse atop Park Lane Apartments, a Depression Modern building on St. Clair Avenue West which curiously adumbrates the performance style Everett-Green described. It is a structure notable, not only for the genius who lived there, but for its own linear rigour and its pragmatic clarity. We could only wish that its influence on the street had been greater.

The area I am talking about stands on both sides of St. Clair, between Yonge Street and Avenue Road—once a smart Easter Parade of stylish apartment blocks, now a stern display of important early experiments in Toronto's postwar architectural Modernism. But if the broad street on the south border of toney Forest Hill and Deer Park has been allowed to change from its former chic to operational, the Park Lane, completed in 1938 by Toronto architects Forsey Page and Steele, continues to hold its own as a fine, modest instance of the high *Moderne,* complete with most of the decorative gestures we look for in deluxe apartment construction in its day.

Project architect Harland Steele clad his symmetrical, U-shaped building with dark-brown brick, streamlined and stripped of ornament, other than firm horizontal courses of raised parallel brickwork binding the exterior all round. The entrance is, predictably, a ceremonial piece confected of chromed steel and fluted concrete posts. To enhance the staid drama of this ensemble, Steele let horizontal sweeps of windows move the eye effectively out of the sheltered, set-back entrance, around the inner corner-curves of the structure, to the straight walls of its two wings, fronting the St. Clair sidewalk. Steele's stripe of windows, varying in size and proportion while keeping to the general horizontal programme of the architecture, creates a melodious counterpoint to the flattish brick facing. (The crisp effect of these windows was muted in 1987, when the glass and horizontal mullions, decreed by Steele to echo the brickwork, were replaced by glazing set in vertical frames.)

The happiest architectural feature of Park Lane is the near-universal trademark of 1930s, the swept-around corner. Whether the object being styled was your neighbourhood Trans-Lux movie theatre, a TWA Dixie Clipper aircraft, a cocktail lounge with a sinuously flowing Flexwood bar

*Glenn Gould entry*

trimmed with opalescent bronze or a Chrysler Airflow sedan, the soft corner was the sign of the deluxe, and of the technologically up-to-date. For the first time in the history of masonry building, and, if only for a moment, the rigidly angled corner was out.

It is difficult to view this apartment block, still neat and smart as a plucked eyebrow, without a twinge of regret. Park Lane stands at the end of the history of opaque, stylishly sophisticated masonry building. In 1938, the style's streamlined external decor and rounded corners, small-scale comfortable living in modern circumstances, were all enjoying their last moments of timeliness. Next would come the era of glass, flat tops and steel frames. Luxurious exterior styling would become a heresy, to be stamped out; and stamped out it was, if the relatively few instances of fine Depression Modern survivals in Toronto are any evidence.

What more appropriate living quarters could have been found by Glenn Gould, this "invisible man" who deserted the concert stage for a life of Garbo-like reclusiveness, than an aloof, exclusive apartment building of the Garbo era? If, as Everett-Green argues, Gould set up "technological filters...between himself and the world," he also chose a domicile constructed as a nearly opaque architectural filter between interior and street—a gesture of construction repugnant to the "democratic" builders of transparent glass and steel slabs who would soon dominate the provision of apartment towers.

Gould was not destined for the revealing eye of the television camera, or for its architectural analogue, the revealing modernist curtain wall of glass. He was born, writes Everett-Green, "for the microphone, and more especially for magnetic tape. His personal distaste for the concert experience, and its potential for accidents, led him naturally toward a technology that invited second thoughts. Editing a bundle of tapes into one performance was not 'cheating,' but putting the studio to its rightful use, which was the creation of an artifact, not an event...

"Gould's instincts led him toward a full-blown ethics of technology. Machines and technology, he wrote, make us better by distancing us from our 'animal response to confrontation.'" As it happened, Glenn Gould lived in an apartment building constructed in the last important style of apartment architecture to propose distance and apartness as existential qualities highly desirable for *wholly intentional* living. At Park Lane, there is simply no question of the free movement of intellectual unequals, of those opportunities for mixing and sociability suggested alike by the windy plazas and cozy, crowded streets beloved by postwar Modernism's theorists and critics alike; any more than there is any tolerance for a dropped hem, or *public* failure of style. Unlike a microphone, Park Lane is an expressive artifact in its own right—declaring in no uncertain terms the distinctiveness of the people who live within from those who live without, and, in its sophisticated and haughty design, their *disdain* for active community with whoever chances to be passing by on the street.

Now we know that in his utopian writings on technology, as opposed to his mandarin performance practice, Gould declared himself on the side of interaction, smudged bounds between artist and audience, and other pieties of the 1960s. "The irony," says Everett-Green, "is that the man who floated the idea of creative anonymity, of blurred boundaries between performer and listener, has been put on a pedestal, and his every recorded note made sacred." But what besides posthumous idolatry could one reasonably expect of an artist who chose to live his last twenty years within *these* stylish and exclusive walls?

# High Styles

*Storm Windows, St. James Cathedral*

# GOTHIC

However tenuous or non-existent one's relation to Christianity, and even if you've never set foot in one, I suspect you'd have no trouble singling out a church on a city street. Scale—the fact that the building is conspicuously bigger than what's around it—is important to the idea of churchliness, but not central. After all, some modern, low churches in the suburbs could easily be mistaken for hockey rinks or Legion halls, were it not for the steeple.

The steeple, then, is crucial to the basic package, and so is more or less strict autonomy of the building on its site. Once a congregation is past the store-front stage, only a free-standing edifice will do, preferably as deluxe as possible. It's curious. I could name several good reasons why a new Christian congregation should think about joining forces with a developer on a mixed commercial/residential/ecclesiastical complex, rather than enthrone an independent church on its own lawn.

A few years ago, a Toronto real-estate developer struck a $3-million purchase and lease-back deal with the Church of the Redeemer, at the corner of Bloor Street West and Avenue Road. As the mixed-use tower went up, it got me wondering why the new building wasn't allowed simply to engulf the piquant 1879 church, including its embellished Victorian interior. As things turned out, the church's Gothic exterior was left to stand primly separate and intact, with the new structure rising behind it.

Most people I know, regardless of their belief or lack thereof, would find the thought of integrating an old church with a new commercial development odd. The contemporary idea of what a church should look and be like, a little informal polling reveals, is extraordinarily rigid, even (and perhaps especially) in the minds of people who give little or no thought to what goes on inside these cherished structures. The model appears to be based on the oldest and most conspicuous ecclesiastical edifices people have grown up with, whether or not they attend the services inside.

In Toronto, that means Victorian Gothic buildings which, while venerated, are not terribly old: the Ohio stone and Toronto brick Cathedral Church of St. James (1849–1874), for example; or St. Michael's Roman Catholic Cathedral (1845–1890), or St. Basil's Church (1856-1895), among others. Myriad older and similarly serious secular bits of Victorian architecture have been demolished without public outcry. These churches, however, will almost certainly stand until their brick facings can no longer be prevented from crumbling into dust.

One could argue, I suppose, that a new country needs such pseudo-ancient edifices—theme parks of geographically remote and presumably unchanging spirituality, as it were—to give it an instant "past," even if the past is stitched together from that of another country. Then there's the argument, more attractive to secular moralizers, that such buildings are necessary, since they serve as visible advertisements for conservative religious conviction and unquestioning loyalty to Crown and country, virtues obviously in quite short supply these days. Viewed from such perspectives, St. James' Cathedral is a hymn in brick to the ethical and social values of the Victorian Empire, from its scrupulously correct imitation of the Collegiate Gothic manner to its magisterial and aloof attitude, and to the top of its exceptionally graceful, lofty spire. One can hardly fail to be impressed by evident dignity, and made to remember the good works of the John Strachan, first bishop of Toronto, who is buried under the altar.

William Thomas's Cathedral of St. Michael provides our best Roman Catholic rehearsal of the same tropes: lofty-minded Englishry, expressed in its conscious mimicry of York Minster, imposing reminders of antique craftsmanship, the loyal mid-Victorian "Gothick" thought to be the true architectural style of the Age of Faith, and clearly meant here to declare the political loyalty of Christians who were still objects of suspicion and prejudice by Protestants.

Do these architectural stylistics really express the triumph of Christian faith and order in the wilderness? I am inclined to believe the answer is no. All these model churches, it is worth remembering, as well as dozens of "Gothic" and "Romanesque" ones which went up at the same time or shortly thereafter in Toronto, were built during the mid-Victorian collapse of popular religious faith. For more than a century before the present fabric of St. James' Cathedral came to be, intellectual, then industrial, modernity had been whittling away at traditional notions of transcendence and Divine Providence. Science was making scepticism and the sceptical method increasingly attractive to the brightest minds of the age, and pressing home the point that humankind had created itself by means of technology and ingenuity, and without help from a benevolent Creator.

But if any event can be said to have announced the city's final changeover from a colonial preserve of Anglican attitudes and proprieties to a profane, modern city, it was the provincial act of 1849 which radically secularized the University of Toronto. For John Strachan, consecrated first bishop of Toronto ten years before, the legislation was a catastrophe and disgrace, and also the immediate occasion of his last great architectural and intellectual project. It was to be the founding of Trinity College, upon what he termed the "clear and unequivocal principle" of loyalty to the Church of England. The college was begun on Queen Street West in 1851 by architect Kivas Tully, who understood well the power of the English Gothic to declare a religious institution's stand in the apocalpytic match between Christian Faith and godless Science. It is no coincidence that the ground was broken for Toronto's most important Gothic buildings in the years just before and just after the University Act of 1849.

Looked at against this background of deepening, rapidly spreading doubt and religious indifference, Toronto's early models for churchliness seem to be desperate rearguard actions rather than declarations of victory, and quite open acknowledgments of just how deep a rift had opened between factory and rectory, the culture of technology and the increasingly non-credible culture of religious institutions. For whatever reasons, Western Christianity failed to understand and confront head-on the nineteenth-century technological and intellectual revolution of secularity, and effectively combat its sweeping claims to universal enlightenment and mental emancipation.

But the struggle is hardly over. Indeed, a principled dislike and disregard for technological modernity, and a persuasive critique of it, seem to be gaining ground in large regions of the world—in the West weakly, under the banner of ecological awareness, architectural preservationism and "Green" consciousness generally; and strongly in those areas dominated by reviving Islam. But whatever the future holds, the present state of Western churches has long been one of retreat and decline, and of reluctant abandonment of cultural leadership—though the churches have continued, despite all, to build refuges from the stuff of Gothic mist, mystery and past architecture carefully studied and reconstructed, and assume the role of dispensing Band-Aids to the victims of mass modernization from the safety of the sidelines. The deliberately archaic Victorian churches in our midst, while beautifying the grey, tight urban fabric, also are signs of a disastrous surrender to a secularizing *Zeitgeist* that now seems not nearly so irresistible or over-whelming as it once did.

## ROMANESQUE

If every city site expresses a state of mind, a literary genre, and a time of day, then Toronto's buildings in the Richardsonian Romanesque style express the irrational and uncanny, romance, and a mystic twilight—all of it pointedly opposed to the noonday rationality symbolized by the Classical. This is a tale of these places of eternal dusk, where massed dark stone volumes loom, and rounded portals and windows deep-cut into walls of quarry-rough rock conceal cool, mysterious rooms within, where a certain grand gloom, compounded of Dark Age barbarity and a sense of rude Christian faith, hangs heavy in the air.

Toronto has many such buildings. But at the time Henry Hobson Richardson died, in 1886, Toronto's Richardsonian moment was still yet to come; and this consummate Romantic architectural imagery was largely a spent force in the United States, its home.

The judgment of Henry-Russell Hitchcock, delivered in 1936 on the occasion of a tribute to Richardson mounted by New York's Museum of Modern Art, still rings true, if harsh, in our ears: "(Richardson) was not the first modern architect: he was the last great traditional architect; a reformer and not an initiator. Dying when he did, his architecture remained entirely within the historic past of traditional masonry archi-tecture, cut off almost entirely from the new cycle which extends from the mid-eighties into the twenties of the present century."

The "great cycle" Hitchcock is talking about is the one set rolling when U.S. and European architects discovered the lightness and great height that could be achieved by the use of steel and elevators. But if this revolution in materials had already doomed the ponderous, costly Richardsonian Romanesque in America by 1886, the expiring style was destined to leave extraordinary marks on Toronto, in the form of a series of highly important Richardsonian buildings put up around 1890. Thus did Toronto become, without meaning to, North America's heaven of the defunct Richardsonian Romanesque, and the style's great epitaph.

At the top of any list of these buildings stands the rose sandstone Provincial Parliament Building, the handiwork of the London-born, Buffalo-based architectural eclectic Richard A. Waite. Majestically heaped on the south end of Queen's Park and glowering officiously down University Avenue like Queen Victoria herself, the vast confection of semi-circular arches (imitations of ancient Syrian church portals), elaborate carving and massed, quarry-rough stone is best visited at the end of a long summer evening, when the dying day makes the sandstone glow, the deep-set windows seem mysterious, and the gargoyles snarl. It is a charmless edifice, and is little liked by Torontonians today. Architectural guide Patricia McHugh has written off our attitude as "the usual city slicker disdain for the country bumpkin," noting the Ontario legislature's historical association with rural interests. Opinion of the building at the time of its unveiling was rather different. Under the curious banner headline "Legislators in Fairyland," an 1893 Toronto *Empire* story trumpeted forth that the opening of Waite's structure "marks an epoch in the history of the province."

Which, of course, it did. With the inauguration of this gigantic seat of government, the low, little but rich and burgeoning provincial capital at last gained a building of metropolitan stature, a monument to eminence it had never before allowed itself. It was also too good a gesture to let stand alone, which brings us to another of Toronto's great

*St. George Street*

Richardsonianisms: Toronto architect E. J. Lennox's Old City Hall, begun in 1889.

It appears necessary for anyone who talks about this building to mention knowingly Richardson's Allegheny County Courthouse, in Pittsburgh, and suggest quietly that Lennox got all his ideas from this 1884–1888 "original." True, the Pittsburgh creation influenced Lennox—it was famous throughout the North American architectural community from the day it was finished—but, as we find just by looking at the Toronto building, Lennox was no mimic. Old City Hall is an asymmetrical Wagnerian fantasia on Romanesque chants, done in brown New Brunswick sandstone and a rose sandstone quarried in Ontario, and markedly different in spirit from Richardson's grave symmetry in Pittsburgh. For reasons both practical and aesthetic—he wanted the pinnacle to dominate the top of Bay Street, our Wall Street—Lennox puts his clocktower off-centre, and makes it gracefully slender, almost Italianate. Richardson's campanile, in contrast, is a stolid affair, squatly centred. Too, Lennox's is made even more operatic by opulent carvings evoking weeds underwater, wildly flourishing capitals, and many an exuberant oddity and surprise—all of it, remote in tone from Richardson's late, overpraised essay. In contrast to their indifference towards the undistinguished provincial legislature, Torontonians have always shown affection for Old City Hall, and have stoutly resisted moves to remove or alter it. Lennox's masterpiece was a superbly archaic, ponderous advertisement for a powerful city muscling its way towards continental prominence—and for Toronto, ever uncertain of its importance and identity, such forthright symbols will always have peculiar importance.

The peculiar pleasures of Toronto's Richardsonian Romanesque is all around us, set in place by builders famous and anonymous. We find an isolated, rude scrap of engraved Richardsonian sandstone under the chin of an oriel at the otherwise dull intersection of St. Clair Avenue West and Old

Weston Road, and many a rough-hewn lintel and flush of weedy carving over the video stores and Vietnamese fast-food joints in the once-stylish neighbourhood of Parkdale. But of all our minor Richardsonian knockoffs, my favourite is the Gladstone House, a hotel erected in 1889 by mainstream architect George M. Miller for business visitors to the industrial outskirts of Parkdale, and still operating as a hotel today, long after most former industries in its neighbourhood have disappeared.

Located on what's become a run-down, hooker-ridden strip of Queen Street West, and home to Bronco's Sports Bar, the Gladstone is a sturdy box transfigured by wonderfully phantasmagorical, eclectic ornament. In some places on this tall building's red-brick façade stand quite respectable Corinthian pilasters, with pretty flounces of vegetation at the capital. Other pilasters shoot up and end with a burst of flickering lizard tongues, or, unaccountably, in a rudely hacked stone stump. Carved, winged dragons cling to the underside of deep windows on the tall, squared-off Italianate tower, and lions roar from perches high up the wall.

The scenario spun by this improbable structure recalls an age of energetic barbarian builders, tacking together an architecture of their own from ornaments and elements left them by the winded, distant Empire—an architecture bent on making up by brute strength what it lacks in tasteful reasonableness. The Gladstone, like so many minor Toronto buildings erected around 1890, suggests a culture awakening to itself, and to its future as cosmopolis.

Until near the end of the last century, Victorian Toronto had styled itself in the manner of the distant patriarchate, typified by the Cathedral Church of St. James, to celebrate conservative intellectual and religious values, and loyalty to Crown and Empire.

The Richardsonian Romanesque, on the other hand, speaks of a new order of things, directing our gaze in two directions. One is back in history, to the system of ornamentation and craftmanship of the north-European Dark Ages, when the rough, formerly subject peoples of Europe found themselves free of Roman rule, yet still in awe of Roman culture. The other direction it points is towards the United States, then enjoying its first ebullient moment of prosperity since the Civil War, the conservatism and opulence of which is ably summed up in the costly, grandiose projects of Henry Hobson Richardson. Here, then, was a style for Canada—then emerging into wealthy, ambitious nationhood, solidly in the new American sphere of economic power, and ready for Richardson's Romanesque, which would proclaim the end of its status as a far-flung colony of the Victorian empire, and its launch towards independence.

## Byzantium and St. Anne's

To Toronto's architectural aficionados, St. Anne's Anglican Church—located on Gladstone Avenue, in a district of west Toronto from which most Anglicans departed generations ago—is famous principally for its remarkable interior, decorated in 1923 under the direction of the Group of Seven's J. E. H. MacDonald.

What MacDonald created is a feast of colour and design. Gold floods across the interior of the great central dome, fifty-five feet in diameter, and glints from the dazzling mosaic behind the plain marble altar. Stencilled designs in blue and rose and gold swarm over pillars and walls and vaulting arches. Within the half-dome arching over the altar, painted grapevines coil and spring, separate and join again in an exuberant illustration of Jesus Christ's simple description of Himself as the vine.

Set among these elaborate decorations are St. Anne's greatest treasures: the large paintings executed by some of the best-known Canadian artists of the twentieth century. Surrounding

the altar are depictions of scenes from the life of Jesus—
including *The Adoration of the Magi* by Frank Carmichael, *The
Transfiguration and the Tempest* by MacDonald, and *The
Raising of Lazarus* by Thoreau MacDonald. High in the dome
are F. H. Varley's large, striking portraits of the Old Testament
figures Moses, Isaiah, Jeremiah and Daniel; and a set of four
medallions, depicting the symbols of the four Evangelists, by
Toronto sculptors Frances Loring and Florence Wyle.

The largest of St. Anne's pictures are the oil paintings
which appear in the triangular areas over the four great pillars
supporting the dome. These works portray the four central
events in the great redemptive drama of the Incarnation. First,
there is Varley's nuanced picture of the Nativity of Jesus, the
finest single painting in the church. (Varley has left us a self-
portrait in the shepherd kneeling to the left of the infant
Jesus.) Next comes the *Crucifixion* by MacDonald, followed
by a dramatic *Resurrection* by H. S. Palmer—Christ seems to
break forward from the picture plane into the church's interior—and, finally, the *Ascension* by H. S. Stansfield, in which
Jesus lifts upward from a thick Canadian forest, past a range
of snowcapped mountains wreathed in cloud.

The story of how St. Anne's came to be such a storehouse
of decoration begins in 1907, when the rapidly expanding
working-class parish decided to demolish its first home—built
on the present site in 1862—to make way for a new and larger
structure. It was then that Lawrence Skey, rector of St. Anne's,
proposed that the design of the new building be imperial
Byzantine. The choice was unusual in Gothic Toronto, but
not eccentric. Anglicanism, which has always believed itself to
be non-papal Catholicism, has been fascinated by the similarly
non-papal Orthodox Church since the century of
Reformation. (The fascination has not been reciprocated.)
Other Toronto Anglicans might worship in stone or brick
churches in the High Medieval-Revival style—but, if Father
Skey got his way, the people of St. Anne's would pray under a

great dome, surrounded by splendid art recalling the glorious triumph of Constantinian Christianity over Roman paganism, and affirming the ecumenical character of Anglican faith and practice.

As matters turned out, the rector got half his way. His Byzantine church, designed by architect Ford Howland to seat 1,400 people, was built in 1908. But Skey had to wait for fifteen years, and the death of a generous parishioner, who left St. Anne's $5,000, to start on the decorations. In 1923, the rector assigned the work of finishing the church's interior to painter and friend J. E. H. MacDonald, and the architect William Rae. When the massive job was finished (in the same year), St. Anne's people found themselves with an stunning interior adorned with paintings by thirteen of Canada's most important contemporary artists.

Some sixty years later, and after an extensive restoration in the 1960s, St. Anne's is still alive, though not exactly thriving. The present rector, like all his recent predecessors, is trying to keep the church going—a worthy task, if only because of the building's unique status as the only project of decoration jointly undertaken by Group of Seven artists. Each artist worked on his own painting in his studio, and each brought to his assigned topic individual treatment—but the colour scheme and the mix of flat, stiff representation borrowed from Byzantium with more subtle modelling taken from the Italian Renaissance was dictated by J. E. H. MacDonald.

The decoration does not always work in harmonious concord. But in a city whose church-folk still clung to the academic English Gothic styles of yesteryear, St. Anne's stands out as a fresh, visually forceful and ecumenical reply to the Edwardian decline of faith into narrow denominationalism, and a restatement of the embracing universality to which Christian witness has always aspired.

## CLASSICAL

Dwellers in cities hardly need to be reminded that we live among buildings decorated with ancient Greek and Roman ornament; the things are everywhere. But while so deeply ingrained into the Toronto cityscape that we just take it for granted, Classicism can still turn up in some surprising places.

One need not look for such surprises in the neighbourhoods of the rich and powerful, since they've always deployed the Classical as a power style. In 1807, when Toronto was little more than a squared-off village in the mud, the near-mythic adventurer and merchant Laurent Quetton St. George classed-up his otherwise blockish house with a Palladian front window and a pedimented portico supported by four graceful Ionic columns. From that time through the 1860s in all antiquarian earnestness, and until the Second World War in the solemn name of academic propriety and "tradition," and again, nowadays, in the playful, gaming spirit of post-Modernism, the columns and Classical orders, have not ceased to appear. (An "order," incidentally, is usually defined as a distinctive ensemble of a column with capital, and, on top of that, a load-bearing superstructure of some kind, called an entablature. A base or pedestal for the column is optional.)

While the Classical vocabulary can be readily detected in most city districts built up more than sixty years ago, the most high-profile uses of this visual language are to be found, of course, in large, noble non-residential structures. Union Station, which opened for business in 1927, exudes businesslike formality from every sweeping, dead-level sculpted line and from every massive Tuscan pillar. As far as the momentous Classical mode is concerned, Toronto's central station cannot be exceeded.

A different tone—still dignified, but less imposing and altogether more celebratory than that of Union Station—is struck by the lofty Ionic columns and elegantly detailed façade of Thomas William Fuller's curving Dominion Public Building (1926–1931), at 1 Front Street West. And speaking of the Ionic Order, my current favourite Toronto building in this traditionally feminine style is the headquarters of the Provincial Ombudsman, formerly the University of Toronto's Lillian Massey Department of Household Science, built between 1908 and 1912 at the intersection of Bloor Street West and Queen's Park. On its west front, this ample, intelligent structure presents an exceptionally fine Ionic portico, whose full columns are echoed by the half-columns in the graceful wings extending from it north and south. No non-monumental Classical building front in Toronto displays such expressive rhythms of light and shade, extrusive ornament and receding aperture, with more harmony or clarity.

But Toronto's noble and important buildings in the classical style have been written up in many textbooks and guidebooks, and so need no further comment. Every city has its columns and pediments and such. I should like to know, however, if every city has so much evidence of the Classical on streets like the one I live on, in an unimportant working-class district which appeared on downtown's west side on the eve of the First World War. Though the factory I live in sports no classical elements, many of the other domiciles along the street do. Were one to tell the neighbours that their front porches are really pedimented porticos supported by pedestalled columns of a simplified Doric order, approaching the stolidity of the Tuscan, and inspired by the Renaissance theories (and misunderstandings) of Andrea Palladio, they might find this news amusing, if not very interesting. But, in any case, that's what they've got, *mutatis mutandis.*

The occurrence of Classical columns and pediments is certainly not limited to my street. That's just where I started noticing it. Nor do I want to suggest that any of the Roman porticos on my street, or those on dozens of other ordinary Toronto steets built up between late Victorian times and the

Depression, are remotely comparable, in beauty, grace or nobility, to those you find adorning the city's great public buildings, or mansions in Rosedale.

But if the builders who gave us working-class and middle-class Toronto around the turn of the century rarely observed the precise proportions and ornamental canons of Classicism, they nevertheless left the city of Toronto haunted by echoes of the ancient architecture of virtue, empire and the gods.

On many old Toronto porches, we find each column resting on a pedestal, just as illustrated in the standard Renaissance manuals on ancient Greek and Roman building—though the Toronto style is, more often than not, to make the pedestal of brick, cap it with a slab of concrete, and run it as much as halfway up to the horizontal superstructure supported by pedestal and column together, i.e. the entablature. Occasionally the column extends the whole distance between floor and entablature, as it sometimes did in Roman times.

The typical Toronto column, standing on the pedestal or on the floor, is almost always of wood, machine turned and mass produced. It is shaped into a semblance of a round, unfluted Doric (or Tuscan) column, with a simple square base and simple square capital, usually devoid of either the volutes of the Ionic style, or the pretty vegetative flourish of the Corinthian. Columns here often present a white shaft with capital and base in some other colour, green and brown being preferred hues on my street.

The entablature is customarily just a horizontal wooden beam, innocent of ornamentation. Supported by the columns and resting on the entablature is the pediment, its triangle defined by the two sloping eaves of the gabled porch. The whole affair is attached to the front of a blocky brick house. On spring and summer evenings, families across old Toronto may be seen visiting in these porticos, whose ancient prototype once served as the ceremonial portal to a god's dwelling place.

Something of this archaeological information may have

been known by those who quickly developed the west-side Toronto neighbourhoods some ninety years ago, though it has long since been lost, if such data ever had a life in popular knowledge. But the history of a culture is largely that of people living in structures whose meanings they do not know, or have forgotten. This amnesia doesn't change the fact that ordinary Toronto neighbourhoods are graced with the most venerable symbolism, which can be brought to life and recollected, given a bit of background and a little imagination.

An ordinary street of working-class houses with plain Doric columns out front then becomes a row of temples sheltering the sacred flame of marriage. As we are told by Vitruvius, the Roman who wrote the only ancient architectural manual that has survived from antiquity, the first Doric temple was dedicated to Hera, the jealous first lady of the gods and guardian of marriage. The Doric columns themselves advertise the sort of people who build such things, as totem poles do. From Vitruvius we learn that the sons of Dorus, a Greek, were a race of conquerors; the writer compares the unadorned Doric columns to naked men—that is, to soldiers (since the Greeks fought naked).

Subsequent architectural authors have always seen in the Doric style a certain militant, plain manliness, as distinct, for example, from the supposed femininity of the more slender, prettier Ionic columns. The Doric ornamentation on countless old Toronto houses thus proclaims them to be the family homes of conquerors, returned from the wars of empire, and the shrines of our era's new hero, the working man.

This is all fantasy, I admit. But it's probably not too different from what many loyal, turn-of-the-century Torontonians of British descent would have found a noble vision indeed. Was this proliferation of innumerable Doric-like columns in Toronto really just happenstance, a matter of builders mindlessly copying out of architectural pattern books? Or were those porticos meant consciously to recall the greatness of

Rome, and the British imperial ideology of the hour?

Such questions inevitably lead not to answers, but to other questions. For while this architectural usage gives a touch of charm and aesthetic elevation to many an otherwise shabby house front, why did it really happen? Why does the spirit of the Classical haunt urban imagination like an unlaid ghost, sometimes quiescent, but always ready to start dispensing plans and comfort again whenever the faith in the current anti-Classicism (Gothic, International Style, or whatever) becomes shaky?

I have no answer, nor a satisfactory explanation. It does little good to say that the business of columns, entablature and so on we have inherited from Classical antiquity is safely beautiful and noble, since Classicism certainly does not ensure the beauty and nobility of the outcome. Though straining mightily for great Classical effect, both the White House and the United States Capitol building, for instance, today look like Victorian mantel clocks with quaint Classical airs.

It would be absurd to argue that New World structures crafted in other revived Old World architectural styles cannot turn out as lovely and high-minded as anything in the Classical mode. One thinks of Toronto's Old City Hall, or the numerous gems of Victorian Gothicizing that dot our downtown; or, for that matter, the Toronto-Dominion Centre, splendid in heroic anti-historicism.

But the fact remains that, for the moment anyway, Modernism is *démodé*. And nobody builds in the palatial Romanesque style of Old City Hall any more, and probably nobody ever will again—while the Classical is with us in new hotels out at the airport, in new condo towers on the lakeshore, in monster houses, and on the columned porches of turn-of-the-century workers' housing that is not monstrous at all. Classicism has never been out of fashion for very long in Europe, or in lands touched by European civilization, since attaining its typical form upwards of 2,500 years or so ago.

The riddle of this durability has exercised the imaginations of many architectural writers, though none has come up with a really convincing solution to it. Quinlan Terry, a contemporary British architect best known for his devotion to reviving architectural antiquity, has written that the Classical Orders—the "timeless and universal recipe for architecture"—were given to Moses by God on Mount Sinai, along with the Ten Commandments. From Moses, this truth of architecture was passed by reverential architects from the Hebrews to the Greeks, and thence to us, via Rome. I do not personally find this explanation particularly helpful, though I do find it colourful.

Less colourful, more modern-sounding and provocative, and conceivably more helpful, is the idea set out by the British art historian John Onians in his 1988 book *Bearers of Meaning*. In this study of the development of the Orders, Onians theorizes that our evolution into humans has predisposed us to like columns, entablature and so on. The forest-dwelling early members of the human family most likely to survive were those primates, naturally, who could discriminate which tracks signalled "food up ahead," and which ones meant danger. Later, the alertness born in the forests was applied to architecture. "Trees and woods have always had a special importance as at once the best source of food and the favourite haunt of enemies," Onians writes. Hence, the persistence in architecture of "tree-like columns and columnar shafts and...capitals which occupied a position similar to that...of the tops of tree trunks."

Are deeply-buried memories of forest hopes and fears, then, the sources of the special pleasure we feel when beholding some contrivance of Classical pillars?

Or could it be, simply, that the Classical style is the most versatile, expressive, desirable and pleasing building style ever devised? The latter view is faintly distasteful, because believing it would mean that a final answer to a problem of the first order—shelter—had been discovered very early in our history; and we Western people *do* like thinking of ourselves as just about the best improvers, inventors and developers humanity has yet produced. But much of this intelligence is inherent in the very stuff of Classical architecture, in the stock ornaments and elements architects receive from the past. Even in the hands of so-so architects, these elements still contain unmistakable sophistication and cultural resonance. Perhaps our admiration for this vocabulary of building has to do with its deeply reassuring unoriginality, and its dependable usefulness as a means of bestowing dignity on the urban streetscape.

## CYBERNETIC

Most city folk who attend a traditional church or synagogue, as well as all outright pagans, would probably have found themselves as bemused as I was by a news release I received early in 1993, promoting an impending trade fair of ecclesiastical technology. The event would be known as Inspiration '93.

Described as "four dynamic days of cutting-edge seminars, workshops, choral readings and exhibits," Inspiration '93 was to feature displays of such unusual worship aids as bass guitars, backdrops, lighting dimmers, "sound effect libraries," "video walls" and audio carts.

Several workshops were advertised. Participants could learn about the "latest in Bible Software," "how to prepare sermons for overhead projectors," and "how a MIDI-equipped organ can become a dynamic instrument in your ministry." (MIDI is the acronym for Musical Instrument Digital Interface. I cannot explain how this device works, or how it could give "unlimited musical possibilities" to an old two-manual wheezer, as promised in the brochure.)

The prospective visitor is also invited to "learn the applications of dimmers, mixers and...gels to change moods and set atmosphere to cover all events," and to discover the mind-expanding possibilities of teleconferencing, "a coming technology that major Religious organizations are looking into."

The most intriguing seminar on the roster, as far as I was concerned, was the one called "Using Pyrotechnics in Religious Settings." That's because, like most people, I love fireworks. But I like thinking up bizarre scenarios even better. Now I have always thought Anglican Evensong—especially when complete with glorious anthems and choral psalms and chants and perhaps a whiff of incense , but even when stripped of all that carry-on—is a quite satisfactory way to pay one's homage to the Most High. It *is* fun to think, however, of what an Evensong would be like with some spark-spitting pinwheels on the chancel railing, air-burst bombs going off high in the nave, criss-crossing fire-trails of sparkle rockets, and a few Red Devil sizzlers in the chancel. While it's hard to see how fireworks would make Evensong better than it is, you can bet your last Roman candle that a service with sizzlers would mark a major break with traditional Anglican practice.

But that appears to be exactly what all the gizmos and workshops at Inspiration '93 were about: inventing popular, eye-catching alternatives to the admittedly low-tech, bookish, predictable services standard in the mainstream churches of North America.

It's no secret that an increasing number of people are finding spiritual bliss, or something akin to it, in the kind of "worship environment" proffered by Inspiration '93, and that old-fashioned religious observance is finding fewer and fewer takers. Hence, the equipment and know-how offered by this fair: all you need to create an iridescent, ever-shifting and enveloping architecture of light, moods and sonorities, insubstantial and pretty as dawn cloud, appropriate to the popular new-time religion.

This evanescent architecture of spectacle is as new as the light and sound technology that's making it possible, and it represents one of the most stunning breaks ever to take place in the history of settings for Christian worship. The architects of these environments, from the earliest days of church-building, have long assumed solidity and a certain grandeur appropriate in their products, to make them identifiable as churches, if for no more important reason. These values have been embodied in many forms, from the Classical and basilical arrangement, through the Romanesque temple and high medieval Gothic cathedral and parish church, to the extraordinary pilgrimage chapel of Notre-Dame-du-Haut, designed by Le Corbusier in 1950 and finished in 1955.

Even in something so "modern" as Notre-Dame-du-Haut, the heavy stuff of churches has traditionally been orchestrated to remind us of the enduring greatness of God, and of those times when the Divinity was, we presume, worshipped more loyally than at the present time. This impulse can go horribly wrong, as it certainly did in my home-town Episcopal church in the American South, put up in the 1950s in English-Gothic style. Among its more amusing features are stained-glass depictions of people receiving baptism, Communion and other ministries of the Church, with all the men uniformed as Confederate officers, and all the women dressed like Scarlett O'Hara—heroes and heroines of the Lost Cause, here turned into saints.

But even if the treatment was newfangled and ultimately silly, the urgency to invoke comfortable cultural traditions was something the architects of this parish church shared with church architects of almost every Christian age and area.

Heavy architecture connects the believer to heavy virtues and loyalties: the electronically produced mood-buildings link the believer with those appliances common in the home, hence to the one haven in a heartless world—television, the family-room, the spectacle of plenty, luxury and leisure. The medieval churches (which dot Toronto) expressed beliefs that were at least as much a part of common English culture as the holly and the ivy. Built in the heyday of Victorian doubt, as optimistic, secular progressivism was becoming the true religion of Toronto's democratic masses, the Victorian Gothic is a visual argument for the traditional mix of piety, duty and Englishry already coming unstuck in Canada. Similarly, the light-and-sound shows of the newer Christian piety appear to be reaching out to a perishing class—this time, a devout middle class, watching its prayers for prosperity and mobility of traditional suburban life go unanswered, as the recession deepens and jobs vanish. I suspect the techniques promoted by Inspiration '93 will do no more to keep religion alive in mass culture, in the long term, than the techniques of the Victorian master-builders.

Be all that as it may, I've decided to go down with the neo-Gothic Anglican ship, clutching my antique Book of Common Prayer to my bosom, and praying that, in the Heaven that surely awaits me, there will be no gels, MIDIs, sound-effect tapes, or teleconferencing devices—though a small fireworks display now and again might prove a nice enhancement of our heavenly work of praise.

# Houses and Home

*Ravine house, Weston*

# AT HOME

These thoughts about home, and its disappearance, began to form in my mind one bright afternoon a few summers ago, after a visit to Toronto's Power Plant gallery, when I decided to hoof the couple of kilometres back to *The Globe and Mail*'s headquarters on Front Street West.

Anyone familiar with Hogtown's deep-downtown geography can visualize the northwesterly route. It went from the waters of the harbour, across high-speed roads and almost unused railway tracks, under the elevated belly of the Gardiner Expressway, up over the Spadina Avenue bridge, and thence to work.

It wouldn't have been a walk worth writing up, had it not been for the discovery of a kind of campsite in the last place one might expect to find one: the dark, sharp angle between the ground and an exit ramp descending from the expressway.

No one was there. To prevent discovery, the occupant had stashed his or her belongings up under the ramp, on a narrow steel ledge. From the looks of the stuff, its owner had been sleeping in this place for some time and was no travelling rich kid, playing poor. The rolled sleeping bag was filthy and ripped, the cooking gear dented, the cans full of the cheapest noodles and stew you can buy. In a nook rendered invisible from the busy roadway nearby by concrete pylons, there were signs of a cooking fire and a scatter of empty cans, plastic bags, booze bottles.

It was, of course, the digs of a homeless person, and merely one among many such sites in downtown Toronto's empty buildings, ravines and dead zones. Nevertheless, it gave me the sense of being an inadvertent trespasser in someone's house—embarrassed, curious, nervous. That feeling of trespass has haunted me since then. How very little it took—just a sleeping bag, a smudge of burnt wood and paper, a couple of battered aluminum pans—to mark that spot as a dwelling place, and to mark me out as an intruder!

The site under the expressway was no home. Home is where the heart is, or, more precisely, the bed. And the human mate we share the bed with, the surly cat who insists on snuggling between us under the duvet every night, the boring religious tome on the bedside table. Home is the familiar faces, objects, personal problems and intimacies to which we return at the end of a day spent in the mutable, impersonal world outside. It need not be always, or altogether, comfortable; it does have to be usual, and as secure as possible against the chops, cheats and changes of contemporary urban reality.

Or so, at least, goes the common wisdom about homes and home-making, and about the things the homeless presumably do not have.

While I have no wish to trivialize the plight and misery of homeless people, the experience under the expressway did leave doubts about the way we speak of "home" and "homelessness," and about just where the line between the two should be drawn.

Just what part, for instance, does *permanence* play in our idea of home? The person who slept under the Gardiner could claim no permanent place of his own. But is anyone cheeky enough to do so today? The idea of endless migration and transition, permanent homelessness—the "starter home," the second home, the third, ad infinitum—is now on hold in Toronto, due to the decline in real-estate prices during the early 1990s. The suspension is temporary; and, before long, city-dwellers will once again be caught up in the churn of selling and buying, moving and moving again.

This is not a phenomenon I can take an unqualified stand against. Virtually every good thing that's come to me in my life has been accompanied by uprooting, temporary rerooting, and moving on. As I grow older, however, home has become intrinsically bound up for me in the specific built entity I now inhabit—one certainly open to architectural experiment and revision, but the place in which I now intend to live, experience the intimacies of human existence, change and learn and, *Deus volens,* die. Everything else is *house*—mere architecture, real estate—whether a Rosedale mansion or a sleeping bag under an expressway ramp.

My convictions about home have not been changed by the gradual awareness that, while I have a dwelling place that is much more secure and comfortable than a cold, muddy spot under a bridge, something of homeness is still lacking in the house I live in. This sense is bound up, somehow, with my house's gradual occupation by impersonal, non-intimate technologies of pleasure. The homeless person's dwelling is vulnerable to the environment, both natural and industrial; my walls no longer stand impermeable, defining the line between private intimacies and the public world of mass-distributed images and noises. The once-solid definitions of home have now got holes in them—a television cable network, pumping in images from the outside world. No family, perhaps, sits together for hours in the dark unspeaking, transfixed by glowing images, as they did in TV's early days. There is a TV for every person's taste, and VCRs, so when the family tires of the various othernesses brought to us by TV, it's easy for us all to rent a video and enjoy exotic mass-produced fantasies, distractions and amusements as we will.

Telephones and the answering machine are always there, dissolving the walls between us and voices in what we used to confidently call the "outside world." With a compact disc player, it is now possible to "stay home" forever, but locked into solitary pleasures created wholly in an outside world. But what exactly are those iridescent discs, if not just more holes in the walls of home, openings to those welcome invaders, the merchandisers of mass-produced simulated experiences?

I do not advocate the course taken by David McDermott and Peter McGough, New York painters who live together in a Manhattan brownstone according to an archaeologically exact Victorianism, with wall-to-wall period decor, only candles and oil lamps for light, and coal for heat. If technology and the rapid spins and displacements of capitalist culture have taken away home forever, turning us all into transients and wanderers, contaminating human intimacy—perhaps even the very idea of the human—with myriad impersonal pleasures, those pleasures are still marvellous, and the well-spring of every urban person's most continual and evocative challenge. "To be modern," literary critic Marshall Berman has written, "is to experience personal and social life as a maelstrom, to find one's world and oneself in perpetual disintegration and renewal, trouble and anguish, ambiguity and contradiction: to be part of a universe in which all that is solid melts into air. To be modernist is to make oneself somehow at home in the maelstrom."

## CASA LOMA

In the last century, many a city too great for such nonsense allowed a monstrosity to be built on its best urban elevation. Paris let Sacré Coeur ruin the summit of Montmartre; Montreal let the pious raise St. Joseph's Oratory on the slopes of Mount Royal—while Toronto gave over a splendid escarpment site to, of all things, the apallingly vast curiosity known as Casa Loma. Built between 1911 and 1914 by Sir Henry Pellatt, an industrialist, at a cost of $3.5 million in Edwardian dollars, this story-book castle is of no historical significance. Nothing important ever happened there, and nobody important ever slept there, though Sir Henry did set aside a suitably opulent guest-room fit for a British royal, should one ever drop by. None ever did.

Leased from the city and operated for charity by the Kiwanis Club since 1936, Casa Loma is more nearly finished than it was in 1923, when Sir Henry's business belly-flopped, his wife died, and the knight moved out. It is a confection of looming ramparts and soaring chimneys out of *Boy's Own* illustrations, a pastiche of gaudily carved wood-panelling and marble and stone veneer, plaster gargoyles and useless towers, among myriad other architectural pomps and fusses and flushes. But despite the romantic insistence of its Walter Scottishness, there is little dour or gloomy or overbearingly *northern* about Casa Loma. Viewed from a standpoint in its cramped grounds, in fact, this busy architectural pastry seems almost too light and frothy—a cardboard fantasia, a set thrown up in a day to serve as the backdrop for a B-movie about knights of yore.

Yet despite its seeming flimsiness, this Moloch required coal costing $25,000 a year to keep it warm. Sir Henry employed a squadron of forty servants to run it, and kept busy nobody knows how many European dealers in baronial junk and pseudo-antiques, the suppliers of the armour and stag-horns and carved, ponderous oaken furniture with which its rooms were once stuffed. These chambers were denuded during the 1923 bankruptcy auction, which lasted five days. Today, in their far more sparsely furnished state, the compartments of Casa Loma seem decently proportioned and detailed—which is what we would expect of E. J. Lennox, its distinguished architect—though they would be just as acceptable in less sensational wrapping.

I think Torontonians make a mistake in dismissing Casa Loma. Whatever else it may be, the grand folly is surely the most conspicuous evidence in our midst of a tendency that's been present in European building a long time—the English *nouveaux-riches* were putting up medieval storybook castles as early as the seventeenth century—but which mutated into a kind of mass neurosis among the North American rich in the decades leading up to the First World War.

Modern military technology had made them obsolete as defences, of course, and advanced communications and industrial rationalization made them look silly as residences. Nevertheless, vast castles proliferated in North Carolina, Ontario, New Jersey, California, all of them staggeringly expensive antiquarian rhapsodies pastiched from a dozen historical sources. Unity of composition was avoided at all costs. Wanted, instead, was what architectural critic Robert Harbison has called "bogus historical scenarios," such as the "neo-Classical" room inserted into the presumably much earlier "Norman" tower at Casa Loma.

But why did this extraordinary event in the history of building take place? While we may just be dealing with the durable human proclivity to pompous nonsense, one senses behind this construction boom in ponderous architectural fictions the quite specifically late nineteenth-century anxiety over loss—the loss of historical bearings, the disintegration of everything once certain and solid and reliable about life. Everywhere in Europe and America, this dissolving of received wisdom and fact by the acid of technological Modernity was proceeding apace. One remedy popular among the very rich, the one chosen by Sir Henry and Lady Pellatt, was to sally forth on an impossible retreat from reality into fantasy, from modern politics into story-hour scenarios of chivalry, from the discomforts of truth into an almost unbelievably expensive prison of pleasing obsolescence. Casa Loma deserves to be considered as a late freak in an era during which the very rich, the only people who could afford such freakishness, made our century's first stand against advancing Modernity. (There would be others; they would not be so harmless.) It deserves membership in that club of such fellow-oddities as Balmoral (1853–1855), King Ludwig II's Neuschwanstein (1868–1886) and Castle Drogo, the monstrous make-believe fort built before and after the First World War by Sir Edwin Lutyens for Julius Drew, a mad tea trader.

The people who operate Casa Loma bristle at the common opinion that Sir Henry was just a colonial Edwardian fat cat with baronial delusions. Their offence is at least partly justified. He was an outstanding and inventive businessman, for at least the first years of his career. He was a lavish philanthropist, a loyal soldier and officer, still fondly remembered by his regiment, the Queen's Own Rifles, which today maintains a display of its memorabilia at Casa Loma. And if he was a pompous man, he was also a tragic one, eventually felled by his doomed attempt to escape the present-day world.

Before his death in 1939, Sir Henry lost just about everything a man can lose, including two wives, his fortune—estimated, at its peak, to have reached $200 million in today's dollars—his farm in nearby King City, his successively smaller houses and apartments. He ended his days in a room in the smudged industrial lakeshore suburb of Mimico. In addition to everything else, he lost his place in Toronto's historical imagination as a pioneer of the city's electrification, and one of Toronto's most fabulously successful industrialists; and is now remembered almost exclusively as the obese, crazy tycoon who built the silly castle high atop the Lake Iroquois escarpment.

But Casa Loma is not the only North American fantasy-castle haunted by a sad story of financial ruin, or untimely death, or lost love. Such miserable tales seem to haunt such structures, which now are vanished, or lying in pathetic ruins, or operated as tourist draws across this continent—as befits their absurd hugeness and their studious anachronism.

But let the soul of Casa Loma's builder rest in peace, and our memory of him be the compound of civic contribution and lunacy he deserves. And let his fantasy be a reminder to us not to condemn those whose extravangance is all that sets them apart from the rest of us, sharers in the same struggle. For there are few of us who do not yearn for safe harbour, a castle of small or great scale, in which the forces of technology, mass communications and mass culture continually dismantling and reorienting life are kept at bay.

## MONSTER HOUSES

If I long avoided writing about the monster houses, all instances of which I hate, it was because I never felt I understood exactly what distinguished this newish architectural type from the ample, eclectic houses I admire. It has mostly to do with television and air-conditioning. Of that, more presently. Right now, some words about the oft-repeated criteria which are said to enable us to recognize the differences between monster and non-monster houses.

One is the aggressive occupation of site, a billowing-out to the property lines on all four sides, dwarfing the older houses on the street. The flagrant violation of street scale is a charge that, I believe, can be made to stick, though the most horrible monster houses I have seen do not stand on little Toronto lots, but on spacious grounds outside town. This very isolation only seems to accentuate the "if you got it, flaunt it" vulgarity, sometimes noted as the most despicable thing about the monster house craze of the 1980s.

Moneyed people, especially those not yet comfortable with wealth, have always gone for the big effect in home-building, with often memorable results. One of the richest spectacles of this sort to be found in Toronto is the George Gooderham house, now the York Club, located just north of the University of Toronto, at the busy corner of St. George and Bloor streets. Put up by a booze tycoon around 1890 in the most deluxe

architectural style of the day—the massive sandstone and terracotta neo-Romanesque associated with the name of
American architect H. H. Richardson—this house proclaims
its occupant's big bucks in every ponderous detail, from its
grand corner tower and soaring chimneys to its deeply shaded
porches and ancient-looking carved arches and windows.

The house is shameless in its advertisement, and wonderful
for its operatic inclination and insistence on effect. While the
contemporary monster house and the Gooderham mansion
share a purely philistine spirit of ostentation, the older building shows off the wealth of its owner with much flair. There
is none of the vulgar archaism of the monster house, the
almost hernia-producing drive to cobble together "period elegance" with the casual. Perhaps the thing that makes monster
houses really monstrous is their *seriousness*—grandiose scale,
and the reckless deployment of ornaments filched from this or
that despotism in the past, and inflated—pediments and
Classical columns from Imperial Rome, boldly rusticated exterior walls composed of real or fake massive blocks of stone separated by deep-cut grooves, from the Florentine Renaissance
or Georgian England.

What makes it possible to be so serious (hence irresponsi-
ble) about mere appearances is that the traditional structures
and ornaments in noble architecture—the ponderous walls,
deeply inset windows, porches and so on—have, with startling
speed, lost all practical usefulness. I suggested earlier that monster-house building has something to do with television and
air-conditioning. That these two technological innovations,
prewar in origin but common everywhere only after the Second
World War, have had a drastic effect on urban life is not an idea
I can take credit for. Marshall Berman, in his book *All That is
Solid Melts into Air,* speaks at some length of the abrupt postwar emptying of the summer streets in his Jewish neighbourhood in New York, as everyone abandoned the porch and the
neighbourly evening stroll to watch TV in cool comfort inside.

This wasn't just a New York phenomenon, of course. I still remember the summer, in the mid-1950s, when TV sets and air-conditioners started arriving in my small home town. Suddenly, nobody was dropping by after dinner for some cool lemonade and leisurely conversation on the south veranda any more. A certain kind of evening talk which traditional Southern families had always enjoyed—rambling, casual, apparently to do with weather, cotton and politics, but really a recital of conversational art for its own sake—came abruptly to an end, and a peculiarly blank silence fell upon the house, never to lift again.

It has taken a while, but, if I'm right, the silence precipitated by the introduction of new technologies has finally found its typical expression in a new architectural style, that of the monster house. It is not the archaism of these buildings that is hateful. Nor is it the mindless exacerbation of old-fashioned ornament I resent—use of the thick walls and heavy overhangs, deep-set windows and so on all for show, without the least attention to the problems these features were designed to address: the bright sun at noon and the long shadows of evening, the direction of breezes in the various seasons, and other weather phenomena. Air-conditioning made this contempt for context possible, even as bad taste, it appears, makes it mandatory.

Perhaps George Gooderham would have built a dull monster-house box, if he'd had the chance. But if he controlled the fates of myriad distillery workers in Toronto, he did not control the Toronto weather. It, not he, dictated the way his house must be built, and accounted for the rich play of exterior variation we find so pleasing in his house, and usually absent in the monster house, except as bits of showoff. The rhythm of porches and cornices, the arrangements of windows, the orientation of portals, and the interplay of house with trees and grounds—all moulded and mandated by the natural elements, by the need for circulating fresh air in the dog days of August, and the corresponding need for shielding from the damp, icy February blasts.

I have less to say about television, since I do not watch it, know little about what people see, and have no interest in finding out. But I do know that watching TV is preferred by many people to having drop-in company after dinner. Hence the tendency of *all* new housing, not just monster housing, to reduce the veranda or porch to the status of disused ornament, degrade the living room to an expensive, purely ceremonial area—a process begun in nineteenth-century domestic architecture with the introduction of the "parlour"—and exalt that zone of sloppy manners and incivility known as the family room.

To my mind, the curious blankness of the monster house is the visual analogue to the barren silence and social blankness created by television, which gathers the family around itself each evening, then forbids conversation, discourages evening callers and regiments life by the clock with a rigidity hitherto known in few places outside Trappist monasteries.

## CASTLE HILL

While not exactly hating Castle Hill, my newspaper has always officially disdained this exclusive Georgian-style residential development at the south-west corner of Spadina and Davenport roads. The paper's dislike, by the way, appears to be casual and habitual, merely a quirk in our corporate culture, not active or vicious. In editorial pronouncements and asides, the phrase Castle Hill often appears with the word kitsch stuck to it, as though the two belonged together, like pea and pod.

I herewith dissent from the prevailing view. In visible contradiction to *The Globe*'s neglect during the half-decade or so since developer Murray Goldman put his ninety-one suites on the market (almost losing his shirt thereby), and in defiance of much else that's made it a hard sell—the slump in Toronto real-estate prices, dismal architectural neighbours (high-tension hydro lines, public parking lots), few fine shops nearby—Castle Hill stands today as one of Toronto's most suggestive recent experiments in high-density, low-rise residential planning.

The design, by the Toronto firm of Gabor & Popper, is a miniaturized paraphrase of the grand-manner Georgian terrace, its long rows of faceted luxury townhouses crisply defining the treed and sidewalked street between them. Gabor & Popper have obeyed the sound Georgian rule for the building line: generally uniform and continuous, but open to quiet differentiation among the various horizontal strata.

Thus, the lowest course in the Castle Hill façade scheme consists of a single storey faced with warm limestone blocks, quarried on the Bruce Peninsula and cut in Cambridge, Ontario, and punctuated by deeply inset entries topped by flat lintels accented by keystones. Above the first storey are the next two storeys, both set behind an uninflected plastered wall tinted light beige. The third, uppermost course is a low, almost white filled balustrade. Again in keeping with the British model, all the railings and fencings on the site are painted black. The insensitive use of the same standardized windows used throughout the project does tend to cast a pall of prefab monotony over Castle Hill. But, in general, the humane visual message created and maintained by the standardized front elevation is one of dignity, stability without ostentation, and sturdy, affluent domesticity.

Unlike an eighteenth-century terraced street, flat on the London mud, however, the Castle Hill site lies on the sloping shoreline of glacial Lake Iroquois, where it drops off below Casa Loma. The architects could have timidly avoided the potential risk to serene Georgian horizontality by orienting their buildings parallel to Davenport. Instead, they forthrightly broke the rules, and stepped their large freehold suites up the hill, emphasizing each "step" with a conspicuous high pilaster, its parts echoing the grey-beige-white upward sequence of the façade.

Among Gabor & Popper's most interesting challenges involved the short north-south stretch of Walmer Road bisecting the site. As the only public street available for architectural definition on both sides—the other two principal boundary roads, Davenport on the north and Spadina on the east, provided no such opportunity—Walmer was their one chance to invoke the distinctive atmosphere of grandeur and intimacy, vista and urbanity which is the glory of the best Georgian thoroughfare. And indeed, they just about did it, albeit on a doll-house scale. The resulting streetscape is stately without being stuffy, exclusive without being forcefully or obviously exclusionary. And perfectly framed by the pleasant ellipse allowed by a concave backup of the building line halfway up Walmer Road, dear and awful old Casa Loma never looked so gracious.

To those observers who think there's something wrong with Castle Hill's old-fashioned styling, because it was developed a couple of centuries ago, I can only say: so what? If you want to kick some architecture, Toronto's full of ugly Tudoroid mansionettes fully deserving a whack. But lay off buildings and street schemes that work. The Georgian town plan worked—for people, for their vehicles, for the eye and for the soul—as well as anything devised in Europe since antiquity.

The problem with Castle Hill, however, is that it's not a town, but only a whisp of alternative urbanism. It's a fragment, a vignette, and not the large, multifarious area implied by its urbane forms, ornament and abbreviated street definitions. There are no ground-floor shops in the complex, none of the variegated amenities that would make the settlement a haven. Castle Hill requires the use of automobiles as much as any Modernist high-rise-in-the-park. Because it is a zone of homogeneously upmarket residences, sharply demarcated from the surroundings, this little, open development is unfortunately pervaded by a whiff of that incompleteness and sterility we sense in suburban American compounds where the rich huddle in their alarmed monster houses behind electrified fences patrolled by armed guards.

Well, Castle Hill, if diminutive, incomplete and flawed, is still not that bad; and it is a notably pleasant, sheltered place to stroll through on a crisp November morning, or windy one in spring. It is also a spot that deserves study by young architectural dreamers able to keep alive the vision of large-scale planning through the current, pitiful design-build drought which developers have visited upon the city fringes. Of all Toronto housing developments I know, Castle Hill is the one I would like to see become bigger, and finally grow up to be the many-streeted town it will not and unfortunately cannot become.

## Sonic City

It would never have occurred to me to write this had it not been for a peculiar thing that happened a couple of years ago, while I recovered at home from minor surgery.

I had lived in cities for the better part of my life, and had taken the urban cacophony for granted, rarely giving much mind to the city's noise makers, other than the particularly terrible jackhammer or siren or cement truck. But during those weeks of convalescence—for reasons nobody has been able to explain satisfactorily—the walls of my house seemed to evaporate, and my hearing briefly became astonishingly, painfully acute.

As long as I was in that state, the most disturbing sounds were not the occasional gruntings of garbage trucks or shrieks of kids playing in the alley, but ambient noises with permanence and dense opacity, like that of brick and cement—the

*Night, February*

steady whine, never louder and never softer, emitted day and night by the toilet factory a block away, for instance; and the great unceasing whirr of innumerable automobile tires rolling on the city's streets.

The noises made by certain household appliances—the high-pitched wheeze of the microwave oven, the buzzing purr of the refrigerator—have something of the same monotonous quality, and were similarly unbearable. Briefly, I took to wearing those hard ear-muffs used by people who guide aircraft to their parking spots; but to little avail. The sounds of the city, and the monotone appliances, came right through their shields of plastic and fibre battings.

Fortunately, this phenomenon was short-lived. Today my hearing and aural tolerance are not appreciably worse or better than anyone else's. But the experience will always be memorable, inasmuch as it made the invisible architecture of urban sounds present to me for the first time—as tangible and complex as the solid architecture of streets and buildings that comprise the central visible fact of our urban dwelling.

Unlike the built city, the sonic city is diffuse, lacking the walls and fences or other strict demarcations that make visible the abstract, modern notion of "real estate." Sound structures blend perversely, puddling and congealing and spreading with no respect for firm boundaries, or for gravity. In the darkness just before dawn, the never-stopping whirr of car tires on pavement washes through streets and lanes and seeps through the windows of my study, being no respecter of legal bounds, such as property lines or walls.

This pervasive noise is joined by the sharper crunching and motor-driven grind of local street work, which in turn mixes with the first rattling of a mechanical operation beginning its day over by the railroad tracks. An early-bird jet on final approach to Toronto's international airport—its business travellers readying themselves for meetings in rooms sonically broadloomed with the grey, muffled stir of air-conditioning,

its engines and down-thrust flaps violently stirring the air outside, showering down its roar, which muddles with the eternal
toilet-factory whine, the incessant gasp of industrial air-intakes
and the slapping flutter of fume exhaust systems. And somewhere far beyond my windows, in a direction I cannot identify, a mechanized chatter of unknown origin has begun its
familiar daily utterance, contributing its strange stutter to the
ramshackle construction of the invisible city of sound.

One of the lessons of my curious convalescence was that,
like the solid, visible city, the unseen, aural one has its distinctive historical architectures, styles, meanings. Lounging on
a deck or patio on a sunny day, or sailing, or sitting near a
window on a rainy afternoon, one can hear the only two
sounds of energy exchange which had any economic significance to urban humankind from the beginning of time until
the mid-eighteenth century: wind, and the rush of water
down the drain spout. Wind power is without importance
nowadays, and falling water's power to drive engines and mills
is much less significant than it used to be; hence their sounds
are now thought by city dwellers to be restful, restorative—
something that would never have occurred to a miller with
wheat to grind under his water-driven wheel, or a farmer with
a crop waiting for rain that does not come.

Most of the non-human sounds we hear come from sites
of energy exchange that are new in the long history of technology—motors, engines, industrial and domestic appliances.
The racket they produce, people still sometimes find strange
and stressful: especially the absolutely steady, unrhythmic
drones, whines, drizzles, grinds and wheezes of such systems
and instruments as electric heating and cooling plants, pumps,
power saws and drills. These are the bricks, so to speak, in the
sound-structure of the late-modern city. But the sonic bricks
of the post-Modern city are with us already, in the form of
eerily banal absences of sound.

Gone from many a workplace are the typewriters that once

saturated the air with the battering of paper by tiny metal bits. And gone from our "industrial parks" are the smoky heaving and pounding that were once conspicuous shapers of the urban soundscape. Computers will be doing more and more of our work, as information becomes the central commodity of the postindustrial age; but we may well find the airless silence in which computers work to be as difficult to live with as the still-new whines of the current era.

The sounds of late industrial modernity and the curious silences of post-Modernism have almost displaced old-fashioned sonic factors in Toronto culture—but not quite. If you happen to be fortunate enough to live near a railway track, you can still hear the clatter of metal wheels hitting the rail-joints, which is perhaps just another sound (like the tick-tock of the Depression-era clock in my kitchen) that is only endearing because of its firmly dated quality. Virtually gone, however, is the hectic, jubilant pulse of car-honks once characteristic of every city's financial district—silenced, partly, by anti-noise laws, but mostly by the tight sealing of recent office buildings against everything outside, including sound.

No writer on urbanism, to my knowledge, has bothered trying to sort out the historical types and forms of urban sounds and their evolution, in the way building types were long ago arranged into a coherent history. Architectural guides to cities concentrate on built artifacts, rarely referring to the network of human use in which these artifacts exist, and never to the unseen net of historical sounds within which we live and work. But if your hearing ever becomes abnormally acute—a fate I wish on no one—or even if you just sit still right now and pay attention to the tableau of sound around you, you will find yourself in the midst of noises as rich in cultural heritage and history as any factory, soaring skyscraper or noble antique edifice.

# *At the Edge*

*Swansea Asphalt*

# HEARTLAND

On the outskirts of every substantial North American city, often near the airport, you find a version of Mississauga's Heartland Business Community, with the same uncanny, new and weightless experiences which technological modernity has brought us.

Laid out on flat Ontario farm country in this far-western Toronto suburb by Orlando Corporation, one of Canada's largest commercial real-estate developers, Heartland is a 1,200-acre zone of broad and curving streets with names that often recall venerable or romantic sites in other countries (Avebury, Venice, Rodeo Drive), and have nothing to do with any local fact or history. The street names appear to have been picked for general effect, as contributions to the scenography or atmospherics of the place, and with the intention of suggesting "tradition." This, in contrast to the names given boulevards of another commercial park in the vicinity, such as Satellite, Orbiter and Shuttle, which long ago lost their their newish-ness and pizazz, becoming tawdry. In Heartland's avenues, no battles are commemorated, no famous people recalled. History, as the collective weight of memory embodied in the names of things, is absent.

The streets in Heartland's developed portions are bordered by enormous vacant lots—one of them the site of a proposed public "sports complex"—and many manicured and primly planted lawns and low, mostly new office buildings and warehouses, curtained with mirrored glass, slabs of concrete or vast sheets of metal. Orlando has put up each of these buildings on more or less the same plan, and with the same internal structurings, but has given each a frosting of architectural stylistics. Some sport delicate green-glazed facades topped by hints of gable and pediment, while others are faced by long horizontal walls of reflective midnight-blue glass, banded with strips of stainless steel. Some are glass all round, while others are blocks of windowless concrete with a glistening glass portico or portal out front.

There is much sameness in this apparent variety, even as the buildings are alike in mystery—their reticence to give away their function—and their air of disuse. In the earlier stages of our industrial era, warehouses looked like warehouses, and factories like factories. Architects believed, as a matter of faith and principle, that this should be the case. And there used to be evidence of *work* everywhere: trash and dirt, smoke and noise, and patches of bare, poisoned dirt. In Heartland, the buildings are immaculate, and very quiet. After several passes around the immense Pepsi Cola building, with its mirrored front and escarpments of windowless concrete, I gave up trying to figure out what happens in it. A process of production, or perhaps of bottling? Or merely of storage and distribution, of marketing and administration? Like everything else in Heartland, it sits, incommunicative, on its clipped, flowered lawn, telling no stories, revealing nothing.

The sky is wide in much of the great semi-circle of postindustrial emplacements surrounding Metropolitan Toronto; but it is nowhere wider than in Heartland. The horizon is low and distant, and the landline would be as dead-flat as a corn field were it not for the huge ziggurats and tumuli of landfill, rising like the sand-covered graves of ancient Mesopotamian cities against the sky. The streets and parking lots are virtually empty on weekends, making it perfect for summer Sunday bicycling and quiet walks. No one lives there, of course. It is thus the exact opposite of the thing represented by Toronto's famously untidy Kensington Market, and an excellent example of a still-strange new urban form created by the car: a market-place emptied and filled, used and abandoned, according to the abstract, arbitrary rhythm of the nine-to-five, Monday to Friday workweek. Heartland seems to rest very, very lightly on its site. A high wind, it seems, could blow away its fragile curtains of glass and new-laid turf and marigold beds. Even the marble-lined, post-Modern *film noir* lobby of Britannia Place, the centrepiece office block of Heartland, seems tentative, theatrical.

But curiously, the postindustrial fantasia of Heartland does recall one historical reality, which is the tale of the very ground it stands on. On weekends, it is as quiet as that former Ontario farmland; on weekdays, as busy. It is a clear space, with the sense of clearing about it, and of keeping things tidy and visually clarified, hence like the land on which it has been installed. I was interested to learn from a commemorative plaque—the surest evidence that true history has passed from popular memory into extinction—that Heartland stands on what was once called Gardner's Clearing, an agricultural community settled in 1821. In late Victorian times, patriotic villagers changed their town's name to Britannia, then left their farms and vanished into the mass of industrial workers clustered around the mills and factories in downtown Toronto. The only reminders of their village is a lovely neo-Gothic United Church, built in 1843, an 1876 schoolhouse and a farm building or two, now used to give Mississauga children a picture-postcard view of Life Before Now.

Someday, as surely as Britannia, Heartland itself will vanish, in the endless process of making and remaking, destroying and emptying and rebuilding and repopulating that have always been the motive forces in urban existence. Will anything of fragile, light Heartland remain, to give schoolkids of the future a taste of life in the age of information, pure surface, mere sheen?

## NOWHERE

Like many people, I often engage in what's laughably called "travel" on behalf of my employer—laughably, because nothing could be more absurdly unlike real travel.

The real thing is moving smoothly, rapidly in a comfortable train coach through Canadian farm country on a wintry afternoon, bewitched by the fleeting tints of last sunlight glancing across the snow. Or it's driving around a bend in Arkansas—hot, sick of being behind the wheel, tired of rap music thumping away on the kid's boom-box in the back seat—and finding the answer to a prayer: Joe Bob's Reptile Ranch and BBQ Pit, with a beehive-hairdoed waitress named Billie, a sleepy old alligator, and a tall glass of iced tea.

Travel, at least of the sort I do, usually by air, is devoid of virtually everything deserving the name. Excitement in the air is not, by the way, what's being asked for. I got enough of that to last a lifetime some twenty years ago over Detroit, when my jet carrier barely escaped mid-air collision with another by performing a disconcerting and unforgettable flip. But getting from place to place by air should have something to do with motion. Paradoxically, this most high-speed means of transport imposes on its users utter immobility, a sense of paralyzed waiting, of being passively processed.

It starts at home, in the dull interval between the panic of packing and the moment the taxi-driver buzzes; and it continues the moment the taxi heads onto the airport-bound expressway, a trip too short to read anything, too familiar to make looking out of the window a revelation.

The descent into boredom continues, quickening, on the airport grounds. Upon entering the precincts of Toronto's

Pearson International, for example, one is immediately disoriented by the tangle of broad highways, forking off in improbable directions, and by a horizon defined by uniformly flat-roofed structures. Even the passenger becomes alert to the omnipresent signage, for fear of being whisked away by the driver to the wrong terminal. Here, in this labyrinth of signs, begins the true onset of that helplessness and routinization typical of every moment of air travel.

That's not to say the airport is an architectural object unworthy of attention. In fact, it is a crucial, focal site of economic and social activity in any city that's got one. Because of this prominence, it has attracted notable interest and homage from writers on urbanism. In his recent book *The 100 Mile City*, British architect Deyan Sudjic hails the contemporary airport as "one of the most intricately interwoven spatial hierarchies to be found anywhere in the world city—as complex as the Forbidden City of Beijing."

Sudjic then describes its four "domains," each one more "forbidden" than the one before. First comes the public concourse, devoted to shops and check-in counters, where anyone can go. Second comes the waiting-room, restricted to passengers who have passed the inspection of their bodies and carry-on luggage for weapons and bombs. Next is the expanse of concrete on which the mighty planes move grandly and park, attended by the scurry of little service vehicles, all of which may be witnessed, but only through windows, by passengers who've been certified weapon-free. Finally, there are the many wholly hidden zones ordinary folk will never see, where baggage is sorted, radar signals are monitored and the movements of those huge machines on the ground and in the air are managed.

As intellectually engaging as I find this description, which I include here for your edification, my actual experience of airports, as a user, remains numbness and impotence, even a kind of degradation. Emotions must be suppressed. When a guard is frisking your crotch for guns with his electronic wand, and the device squeals hysterically because it's sensed a dollar-coin in your pocket, you dare not show your disgust, for fear of being forbidden entry to the yet-more inner sanctum. One must take pains to act and look "normal," by reason of the same fear—a reasonable one, incidentally, since there's a sign suggesting that the guards are on the lookout for people who are not behaving normally. Nothing spells out what "normal" is, and you dare not ask. The important thing is to catch one's plane. To do so requires the adoption of an attitude as sedate, standardized and abject as the chrome and plastic seating, the broadloom, the soporific colour scheme—the adoption of the visible pose of a person who is patient, resigned, passive and stupidly happy with the prospect of air travel.

This prospect is not what it was. Once deluxe, streamlined and "special," the contemporary passenger aircraft has become merely an extension of the airport lounge: a cylinder, instead of a box, for waiting. One moves in an airplane, but does not travel, since there is virtually nothing to see (except worthless movies) and nothing to do, except try to read, between interruptions by service personnel at drink time, feeding time, hot-towel time, and the time it takes the captain to tell us it's going to be smooth flying all the way.

The passenger waits as the plane taxis and takes off; of course, one is supposed to read, or look at the pictures in, the brochure indicating what to do should your B-767M aircraft dive into the water or crash-land. I don't read these things, since I am convinced that they are meant merely to make me feel better. I prefer realism. In case of accident, I'm doomed.

Then one waits a certain period aloft and waits to land, waits to be taxied to the terminal, waits to exit the plane and to enter a terminal identical in almost every respect to the one he or she has left. Terminal, plane, terminal become a single and continuous site of waiting.

This is not the alert, wholly human waiting one learns in the spiritual practices of all great religions. It's not the exhilarating wait for a lover to arrive at the front door, nor the expectant waiting for death's release and peace after a grave illness. The waiting that air transit enforces is a training in blandness, anonymity, insignificance, in putting up with bad food and cramped quarters. How did it happen that the one conspicuous moment of public immobility our high-speed technical culture allows us has to be so stupid? Why can't every airport, and at least one or two take-offs in life, be just a little more like the final scene in *Casablanca*?

## PROSPECTS FOR THE MIDDLE

Young architects hardly need reminding that they face a dim future. They know better than anyone about the decline of the three great forces that have traditionally provided marvellous opportunities for young architects to recast great European and American cities boldly and memorably.

One is hostile aerial bombardment, which, in a few hours, can level many square kilometres and a half-dozen centuries of pompous building, as it did in Germany a half-century ago. But perhaps it's just as well this sort of radical urban renewal is currently out of fashion in most parts of Europe, and everywhere in North America. As the banal rebuilt downtowns of Frankfurt, Kassel and Cologne abundantly testify, few imaginative planners or architects got the chance to build on the empty lots opened by such sweeping demolition.

Too, megalomaniacal visionaries—with armies of work-gangs and strong sympathetic governments behind them—are in notably short supply in our mass-democratic times. Where are the enlightened, autocratic vandals who, every hundred years or so, used to sweep away old Berlin, and raise a new city in its place? And just when smart young architects need him, where is the Toronto or Vancouver rendition of Georges-Eugene Haussmann (1809–1891), the remorseless destroyer and reshaper of Napoleon III's Paris?

Last, and perhaps most important for their future as changers of the cityscape, architecture grads must discount earthquakes, fires and windstorms, all traditional allies in their quest for interesting commissions. The tall building, glory of urban culture in our time, would quite possibly have never arisen and flourished in Chicago had not the city's central clutter been cleared by the fire of 1871. And, long before the human-inspired devastation of central Toronto in the 1960s and 1970s, important fires in 1849 and again in 1904 gave local architects extraordinary chances to ply their trade, try their ideas, make over the city centre in the current image of the New.

I had harboured hopes that such an opportunity for Toronto architects might arise again one day. Not in the wake of earthquake or fire, mind you, but in the natural, slow course of things. By reducing the threat of widespread devastation by meteorological or geological powers, structural engineering during the past century has proved to be a mixed blessing for architects at best, and, at worst, a grounds for their elimination. But even the best-engineered tall buildings (I told myself) grow old, become weather-beaten and worn, and must be taken down, to make way for something new.

Or so I thought, until a visit to the Scarborough headquarters of Dowdell Pal Ellis Shim Consulting Engineers. Founder and senior partner Gordon Dowdell—whose projects include Ontario Place and the Sherway Gardens shopping plaza in Etobicoke—quickly put one of these thoughts out of my head. If maintenance is kept up, the steel-framed tall buildings that define our skyline, says Dowdell, should last. "We don't have a problem of deterioration with time. There are wind and earthquake stresses, and a building moves all the time. But if the whole exterior cladding is designed to withstand such forces, you have no problem."

If the load-bearing metal cage of a tall building is indefinitely reliable, in theory anyway, little else about it is. At the end of a particularly severe test of nineteenth-century construction techniques—the San Francisco earthquake and fire of April 18, 1906—the steel-framed, curtain-walled edifices were among the few built things to survive. But as the panoramic photos recently shown at Montreal's Canadian Centre for Architecture reveal, that's about all that did survive: gone was the glass, the furniture, the people—everything, in fact, *but* the frame.

Given the frailty of cladding commonly in use these days, Dowdell is concerned about what will happen to Toronto's tall glass-walled structures in the entirely possible (through statistically improbable) event of a significant earthquake. His more immediate worries, however, have to do with a long-term failure to maintain buildings against more subtle threats to their existence. "Many of our tall buildings have precast concrete panels tied onto the surface, anchored back into the building. The anchorage is supposed to be corrosion-resistant, but I question this. Our weather is becoming more and more corrosive. Too, glass ages and becomes more brittle with time. The other snag is that glass can tolerate very little distortion." The problem will always be one of maintenance—of just how long, that is, the owners can afford to pay for upkeep against the slowly declining structural reliability of a given high building. Abandon this pricey, permanently necessary maintenance, and, even if it won't fall down, a tall building becomes a dangerous proposition.

The precast concrete apartment buildings built all over Metro since the 1950s are another story, says Dowdell. Long before the high office towers are done for, atmospheric corrosion and crumble, salt damage (especially in the underground parking garages), and the natural shrinkage of all poured stone, known as "creep," will necessitate the demolition of apartments, which were produced faster and with less structural resistance to the elements than their commercial cousins. Current life expectancy of these buildings: about twenty-five years.

So here's my advice to architecture students who hope to build something on the Toronto city site before the middle of the next century. Forget about 150 storeys of deluxe office space, glistening towers piercing the golden mists of a summer morning, monumental spectacles of steel and glass punctuating the city's low horizon. Start thinking up something new to do with the family room.

EDGE CITIES

Lest this seems an unnecessarily gloomy and apocalyptic vision to lay on a young architect, I hasten to add that there is an alternative scenario on the horizon; and, if it comes into play on the urban stage, future designers will have their hands full indeed.

This more hopeful prognosis first began to form in my head in early 1993, when several birds of distinctly unlike feather—vulture developers, gentle spotted environmentalists, red-crested socialists and unionists, and wattled grey entrepreneurs—hopped on the same snowy branch and together began twittering the praises of the Ontario government's new $2.5-billion mass-transit plan for the greater Toronto area.

Not joining the noisy perch-in, however, was *The Globe and Mail*'s resident Raven of Doom, Colin Vaughan. He took one look at the plan and its proposed funding formula for the big projects—a pooling of provincial and municipal tax money with $500 million from private pockets—rustled his black feathers on his lofty rafter, and solemnly quoth: Nevermore!

On the off-chance you haven't heard what lies in the future for us mobile Torontonians, here's a quick summary. A new 5.4-km subway line, burrowed eastward from the north-south Yonge line into the settled, upmarket suburbia around Sheppard Avenue East and Don Mills Road. A 4.4-km subway, run out from Eglinton West station to a currently unpopulated wasteland, on whose dank flats is destined to rise the commercial, residential and governmental towers of the new York City Centre.

The Spadina Subway—always called that, despite the fact that most of its track lies above ground (and not under or along Spadina Avenue)—will be pushed north-west 5.2 km to York University, at last hard-wiring the farflung campus into the urban transportation grid.

The Scarborough Rapid Transit line will be extended 3.4 km farther into the largely unexplored forests of north-east Metro, where wolves and a few residual pioneers have been sighted in recent years. Finally, dedicated express lanes will be built on the margins of the west-suburban superhighway 403 to accommodate fast bus travel for the huge numbers of people always in a great rush, I've noticed, getting from nowhere to nowhere in northern Mississauga.

"The outlook is grim," croaked Vaughan. The biggest bone sticking in his craw was the predicted private-sector involvement. Vaughan was aflutter, specifically, at the thought of developer Murray Frum dropping a few million into the pot for the Scarborough Rapid Transit extension, which happens to be going out where he has land, presumably in hopes of turning a profit.

Now for those, like this writer, who would like to see all public utilities and most government services, including the streets and mass-transit system, sold off to private investors, the Frum involvement will probably seem like a very tiny step indeed in the right direction. But for Vaughan, it would be the first step on the slippery slope to perdition. "The cheque book has become the keystone of the new urban order in Ontario," he lamented. "To hell with the planning priorities....Sadly, we can only wait for the horror stories to emerge."

But why wait? From Vaughan's perspective, the shape of things to come is already plain, and plainly unacceptable.

Magnified urban sprawl. The hastened flight of populations from urbia to suburbia. The final quenching of Toronto's downtown seethe, and the surrender of our once-busy city to drug fiends and prostitutes, and desertion by the kindly and decent.

Missing from this dark view is, first, the acknowledgement that subways run two ways. If everybody's hurtling downtown to work every morning now, who's to say that they'll be hurtling in the same direction forever? In my crystal ball, I see the future toiling masses of Information City—for so Toronto has already become—living right downtown, in increasingly compact, enjoyable high-rise and low-rise circumstances, and scattering on outbound subways to the several neo-urban centres of commerce, industry and high-tech work that will then stand, like beacons, on the city's periphery. These neo-urbanisms will perhaps (or perhaps not) re-create, on a little scale, the traditional metropolitan mountain, with skyscrapers at the centre, lower industrial/commercial blocks beyond, and, beyond them, yet lower residential neighbourhoods. (After all, there's no law that says every city must have the same sort of skyline forever.)

A jet traveller landing at Pearson International in fifty years, for instance, may well see a rumpled carpet of high and low housing and amenities where the old high city core of Toronto used to be, before we took a few skyscrapers down. On the far eastern, western and northern horizons, the same traveller glimpses things that seem to belong to a former time: a scatter of widely separated vertical points composed (on closer view) of numerous compact tall and low buildings. These neo-urban units would house our workplaces, our workshops, factories and offices. Though broadly spaced, each would be connected to each other and to the residential downtown by even more marvellous electronic gadgetry than we have today, and by the branching mass-transit system already in place, and about to be given a nudge by the Ontario government and its capitalist allies.

Only after this fantasy came to me did I discover, not to my surprise, that architects and urbanists had already begun drawing up plans for the diffused city. In 1991, the University of Texas's Center for American Architecture and Design held a symposium in Austin called "New Centers on the Periphery: the Case of Four Texas Metropolitan Areas." Several talking-points, later published in the Center's journal, struck me as provocative, but none more than the assertion that we've always had it wrong about North American cities. They've never been uniformly centred, with lessening densities from the inside out. "In fact," said Texas architectural historian Robert Bruegmann, "the American city has been decentralizing and re-centering virtually as long as there has been an American city." While acknowledging the near-universal hatred of edge-towns by academics and upholders of the high-density downtown ideal, Bruegmann urged his colleagues to think *diffusion,* since so little is really known about this phenomenon. "It may be daunting, but what a challenge: to try to understand urban systems at the moment that they are fundamentally transforming themselves before our very eyes."

And, anyway, what have we got to lose? Pick a centre on the edge—any one will do—and try to understand how it works, *if* it works, how people use and move and respond to each other within it. Your spot may be far removed from downtown Toronto, but it need not be. I'm interested in the mixed-use York City Centre, the new focus of the constituent Metro city, and a proposed terminus of a new spur off the Spadina line. From the imaginary pictures made by its planners, it appears that this place will feature rather old-fashioned skyscrapers, showing more stone than steel and glass, hence more intimate than the distinct "tall building" of classic postwar Modernism. Moreover, as if intent on declaring the centre's theme to be proximity rather of purity, the principal York skyscrapers will be linked near the top by dramatic flying bridges and, near the bottom, by what appears to be a lofty atrium or mall.

When completed, of course, York City Centre may not function as planned. But if it doesn't, it can be written off as yet another experiment in the long attempts of urban populations to adjust to the inevitable arising of concentrated but widely spaced urbanism. Some day, it's to be hoped, the planners and developers will get the formula right, and start consciously creating fringe-cities architecturally responsive to the opportunities for scatter opened by contemporary communications technology, transport systems, and social desire.


## YORK

In the waning days of 1993, I suddenly recalled that Toronto's bicentennial was rapidly slipping away, and that I'd not done so much as raise a glass of Diet Coke to my adopted home town. Whereupon I resolved to pay a visit to pay an honorific visit to the spot my city got its start.

First, I had to find it. Of the civilian town called York—the town site's name until its incorporation in 1834—nothing has survived except a patch of rigid street-plan. To the best of my knowledge, no persisting architectural marker indicates the town's original boundaries. When I sat down with a city map and thought about exactly where York had been—something anyone who'd lived in Toronto a quarter-century *should* know—I was surprised to find the whole business a bafflement. All I knew was that York was somewhere quite downtown, and east of Yonge Street, but north of Front Street, simply because that was the shoreline of Lake Ontario until nineteenth-century landfill pushed the docklands far south.

Getting this bit of information was easy. Eric Arthur's *Toronto No Mean City*, shows the civilian town as a tiny rectangle bounded by present-day George, Berkeley, Adelaide and Front streets. Even if one knows where the borders are, however, they are bound to seem arbitrary. The territory they enclose is an especially undistinguished swatch of east down-town, with the usual gaps of parking lots, a few tottering late Victorians somebody forgot to demolish, and many Vic-but-renovated and twentieth-century buildings. But this very non-descriptness has a venerable history. Right from 1793, what Arthur calls the "practical but indescribably mean and unimaginative" plan of York never had architectural focus or definition. "Had there been provision for a school, a church, or, more particularly, a village green, the plan of Toronto today would have been different," he bewails. "It also lacked direction, so that when expansion was inevitable, the town grew merely by adding more squares."

The tight plan Arthur so disliked was the brainchild of one Alexander Aitkin, who drew it off for Lieutenant-Governor Simcoe in 1793. Aitkin hardly deserves such harsh condemnation. He was, after all, a military engineer, not a visionary; and his checkerboard of streets was, and is, the most common ever devised to lay out a new city intended to serve as a trading, industrial, administrative or military centre. It was introduced early into Britain's American colonies, and thereafter never lost its utility, or its appeal to planners.

The grid proposed by Thomas Hulme for Philadelphia in 1682, for example, provided no more common space than the 1793 plan for York. Following the example of Hulme and new-town planners like him, Aitkin simply ignored the bumps and dips in the land which, in Toronto's case, included swampy beaver ponds, deep hardwood forests, meandering creeks and gullies cut in the clay. Beginning with Aristotle and finding especially fertile ground among radical philosophers of habitation in our own century, this imposition of rectilinear order on wiggly Nature has always been a persistently popular idea in serious Western urbanism. Unless Western civic idealism is coming permanently unstuck, the grid will return to favour—though it should be said that, for some time, it has been in deep disfavour indeed. Visiting Hulme's Philadelphia in 1842, Charles Dickens complained of the city's "distract-ingly regular" layout: "After walking about it for an hour or two, I felt that I would have given the world for a crooked street." Eric Arthur, Dickens's latter-day soul mate, is then voicing no new gripe against the old gridiron, when he con-demns the Toronto street-plan "with which we have had to cope for almost two hundred years and with which posterity will have to deal till the end of time."

Sure enough, addition of new city blocks became quickly necessary after 1793, since Aitken had plunked York too close to the great, foggy swamp that, 125 years later, would be filled and become the Port Industrial District. Within only a few years of tiny York's creation, the more important colonial citi-zenry had begun to move their homes and businesses, and hence the centre of town, westward, in the direction of the financial district focusing the financial and corporate city today. (As late as 1834, the middle of the city still was no far-ther west than the corner of King and Frederick, and Queen Street had not been pushed as far west as Yonge Street.) Old York, which could have been our Boston Common or Wall Street, had it presented a suitable focus, was swiftly abandoned to an ignominious fate as a Victorian warehousing and factory zone, of no further immediate importance to the growing metropolis.

After reading Arthur's dismissive account, it seemed unfit-ting to visit this ill-starred place only by day, when it would be swarming with trucks and haulers and office workers, busy with their metropolitan day-jobs. Alexander Aitkin's York *is* the cemetery of a noble, unpopular historical idea in town planning, applied here with the same nonchalant disregard for topographical reality as elsewhere. So I decided to pace off York's emptied lanes and streets in the hours long before dawn one winter's night, when even the unsleeping city nods off just a little, and a certain pensive quiet dawns in the downtown lanes.

On the principal streets, of course, darkness had long been vanquished by unblinking lamps—though in the dark alleys hidden among tall buildings, the chilling dank gloom that once shrouded the little wooden houses of eighteenth-century York could still be felt. I love downtown night laneways such as these—very still, littered with the detritus of industry, at times shadowed thick as ink, at other times turned into a mad fantasia of black and bright white by a glaring light-bulb installed on a rear wall. Due to the clay on which it was built, "Muddy York" deserved its early nickname—though the point is driven home with special force when, making your way over the icy, broken pavement of an alley and trying not to seem snoopy about the deal going down between the hooker and john a few metres down the lane, you put your foot into a deep pot-hole filled with that oily, never-draining water that gave York its odd handle.

If the site lacks a central square, or anything else that would have kept the burgeoning city anchored there, it does have one accidental peculiarity that I'd never noticed before my wintry night prowl. An outsized number of the businesses installed in the old warehouses and new, short towers have to do with communications and transportation; and all are bathed in the faint electric buzz and sublimnal vibratory haze characteristic of such structures. The large office building and printing plant of *The Toronto Sun*—its lunchroom empty, its ground-floor editorial nooks flooding the dark, damp sidewalk outside with glaring fluorescent light—stands upon the site of old York, along with the headquarters of *Saturday Night* magazine, and Greyhound's parcel-handling facility. There are innumerable copy shops, their machinery hooded in plastic at night, and countless design firms, ad agencies, little publishing outfits and printing companies.

If old York did not become our geographical urban centre, it did become the forum of Toronto's key industry in the late twentieth century, which is information. In this place are monuments to Toronto's essential existence, though hidden from sight: a thick web of wires wriggling through walls and under the streets, telecommunications and data-processing equipment glowing and pulsing, receiving and sending; and whole buildings whose human staff is organized by its computers and cybernetic gadgetry. Without meaning to, Old York today typifies what Toronto seems always destined to become, and which many students of cities now appear deeply uneasy about: an urban complex much poorer in focused, stately, famous architectural space and construction than Eric Arthur would have liked, without greatness as a manufacturing centre or port, yet dense and busy with the electric impulses, data, words, texts, stories, movements, service exchanges and flying numbers which together constitute whatever significance it has, and whatever its claim to the name *cosmopolis*. I am not downplaying the importance of our architectural monuments in brick, stone and glass; I do not need to do so. Long before I sat down to write the columns on which this book is based, the solvent of high technology had already dissolved the historic substantiality of the modern city, leaving behind only the Cheshire Cat's mercurial smile—the information and ornamentation, the evanescent visual and sensuous codes which are now the central facts of contemporary urban experience and, by an interesting historical irony, the principal products being made today in Old York.

But fear not: I am not about to launch into a happy-faced hymn to the "information highway"—the most vulgar buzzword so far invented by the futurologists of the 1990s—or claim Old York to be a particularly key crossroads in it. Though I believe the city as we have known it is vanishing, and a new city as we have *not* known it is coming to be— which makes it utterly beyond words, hence beyond thought—I find much joy in contemplating the evidence of the historic Western idea of urbanism as stolid, choreographic, disciplined. A number of buildings in the Old York district,

*Near Dupont Street, Evening*

for example, have what is known as "historic interest," a polite way to say they have become ideologically obsolete—dear, discarded shells left as the city became something new. Among the oldest extant buildings is also the most lovely: the august structure at 252 Adelaide Street East, originally the Bank of Upper Canada and now a restored "period" post office, built in the late 1820s. There are also a few other brick Victorian churches and commercial and industrial buildings, and a nice ultra-*moderne* one or two, standing among the parking lots, pocks and pot-holes, now decidedly beyond the eastern edge of the gleam-zone of our financial and banking skyscrapers.

Because I find "architectural tours" too tightly aesthetic and sentimental, and invariably unconscious of urban context and the dissolving process that turns discreet buildings into city sites—from *things* into fields over which meaning flickers and dances—I've made the acquaintance of these buildings on my own over the years. Visiting them should be, and is, like dropping in on elderly friends, retired actors in a long-running play, now closed. My gradual learning has usually come after admiring, by chance, the grace of a porch or column, the polite or haughty or faintly overbearing ways the façades address the street, the way they silently request the passer-by to realign her posture or straighten his tie.

Most of the buildings and occurrences in the district do not remind us of terribly serious matters, only interesting and intellectually vivifying ones. Not so—at least for this walker in the city—the sight of St. James' Cathedral, and the sounds of its bells, pealing over the city. I know as well as any Torontonian that St. James is destined forever to be one of the top ten stops on any architectural guide's tour of Ye Olde Toronto. Surely because I am a Christian believer, this church is an abrupt comeuppance to thoughts adrift on the intellectual draughts and alluring currents I'm habitually drawn to. For if the city is changing into something new, and seems to be tending in directions hardly thinkable in traditional categories, I am not.

This point came home to me on a Saturday just before I finished this book, when walking the streets of Old York, I heard
the bells of St. James. Almost without thinking, I dropped in
on the noontime Eucharist, which, to my surprise and pleasure, was being celebrated by a priest I had not seen in some
time. As she offered the bread and wine to God, using the
ancient words of thanksgiving, I was reminded of the men and
women who had been bringing to this place, for two centuries,
the little-changing sorrows, dreads and joys and exaltations of
human existence. These experiences know no ethnic boundaries, no limits of time. Perhaps at the very heart of our historic need to live in cities is this longing not to be alone—to
be continually aware that we are surrounded by a cloud of witnesses, living and dead and yet unborn, to the immense richness and endless discovery of urban experience.

"Heritage" concentrates on the dead merely, making them
seem remote in their quaint costumes and antique surroundings. The service at St. James, however, called to mind the persistent issues and needs, and the nearness of the long-dead to
our own condition, and our enduring community with them.
Frankly, that plain Saturday celebration of the Holy
Communion was the first occasion on which I had felt good
about the Toronto bicentennial, simply because it was the first
time I felt proper gratitude for Toronto, this experiment in
urbanity begun two hundred years before. It was also a
moment of thanksgiving for those who will come after this
book and its author, and all those now living, have been forgotten—our children and newcomers, who will be drawn by
the lights of the Emerald City, and decide to inhabit this place,
pace it off and consider it anew, learn from and build it again,
forever.

# SOURCES

## AND

## RESOURCES

## *Thinking Places*

Banham, Reyner. *A Concrete Atlantis: U.S. Industrial Building and European Modern Architecture 1900–1925*. Cambridge, Mass.: The MIT Press, 1986.

Canadian Auto Workers Local 303 Heritage Committee. *You Can't Bring Back Yesterday*. Toronto: CAW Local 303, 1993.

Charles, Prince of Wales, quoted by Jonathan Bate in *Times Literary Supplement*, June 12, 1992.

Le Corbusier. "Three Reminders to Architects, (I): Mass," in *Towards a New Architecture*. New York: Dover Publications, 1986.

Macaulay, Rose. *Pleasure of Ruins*. London: Thames and Hudson, 1984.

Roberts, V.M. "Toronto Harbour," *Canadian Geographical Journal*, Vol. XV, No. 2 (August, 1937).

Ruskin, John. *The Seven Lamps of Architecture*. London: George Routledge & Sons, 1907.

Sobel, David. *The Moving Past: A Presentation of Archival Work Films*. Toronto: Labour History Imagers Group, n.d.

Sobel, David, and Susan Meurer. *Working at Inglis: The Story of a Toronto Factory*. Toronto: James Lorimer and Co., 1994.

Stinson, Jeffrey. *The Heritage of the Port Industrial District*, Vol. I. Toronto: The Toronto Harbour Commissioners, 1990. See also Suzanne Barrett and Joanna Kidd, *East Bayfront and Port Industrial Area: Pathways: Towards an Ecosystem Approach, A Report to the Royal Commission on the Future of the Toronto Waterfront*. Ottawa: Minister of Supply and Services Canada, 1991.

## On the Land

Gregory, Dan, and Roderick MacKenzie. *Toronto's Backyard: A Guide to Selected Nature Walks.* Vancouver and Toronto: Douglas & McIntyre, 1986.

Moore, Charles W., William J. Mitchell, William Turnbull, Jr. *The Poetics of Gardens.* Cambridge, Mass.: The MIT Press, 1988.

Pielou, E.C. *After the Ice Age: The Return of Life to Glaciated North America.* Chicago and London: The University of Chicago Press, 1991.

Solomon, Barbara Stauffacher. *Green Architecture: Notes on the Common Ground (Design Quarterly 120).* Minneapolis: Walker Art Center, 1982.

## Binding and Loosing the Waters

Hough, Michael. *City Form and Natural Process.* London and New York: Routledge, 1991.

McGlade, Terry, James Brown, Whitney Smith. "The Garrison Creek Community Project." Grant application, n.d.

The Task Force to Bring Back the Don. *Bringing Back the Don.* Toronto: City of Toronto Planning and Development Department, 1991.

## Tales of the Pioneers

Beck, Julia, and Alec Keefer, eds. *Vernacular Architecture in Ontario.* Toronto: The Architectural Conservancy of Ontario, 1993.

Benn, Carl. *Historic Fort York 1793–1993.* Toronto: Natural Heritage/Natural History, Inc., 1993.

Brunskill, R.W. *Illustrated Handbook of Vernacular Architecture.* London and Boston: Faber and Faber, 1987.

Duncan, Dorothy. *Life in the Past Lane.* Toronto: Metropolitan Toronto & Region Conservation Foundation, n.d.

Mika, Nick, Helma Mika and Gary Thomson. *Black Creek Pioneer Village.* Belleville: Mika Publishing Co., 1988.

*A Pictorial History of Weston.* Toronto: The Weston Historical Society, 1981.

Rempel, John I. *Building with Wood.* Toronto: University of Toronto Press, 1980.

Stacey, C.P. *The Undefended Border: The Myth and the Reality.* Ottawa: The Canadian Historical Association, 1967.

The Town Project. "Railways in Weston," "Churches in Weston" and other publications, n.d.

## Pleasures in Places

Colvin, Howard. *Architecture and the After-Life.* New Haven: Yale University Press, 1992.

Etlin, Richard A. *The Architecture of Death: The Transformation of the Cemetery in Eighteenth-Century Paris.* Cambridge, Mass.: The MIT Press, 1987.

Filey, Mike. *Mount Pleasant Cemetery: An Illustrated Guide.* Toronto: Firefly Books, 1990.

Francis, Mark, and Randolph T. Hester, Jr. *The Meaning of Gardens: Idea, Place and Action.* Cambridge, Mass.: The MIT Press, 1990.

Harris, Neil, and Benjamin Portis. *Civic Visions, World's Fairs.* Exhibition catalogue. Montreal: The Canadian Centre for Architecture, 1993.

Ring, Dan, Guy Vanderhaeghe and George Melnyk. *The Urban Prairie.* Exhibition catalogue. Saskatoon: Mendel Art Gallery and Fifth House Publishers, 1993.

Robinson, John. *Once Upon a Century: 100 Year History of the 'Ex.'* Toronto: privately printed, 1978.

Rybczynski, Witold. "Building the City Beautiful." *Times Literary Supplement,* November 20, 1992.

Toronto Historical Board. "Colborne Lodge, 1837." Mimeographed handout, n.d.

Webster, Donald. "Colborne Lodge Furnishings." Mimeographed training text. Toronto Historical Board, n.d.

## Modern

Dal Co, Francesco. *Figures of Architecture and Thought: German Architecture Culture 1880–1920.* New York: Rizzoli, 1990.

Fenton, Joseph. *Hybrid Buildings (Pamphlet Architecture 11).* 2nd ed. Princeton: Princeton Architectural Press, 1985.

Ferriss, Hugh. *The Metropolis of Tomorrow.* New York: Ives Wasburn, 1929.

Frith, Valerie, ed. *Toronto Modern: Architecture 1945–1965.* Toronto: Coach House Press and the Bureau of Architecture and Urbanism, 1987.

Huxtable, Ada Louise. *Architecture, Anyone? Cautionary Tales of the Building Art.* Berkeley and Los Angeles: University of California Press, 1986.

Jacobs, Jane. *The Death and Life of Great American Cities.* New York: Random House, 1961.

Jencks, Charles. *Modern Movements in Architecture.* Harmondsworth: Penguin Books, 1982.

The Royal Commission on the Future of Toronto. *Regeneration.* Ottawa: Minister of Supply and Services Canada, 1992.

## Shopping

Cappe, Lorne, *Window on Toronto.* City of Toronto Planning and Development Department, 1990.

Laycock, Margaret, and Barbara Myrvold. *Parkdale in Pictures: Its Development to 1889.* Toronto Public Library Board, 1991.

Little, Bruce. "Retail Sales? It's not our department." *The Globe and Mail,* November 1, 1993.

Pevsner, Nikolaus. *A History of Building Types.* Princeton: Princeton University Press, 1989.

Sorkin, Michael, ed. *Variations on a Theme Park: The New American City and the End of Public Space.* New York: The Noonday Press, 1992.

Wills, Garry. "Chicago Underground." *The New York Review of Books,* October 21, 1993.

## Suburban Idylls

Adorno, Theodor. "Culture and Administration." Trans. by Wes Blomster, in Dennis Crow, ed. *Philosophical Streets: New Approaches to Urbanism.* Washington, D.C.: Maisonneuve Press, 1990.

Bonis, Robert R., ed. *A History of Scarborough.* Toronto: Scarborough Public Library, 1968.

Le Corbusier. "The Hours of Repose," in *The City of To-Morrow and its Planning.* Mineola, N.Y.: Dover Publications, 1987.

Sewell, John. *The Shape of the City: Toronto Struggles with Modern Planning.* Toronto: University of Toronto Press, 1993.

Spain, Daphne. *Gendered Spaces.* Chapel Hill and London: The University of North Carolina Press, 1992.

Teshima, Ted, et al. "Moriyama & Teshima: Architecture as a Work of Life." *Process: Architecture* No. 107 (December, 1992).

Wilson Alexander. *The Culture of Nature: North American Landscape from Disney to the Exxon Valdez.* Toronto: Between the Lines, 1991.

## Concrete Dreams

Billington, David P. *The Tower and the Bridge: The New Art of Structural Engineering.* Princeton: Princeton University Press, 1983.

Brown, David J. *Bridges: Three Thousand Years of Defying Nature.* London: Mitchell Beazley, 1993.

McKillop, David. *The Motel Strip Study.* Toronto: City of Etobicoke Planning Department, 1986.

Zwarts, Moshé. "Why Are Car Parks So Ugly?" In Maarten Kloos, ed. *Architecture Now: A Compilation of Comments on the State of Contemporary Architecture.* Amsterdam: Architectura & Natura, 1991.

## Streets

Cameron, C.J. *Foreigners or Canadians?*, quoted in text accompanying "The Magic Assembling: Metropolitan Toronto Storefronts and Street Scenes," an exhibition organized by Michael McMahon and Lillian Petroff for the Metropolitan Toronto Archives, March, 1993.

Dendy, William. *Lost Toronto: Images of the City's Past.* rev. ed. Toronto: McClelland & Stewart, 1993.

Donegan, Rosemary, introduction by Rick Salutin. *Spadina Avenue.* Vancouver: Douglas and McIntyre, 1985.

Kostof, Spiro. *The City Assembled: The Elements of Urban Form Through History.* Boston: Little, Brown and Company, 1992.

Myrvold, Barbara. *Historical Walking Tour of Kensington Market and College Street.* Toronto: Toronto Public Library Board, 1993.

## Gardens

Baraness, Marc, and Larry Richards. *Toronto Places: A Context for Urban Design.* Toronto: University of Toronto Press, 1992.

Brown, Jane. *Gardens of a Golden Afternoon: The Story of a Partnership, Edwin Luytens and Gertrude Jekyll.* New York: Van Nostrand Reinhold, 1982.

Ellacombe, Canon Henry N. *In a Gloucestershire Garden.* London: Century Hutchinson, 1986.

Holl, Stephen. "Double House." *Rural and Urban House Types in North America (Pamphlet Architecture 9).* Princeton: Princeton Architectural Press, 1983.

Pavord, Anna. "Back to the fuchsia." *Times Literary Supplement,* July 17, 1992.

Pollan, Michael. "Why Mow? The Case Against Lawns." *The New York Times Magazine,* May 28, 1989.

Sackville-West, Vita. *V. Sackville-West's Garden Book.* Edited by Philippa Nicolson. London: Michael Joseph, 1989.

## Moral Management

Campbell, Mary, and Barbara Myrvold. *The Beach in Pictures 1793–1932*. Toronto: Toronto Public Library Board, 1988.

Conway, Hazel. *People's Parks: The Design and Development of Victorian Parks in Britain*. Cambridge: Cambridge University Press, 1992.

Department of Parks and Recreation, City of Toronto. "High Park: Past to Present." Toronto, n.d.

Foucault, Michel. *Discipline and Punish: The Birth of the Prison*. Trans. by Alan Sheridan. New York, 1977. See also Joseph Masheck. *Building-Art: Modern Architecture Under Cultural Construction*. Cambridge: Cambridge University Press, 1993.

Rosenzweig, Roy and Elizabeth Blackmar. *The Park and the People: A History of Central Park*. Ithaca: Cornell University Press, 1993.

## Moderne *Variations*

Bliss, Michael. "The Historical Significance of Maple Leaf Gardens." Memorandum submitted to the Toronto Historical Board, November 26, 1989.

Fleming, Keith R. *Power at Cost: Ontario Hydro and Rural Electrification 1911–1958*. Montreal and Kingston: McGill-Queen's University Press, 1992.

Greif, Martin. *Depression Modern: The Thirties Style in America*. New York: Universe Books, 1988.

Hawes, Elizabeth. *New York, New York: How the Apartment House Transformed the Life of the City (1869–1930)*. New York: Alfred A. Knopf, 1993.

Holl, Stephen. *The Alphabetical City (Pamphlet Architecture 5)*, 2nd ed. Princeton: Princeton Architectural Press, 1980.

Huxtable, Ada Louise. *The Tall Building Artistically Considered: The Search for a Skyscraper Style*. Berkeley and Los Angeles: University of California Press, 1992.

Toronto Historical Board. "Heritage Property Report: Maple Leaf Gardens, 438 Church Street." December 1989.

## High Styles

Hersey, George. *The Lost Meaning of Classical Architecture: Speculations on Ornament from Vitruvius to Venturi*. Cambridge, Mass.: The MIT Press, 1988.

Hersey, George, and Richard Freedman. *Possible Palladian Villas*. Cambridge, Mass.: The MIT Press, 1992.

Hitchcock, Henry-Russell. *The Architecture of H.H. Richardson and his Times*. rev. ed. Cambridge, Mass.: The MIT Press, 1986.

Onians, John. *Bearers of Meaning: The Classical Orders in Antiquity, the Middle Ages and the Renaissance*. Princeton: Princeton University Press, 1988.

Pelt, Robert Jan van, and Carroll William Westfall. *Architectural Principles in the Age of Historicism*. New Haven: Yale University Press, 1993.

Summerson, John. *The Classical Language of Architecture*. rev. ed. London: Thames and Hudson, 1980.

## Houses and Home

Berman, Marshall. *All That is Solid Melts into Air: The Experience of Modernity*. New York: Simon and Shuster, 1982.

Denison, John. *Casa Loma and the Man who Built it*. Erin, Ont.: The Boston Mills Press, 1982.

Harbison, Robert. *The Built, the Unbuilt and the Unbuildable: In Pursuit of Architectural Meaning*. Cambridge, Mass.: The MIT Press, 1991.

Kolb, David. *Postmodern Sophistications: Philosophy, Architecture and Tradition*. Chicago: The University of Chicago Press, 1992.

Rybczynski, Witold. *Looking Around: A Journey Through Architecture*. Toronto: HarperCollins, 1993.

## *At the Edge*

Adams, James L. *Flying Buttresses, Entropy, and O-Rings: The World of an Engineer.* Cambridge, Mass.: Harvard University Press, 1991.

Bergh, Wim van den. "Mental Transparency." In Maarten Kloos, ed. *Architecture Now: A Compilation of Comments on the State of Contemporary Architecture.* Amsterdam: Architecture & Natura, 1991.

Bruegmann, Robert, and Tim Davis, "New Centers on the Periphery." *Center,* Vol. 7, 1992. See also Mildred Friedman. *Edge of a City (Pamphlet Architecture 13),* Princeton: Princeton Architectural Press, 1991.

Elliot, Cecil D. *Technics and Architecture: The Development of Materials and Systems for Buildings.* Cambridge, Mass.: The MIT Press, 1992.

Isin, Engin F. *Cities without Citizens: Modernity of the City as a Corporation.* Montreal and New York: Black Rose Books, 1992.

Kelly, Colleen. *Cabbagetown in Pictures.* Toronto: Toronto Public Library Board, 1984.

Kostof, Spiro. *The City Shaped: Urban Patterns and Meanings Through History.* Boston, Toronto and London: Little, Brown and Company, 1991.

Macrae-Gibson, Gavin. *The Secret Life of Buildings: An American Mythology for Modern Architecture.* Cambridge, Mass.: The MIT Press, 1988.

Sudjic, Deyan. *The 100 Mile City.* London: Andre Deutsch, 1992.